Voices of
America Past and Present

Volume II

PEARSON
Longman

New York   Boston   San Francisco
London   Toronto   Sydney   Tokyo   Singapore   Madrid
Mexico City   Munich   Paris   Cape Town   Hong Kong   Montreal

Executive Editor: Michael Boezi
Supplements Editor: Brian Belardi
Cover Design: Teresa Ward
Electronic Page Makeup: Lorraine Patsco

Voices of America Past and Present, Volume II

Copyright © 2007 Pearson Education, Inc.

Please visit our Web site at: www.ablongman.com

ISBN 0-205-52152-5

3 4 5 6 7 8 9 10—DOC—12 11 10 09

Contents

Preface   vii

Chapter 16—The Agony of Reconstruction   1
- Abraham Lincoln, Second Inaugural Address (1865)   3
- Mississippi Black Codes (1865)   5
- A Sharecrop Contract (1882)   8
- *Civil Rights Cases* (1883)   11
- Congressional Testimony on the Actions of the Ku Klux Klan (1872)   14
- Henry Grady, "The New South" (1886)   18

Chapter 17—The West: Exploiting an Empire   23
- Helen Hunt Jackson, from *A Century of Dishonor* (1881)   24
- Frederick Jackson Turner, "The Significance of the Frontier in
  American History" (1893)   28

Chapter 18—The Industrial Society   33
- Andrew Carnegie, from "The Gospel of Wealth" (1889)   35
- Russell Conwell, from "Acres of Diamonds" (1915)   38
- Terence V. Powderly, Preamble to the Constitution of the Knights
  of Labor (1878)   41
- Chinese Exclusion Act (1881)   43

Chapter 19—Toward an Urban Society, 1877–1900   47
- Edward Bellamy, from *Looking Backward* (1888)   49
- From *Plessy v. Ferguson* (1896)   52
- Booker T. Washington, Atlanta Exposition Address (1895)   54
- W. E. B. Du Bois, from "Of Mr. Booker T. Washington
  and Others" (1903)   56
- Lee Chew, from *Life of a Chinese Immigrant* (1903)   58
- The Secret Oath of the American Protective Association (1893)   61
- George Waring, Sanitary Conditions in New York (1897)   63

Chapter 20—Political Realignments in the 1890s   67

- The Omaha Platform of the Populist Party (1892)   68
- William Allen White, What's the Matter with Kansas? (1896)   71
- Theodore Dreiser, from *Sister Carrie* (1900)   74

Chapter 21—Toward Empire   79

- Josiah Strong, from *Our Country* (1885)   81
- Albert Beveridge, "The March of the Flag" (1898)   84
- William Graham Sumner, from "On Empire and the Philippines" (1898)   86
- William McKinley, "Decision on the Philippines" (1900)   88

Chapter 22—The Progressive Era   91

- Ida M. Tarbell, from *The History of the Standard Oil Company* (1904)   93
- William L. Riordon, from *Plunkitt of Tammany Hall* (1905)   97
- Ida B. Wells-Barnett, from *A Red Record* (1895)   99
- Jane Addams, from *Twenty Years at Hull House* (1909)   102

Chapter 23—From Roosevelt to Wilson in the Age of Progressivism   107

- Theodore Roosevelt, from *The New Nationalism* (1910)   109
- Woodrow Wilson, from *The New Freedom* (1913)   111
- National American Woman Suffrage Association, Mother's Day Letter (1912)   113

Chapter 24—The Nation at War   117

- The Roosevelt Corollary to the Monroe Doctrine (1904)   119
- Boy Scouts of America, from "Boy Scouts Support the War Effort" (1917)   121
- Newton D. Baker, "The Treatment of German-Americans" (1918)   124
- Eugene Kennedy, A "Doughboy" Describes the Fighting Front (1918)   126
- Eugene V. Debs, Statement to the Court (1918)   129
- Woodrow Wilson, The Fourteen Points (1918)   132

Chapter 25—Transition to Modern America   137

- A. Mitchell Palmer, "The Case Against the Reds" (1920)   139
- Comprehensive Immigration Law (1924)   141
- Calvin Coolidge, Honoring Charles Lindbergh (1927)   144
- Marcus Garvey, Aims and Objectives of the UNIA (1923)   147

Chapter 26—Franklin D. Roosevelt and the New Deal   153
- Franklin D. Roosevelt, First Inaugural Address (1933)   155
- Huey Long, "Share Our Wealth" (1935)   159
- Eleanor Roosevelt, from "My Day" Columns (1939)   161

Chapter 27—America and the World, 1921–1945   165
- Albert Einstein, Letter to President Roosevelt (1939)   167
- Franklin D. Roosevelt, The Four Freedoms (1941)   170
- Charles A. Lindbergh, from Des Moines Speech (1941)   173
- A. Philip Randolph, "Why Should We March?" (1942)   177
- *Korematsu v. United States* (1944)   180

Chapter 28—The Onset of the Cold War   185
- Harry S Truman, The Truman Doctrine (1947)   187
- George Marshall, The Marshall Plan (1947)   189
- Joseph R. McCarthy, from Speech Delivered to the Women's
  Club of Wheeling, West Virginia (1950)   191
- Margaret Chase Smith, from "Declaration of Conscience" (1950)   193
- Whittaker Chambers, from Foreword to *Witness* (1952)   196

Chapter 29—Affluence and Anxiety   201
- *Brown v. Board of Education* (1954)   203
- The Southern Manifesto (1956)   206
- Jo Ann Gibson Robinson, The Montgomery Bus Boycott (1955)   209

Chapter 30—The Turbulent Sixties   213
- From John F. Kennedy, Cuban Missile Address (1962)   216
- The Tonkin Gulf Incident (1964)   218
- Lyndon Johnson, The War on Poverty (1964)   221
- Students for a Democratic Society, Port Huron Statement (1962)   223
- Curtis Sitcomer, "Harvest of Discontent" (1967)   225
- National Organization for Women, Statement of Purpose (1966)   228

Chapter 31 – To a New Conservatism, 1969-1988   233
- Kevin MacCauley, Oral History on the 1968 Siege of Khe Sanh   235
- Richard M. Nixon, Speech on Vietnamization Policy (1969)   238
- House Judiciary Committee, Conclusion on Impeachment Resolutions (1974)   242
- *Roe v. Wade* (1973)   245
- Ronald Reagan, Speech to the House of Commons (1982)   248
- David Wildom, The Conscience of a Conservative Christian (1985)   250

Chapter 32 – To the Twenty-first Century, 1989-2006   254

- George H.W. Bush, Address to the Nation Announcing Allied Military
  Action in the Persian Gulf (1991)   256
- Articles of Impeachment Against William Jefferson Clinton (1998)   260
- Barbara Lee, Speech in Opposition to Authorizing the U.S. War in
  Afghanistan (2001)   264
- Owen Burdick, Witnessing the 9-11 Terrorist Attack in New York (2001)   266
- Wayne Allard, Testifying in Favor of the Federal Marriage Amendment
  (2004)   269

Credits   273

Preface

Selected to complement the *America: Past and Present* textbook, the documents in this reader are crucial resources in the quest to understand and interpret American history. Their purpose is to introduce some of the voices from the American past, to impart a sense of how historians write history, and to hint at some of the complexities of writing the past.

Several features make the documents accessible and assist in their analysis. Chapter introductions place the selections within a broadly drawn historical context, and each document is accompanied by a headnote which describes the author of the selection and the circumstances under which the document was written. Analysis questions follow each document, suggesting lines of inquiry to help better understand the documents themselves or how they fit into the wider historical context. Study questions at the end of each chapter direct the reader to points of special note and suggest comparisons and opportunities for further inquiry.

Sixteen

The Agony of Reconstruction

By the fall of 1864, after three bloody years of Civil War, the North was finally winning decisively. Abraham Lincoln won re-election that November and supporters of the Union cheered additional battle victories and territorial gains over the next few months. In March of 1865, with the war nearly won, Lincoln took the oath of office for a second term. In that inaugural address, he offered his hopes for quickly reuniting the nation.

At the end of Civil War, the nation remained in crisis. The most pressing questions involved reconstructing the Union—what should be done with the newly emancipated slaves and in what capacity and under what conditions should the rebellious states be readmitted? While these issues were debated nationally, the South quickly attempted to find solutions for the economic and social disruptions that had occurred as a result of the war.

Based upon an agrarian economy, the South had depended on the land and slave labor for its wealth. The war had destroyed much of the land and had eliminated the institution of slavery. In the first years after the war ended, the white power structure devised new political and economic arrangements to revive the economy. Black Codes were instituted by some southern legislatures immediately following the war as a means of reestablishing white dominance and assuaging white fear. These laws defined the relationship between African American and white Southerners, describing exactly what rights newly emancipated slaves were entitled to.

The continued dependence on an agricultural economy and the loss of the dependable labor pool provided by slavery forced the South to look for a replacement, while the freedmen did not have the necessary capital to develop an independent farming system. As a result, legal slavery was replaced throughout the South with the economic bondage known as sharecropping. Included in this chapter is a typical contractual agreement between a landowner and a sharecropper.

1

The Radical Republicans reacted quickly to the legal and economic changes being made in the South. Unlike the executive branch, which believed a quick and expedient readmission of the South to the Union was possible, these legislators thought that the white South was insufficiently repentant for the war and deserved punishment. They attempted to institute their own plans for Reconstruction, which included federal protection for the freedmen. The Fourteenth Amendment was intended to guarantee the political rights of freedmen and punish white Southerners who had actively participated in war. Congress secured ratification by making readmission to the Union dependent upon it.

During the period in which the federal government controlled the South, some white Southerners sought extralegal ways to maintain control. Among the organizations that developed was the Ku Klux Klan, a quasi-secret society dedicated to using violence to intimidate and influence the political actions of the freedmen. Included here is an excerpt from a congressional report on the Ku Klux Klan, published in 1872. This document is an example of the intimidation tactics used by the Klan and other groups to thwart Republican power in Southern states.

By the mid-1870s, Congress and the Northern public had tired of the focus on the post-war reconstruction of the South. As one final attempt to protect the freed slaves, however, Congress passed the Civil Rights Act of 1875, aimed at enforcing the equal protection clause of the Fourteenth Amendment by penalizing those who discriminated against blacks. In 1883, however, the U.S. Supreme Court overturned the Civil Rights Act of 1875 in a decision known as the *Civil Rights Cases*. The document here provides an excerpt from the majority opinion as well as the opinion of one dissenting judge.

In the decades immediately following the Civil War, many business and civic leaders in the former Confederacy championed what they called the "New South." What they meant by this was the move to industrialize and modernize the South, actively luring Northern capital to build iron and steel industries, textile mills, a more extensive railroad system, and other large-scale businesses. One of the leaders of this "New South" movement was Henry Grady, editor of the *Atlanta Constitution*. In a speech Grady gave in New York in 1886, excerpted below, he emphasized the progress already made in his native region. Grady overstated the speed with which the South was actually being transformed, but gradual improvement was taking place.

Abraham Lincoln, Second Inaugural Address (1865)

In March of 1865, the Civil War was almost over. The Confederacy had held out for longer than most expected, but much of the South was now under Union control and General Robert E. Lee's forces were losing ground in Virginia at last. With victory in sight, Abraham Lincoln gave a brief speech to commemorate his inauguration for a second term as President. In this speech, he laid out his hopes for a better nation emerging from the end of the war. Only six weeks after this speech, Lee would surrender, the Union would celebrate victory, and Lincoln would be assassinated.*

*F*ellow-countrymen:

At this second appearing to take the oath of the presidential office, there is less occasion for an extended address than there was at the first. Then a statement, somewhat in detail, of a course to be pursued, seemed fitting and proper. Now, at the expiration of four years, during which public declarations have been constantly called forth on every point and phase of the great contest which still absorbs the attention and engrosses the energies of the nation, little that is new could be presented. The progress of our arms, upon which all else chiefly depends, is as well known to the public as to myself; and it is, I trust, reasonably satisfactory and encouraging to all. With high hope for the future, no prediction in regard to it is ventured.

On the occasion corresponding to this four years ago, all thoughts were anxiously directed to an impending civil war. All dreaded it—all sought to avert it. While the inaugural address was being delivered from this place, devoted altogether to saving the Union without war, insurgent agents were in the city seeking to destroy it without

* From Abraham Lincoln, Second Inaugural Address, March 4, 1865, accessible online at http://www.ourdocuments.gov/doc.php?doc=38 or at http://wps.ablongman.com/wps/media/objects/1676/1716309/documents/doc_d16d01.html.

war—seeking to dissolve the Union, and divide effects, by negotiation. Both parties deprecated war; but one of them would make war rather than let the nation survive; and the other would accept war rather than let it perish. And the war came.

One-eighth of the whole population were colored slaves, not distributed generally over the Union, but localized in the Southern part of it. These slaves constituted a peculiar and powerful interest. All knew that this interest was, somehow, the cause of the war. To strengthen, perpetuate, and extend this interest was the object for which the insurgents would rend the Union, even by war; while the government claimed no right to do more than to restrict the territorial enlargement of it.

Neither party expected for the war the magnitude or the duration which it has already attained. Neither anticipated that the cause of the conflict might cease with, or even before, the conflict itself should cease. Each looked for an easier triumph, and a result less fundamental and astounding. Both read the same Bible, and pray to the same God; and each invokes his aid against the other. It may seem strange that any men should dare to ask a just God's assistance in wringing their bread from the sweat of other men's faces; but let us judge not, that we be not judged. The prayers of both could not be answered—that of neither has been answered fully.

The Almighty has his own purposes. "Woe into the world because of offenses! for it must needs be that offenses come; but woe to that man by whom the offense cometh." If we shall suppose that American slavery is one of those offenses which, in the providence of God, must needs come, but which, having continued through his appointed time, he now wills to remove, and that he gives to both North and South this terrible war, as the woe due to those by whom the offense came, shall we discern therein any departure from those divine attributes which the believers in a living God always ascribe to him? Fondly do we hope—fervently do we pray—that this mighty scourge of war may speedily pass away. Yet, if God wills that it continue until all the wealth piled by the bondman's two hundred and fifty years of unrequited toil shall be sunk, and until every drop of blood drawn with the lash shall be paid by another drawn with the sword, as was said three thousand years ago, so still it must be said, "The judgments of the Lord are true and righteous altogether."

With malice toward none; with charity for all; with firmness in the right, as God gives us to see the right, let us strive on to finish the work we are in; to bind up the nation's wounds; to care for him who shall have borne the battle, and for his widow, and his orphan—to do all which may achieve and cherish a just and lasting peace among ourselves, and will all nations.

DOCUMENT ANALYSIS

1. What does Lincoln say about slavery in his second inaugural address?

2. In what ways does Lincoln invoke God's power and judgment in the course of this speech? Do his religious references appeal to you or not? Explain.

Mississippi Black Codes (1865)

The Mississippi Black Codes are an example of the manner by which the old order was maintained in the South while African Americans were given limited new rights. Many in the North and the Republicans in Congress were alarmed by the Black Codes. Reaction to the codes helped to radicalize Congress and catalyzed its attempt to seize control of Reconstruction from the president. *

The Civil Rights of Freedmen in Mississippi

Section 1. Be it enacted by the legislature of the State of Mississippi, That all freedmen, free Negroes, and mulattoes may sue and be sued, implead and be impleaded in all the courts of law and equity of this state, and may acquire personal property and chooses in action, by descent or purchase, and may dispose of the same, in the same manner, and to the same extent that white persons may: Provided that the provisions of this section shall not be so construed as to allow any freedman, free Negro, or mulatto to rent or lease any lands or tenements, except in incorporated town or cities in which places the corporate authorities shall control the same.

Sec. 2. Be it further enacted, That all freedmen, free Negroes, and mulattoes may intermarry with each other, in the same manner and under the same regulations that are provided by law for white persons: Provided, that the clerk of probate shall keep separate records of the same.

Sec. 3. Be it further enacted, That all freedmen, free Negroes, and mulattoes, who do now and have heretofore lived and cohabited together as husband and wife shall be taken and held in law as legally married, and the issue shall be taken and held as legiti-

* From *Mississippi, Laws of the State…*,1865 (Jackson, Miss., 1896), 82–96.

mate for all purposes. That it shall not be lawful for any freedman, free Negro, or mulatto to intermarry with any white person; nor for any white person to intermarry with any freedman, free Negro, or mulatto; any person who shall so intermarry shall be deemed guilty of felony and, on conviction thereof, shall be confined in the state penitentiary for life; and those shall be deemed freedmen, free Negroes, and mulattoes who are of pure Negro blood, and those descended from a Negro to the third generation inclusive, though one ancestor of each generation may have been a white person.

Sec. 4. Be it further enacted, That in addition to cases in which freedmen, free Negroes, and mulattoes are now by law competent witnesses, freedmen, free Negroes, or mulattoes shall be competent in civil cases when a party or parties to the suit, either plaintiff or plaintiffs, defendant or defendants, also in cases where freedmen, free Negroes, and mulattoes is or are either plaintiff or plaintiffs, defendant or defendants, and a white person or white persons is or are the opposing party or parties, plaintiff or plaintiffs, defendant or defendants. They shall also be competent witnesses in all criminal prosecutions where the crime charged is alleged to have been committed by a white person upon or against the person or property of a freedman, free Negro, or mulatto: Provided that in all cases said witnesses shall be examined in open court on the stand, except, however, they may be examined before the grand jury, and shall in all cases be subject to the rules and tests of the common law as to competency and credibility.

Sec. 5. Be it further enacted, That every freedman, free Negro, and mulatto shall, on the second Monday of January, one thousand eight hundred and sixty-six, and annually thereafter, have a lawful home or employment....

Sec. 6. Be it further enacted, That all contracts for labor made with freedmen, free Negroes, and mulattoes for a longer period than one month shall be in writing and in duplicate, attested and read to said freedman, free Negro, or mulatto, by a beat, city or county officers, or two disinterested white persons of the country in which the labor is to be performed, of which each party shall have one; and said contracts shall be taken and held as entire contracts, and if the laborer shall quit the service of the employer, before expiration of his term of service, without good cause, he shall forfeit his wages for that year, up to the time of quitting.

Sec. 7. Be it further enacted, That every civil officer shall, and every person may, arrest and carry back to his or her legal employer any freedman, free Negro, or mulatto who shall have quit the service of his or her employer before the expiration of his or her term of service without good cause, and said officer and person shall be entitled to receive for arresting and carrying back every deserting employee aforesaid, the sum of five dollars, and ten cents per mile from the place of arrest to the place of delivery, and the same shall be paid by the employer, and held as a set-off for so much against the wages of said deserting employee.

Sec. 8. Be it further enacted, That upon affidavit made by the employer of any freedman, free Negro, or mulatto, or other credible person, before any justice of the peace or member of the board of police, that any freedman, free Negro, or mulatto, legally employed by said employer, has illegally deserted said employment, such justice of the peace or member of the board of police shall issue his warrant or warrants, returnable before himself, or other such officer, directed to any sheriff, constable, or special deputy, commanding him to arrest said deserter and return him or her to said employer, and the like proceedings shall be had as provided in the preceding section....

Sec. 9. Be it further enacted, That if any person shall persuade or attempt to persuade, entice, or cause any freedman, free Negro, or mulatto to desert from the legal employment of any person, before the expiration of his or her term of service, or shall knowingly employ any such deserting freedman, free Negro, or mulatto, or shall knowingly give or sell to any such deserting freedman, free Negro, or mulatto, any food, raiment, or other thing, he or she shall be guilty of a misdemeanor and, upon conviction, shall be fined not less than twenty-five dollars and not more then two hundred dollars and the costs, and, if said fine and costs shall not be immediately paid, the court shall sentence said convict to not exceeding two months' imprisonment in the county jail, and he or she shall moreover be liable to the party injured in damages....

Sec. 10. Be it further enacted, That it shall be lawful for any freedman, free Negro, or mulatto to charge any white person, freedman, free Negro, or mulatto, by affidavit, with any criminal offense against his or her person or property and upon such affidavit the proper process shall be issued and executed as if said affidavit was made by a white person, and it shall be lawful for any freedman, free Negro, or mulatto, in any action, suit, or controversy pending, or about to be instituted, in any court of law or equity of this state, to make all needful and lawful affidavits, as shall be necessary for the institution, prosecution, or defense of such suit or controversy.

Sec. 11. Be it further enacted, That the penal laws of this state, in all cases not otherwise specially provided for, shall apply and extend to all freedmen, free Negroes, and mulattoes....

Approved November 25, 1865

DOCUMENT ANALYSIS

1. How was the post–Civil War relationship between whites and blacks in Mississippi defined by the Black Codes?
2. What privileges did freedmen gain and lose in the Black Codes?

A Sharecrop Contract
(1882)

*This is a typical contractual agreement between a landowner and sharecropper. The system
ensured that the sharecropper remained poor and in debt to the owner and that the sharecropper might never become an independent farmer.* *

To every one applying to rent land upon shares, the following conditions must be
read, and agreed to.

To every 30 and 35 acres, I agree to furnish the team, plow, and farming implements,
except cotton planters, and I do not agree to furnish a cart to every cropper. The croppers are to have half of the cotton, corn, and fodder (and peas and pumpkins and potatoes if any are planted) if the following conditions are complied with, but—if not—they
are to have only two-fifths (⅖). Croppers are to have no part or interest in the cotton
seed raised from the crop planted and worked by them. No vine crops of any description, that is, no watermelons, muskmelons,…squashes or anything of that kind, except
peas and pumpkins, and potatoes, are to be planted in the cotton or corn. All must
work under my direction. All plantation work to be done by the croppers. My part of the
crop to be housed by them, and the fodder and oats to be hauled and put in the house.
All the cotton must be topped about 1st August. If any cropper fails from any cause to
save all the fodder from his crop, I am to have enough fodder to make it equal to one-
half of the whole if the whole amount of fodder had been saved.

For every mule or horse furnished by me there must be 1000 good sized
rails…hauled, and the fence repaired as far as they will go, the fence to be torn down
and put up from the bottom if I so direct. All croppers to haul rails and work on fence
whenever I may order. Rails to be split when I may say. Each cropper to clean out every
ditch in his crop, and where a ditch runs between two croppers, the cleaning out of that

* From *Grimes Family Papers* (#3357), 1882. Held in the Southern Historical Collection, University of
North Carolina, Chapel Hill.

ditch is to be divided equally between them. Every ditch bank in the crop must be shrubbed down and cleaned off before the crop is planted and must be cut down every time the land is worked with his hoe and when the crop is "laid by," the ditch banks must be left clean of bushes, weeds, and seeds. The cleaning out of all ditches must be done by the first of October. The rails must be split and the fence repaired before corn is planted.

Each cropper must keep in good repair all bridges in his crop or over ditches that he has to clean out and when a bridge needs repairing that is outside of all their crops, then any one that I call on must repair it.

Fence jams to be done as ditch banks. If any cotton is planted on the land outside of the plantation fence, I am to have three-fourths of all the cotton made in those patches, that is to say, no cotton must be planted by croppers in their home patches.

All croppers must clean out stable and fill them with straw, and haul straw in front of stable whenever I direct. All the cotton must be manured, and enough fertilizer must be brought to manure each crop highly, the croppers to pay for one-half of all manure bought, the quantity to be purchased for each crop must be left to me.

No cropper is to work off the plantation when there is any work to be done on the land he has rented, or when his work is needed by me or other croppers. Trees to be cut down on Orchard, house field, & Evanson fences, leaving such as I may designate.

Road field is to be planted from the very edge of the ditch to the fence, and all the land to be planted close up to the ditches and fences. No stock of any kind belonging to croppers to run in the plantation after crops are gathered.

If the fence should be blown down, or if trees should fall on the fence outside of the land planted by any of the croppers, any one or all that I may call upon must put it up and repair it. Every cropper must feed or have fed, the team he works, Saturday nights, Sundays, and every morning before going to work, beginning to feed his team (morning, noon, and night every day in the week) on the day he rents and feeding it to including the 31st day of December. If any cropper shall from any cause fail to repair his fence as far as 1000 rails will go, or shall fail to clean out any part of his ditches, or shall fail to leave his ditch banks, any part of them, well shrubbed and clean when his crop is laid by, or shall fail to clean out stables, fill them up and haul straw in front of them whenever he is told, he shall have only two-fifths ($\frac{2}{5}$) of the cotton, corn, fodder, peas, and pumpkins made on the land he cultivates.

If any cropper shall fail to feed his team Saturday nights, all day Sunday and all the rest of the week, morning/noon, and night, for every time he so fails he must pay me five cents.

No corn or cotton stalks must be burned, but must be cut down, cut up and plowed in. Nothing must be burned off the land except when it is impossible to plow it in.

Every cropper must be responsible for all gear and farming implements placed in his hands, and if not returned must be paid for unless it is worn out by use.

Croppers must sow & plow in oats and haul them to the crib, but must have no part of them. Nothing to be sold from their crops, nor fodder nor corn to be carried out of the fields until my rent is all paid, and all amounts they owe me and for which I am responsible are paid in full.

I am to gin & pack all the cotton and charge every cropper an eighteenth of his part, the cropper to furnish his part of the bagging, ties, & twine.

The sale of every cropper's part of the cotton to be made by me when and where I choose to sell, and after deducting all they owe me and all sums that I may be responsible for on their accounts, to pay them their half of the net proceeds. Work of every description, particularly the work on fences and ditches, to be done to my satisfaction, and must be done over until I am satisfied that it is done as it should be.

No wood to burn, nor light wood, nor poles, nor timber for boards, nor wood for any purpose whatever must be gotten above the house occupied by Henry Beasley—nor must any trees be cut down nor any wood used for any purpose, except for firewood, without my permission.

DOCUMENT ANALYSIS

1. How did the sharecropping system differ from slavery?

Sixteen.4

Civil Rights Cases
(1883)

The last major piece of Reconstruction legislation passed by Congress was the Civil Rights Act of 1875. It was aimed at preventing discrimination based upon race in public accommodations, such as railroads, hotels, restaurants, music halls, etc. Congress was tiring of Reconstruction by the time this law was passed, but this legislation was aimed at protecting the freed slaves against possible abuse, and Congress felt it was merely enforcing the equal protection clause of the Fourteenth Amendment, which had already gone into effect. In reviewing a series of cases in 1883, the U.S. Supreme Court ruled the Civil Rights Act of 1875 was unconstitutional, thus establishing a precedent for their ruling in 1896 in Plessy v. Ferguson.*

Justice Bradley delivered the opinion of the Court.

Has Congress constitutional power to make such a law? Of course, no one will contend that the power to pass it was contained in the Constitution before the adoption of the last three amendments. The power is sought, first, in the 14th Amendment. It is State action of a particular character that is prohibited....Individual invasion of individual rights is not the subject-matter of the amendment. It nullifies and makes void all State legislation, and State action of every kind, which impairs the privileges and immunities of citizens of the United States, or which injures them in life, liberty or property without due process of law, or which denies to any of them the equal protection of the laws. The last section of the amendment invests Congress with power to enforce it by appropriate legislation. To enforce what? To enforce the prohibition. To adopt appropriate legislation for correcting the effects of such prohibited State laws and State acts, and thus to render them effectually null, void, and innocuous. This is the legislative power conferred upon Congress, and this is the whole of it. It does not invest Congress with power to legislate upon subjects which are within the domain of State legislation;

* From 109 U.S. 3 (1883).

but to provide modes of relief against State legislation, or State action, of the kind referred to. It does not authorize Congress to create a code of municipal law for the regulation of private rights; but to provide modes of redress against the operation of State laws, and the action of State officers executive or judicial, when these are subversive of the fundamental rights specified in the amendment. And so in the present case, until some State law has been passed, or some State action through its officers or agents has been taken, adverse to the rights of citizens sought to be protected by the 14th Amendment, no legislation of the United States under said amendment, nor any proceeding under such legislation, can be called into activity: for the prohibitions of the amendment are against State laws and acts done under State authority....

An inspection of the law shows that it proceeds *ex directo* to declare that certain acts committed by individuals shall be deemed offences, and shall be prosecuted and punished by proceedings in the courts of the United States. It does not profess to be corrective of any constitutional wrong committed by the States; it applies equally to cases arising in States which have the justest laws respecting the personal rights of citizens, and whose authorities are ever ready to enforce such laws, as to those which arise in States that may have violated the prohibition of the amendment. In other words, it steps into the domain of local jurisprudence, and lays down rules for the conduct of individuals in society towards each other, and imposes sanctions for the enforcement of those rules, without referring in any manner to any supposed action of the State or its authorities.

Civil rights, such as are guaranteed by the Constitution against State aggression, cannot be impaired by the wrongful acts of individuals, unsupported by State authority in the shape of laws, customs, or judicial or executive proceedings. The wrongful act of an individual, unsupported by any such authority, is simply a private wrong, or a crime of that individual....The abrogation and denial of rights, for which the States alone were or could be responsible, was the great seminal and fundamental wrong which was intended to be remedied. And the remedy to be provided must necessarily be predicated upon that wrong. Of course, these remarks do not apply to those cases in which Congress is clothed with direct and plenary powers of legislation over the whole subject as in the regulation of commerce. It is clear that the law in question cannot be sustained by any grant of legislative power made to Congress by the 14th Amendment. This is not corrective legislation; it is primary and direct....

But the power of Congress to adopt direct and primary, as distinguished from corrective legislation on the subject in hand, is sought, in the second place, from the Thirteenth Amendment. Such legislation may be primary and direct in its character; for the amendment is not a mere prohibition of State laws establishing or upholding slavery, but an absolute declaration that slavery or involuntary servitude shall not exist in any part of the United States....

It would be running the slavery argument into the ground to make it apply to every act of discrimination which a person may see fit to make as to the guests he will entertain, or as to the people he will take into his coach or cab or car, or admit to his concert or theatre, or deal with in other matters of intercourse or business. Innkeepers and public carriers, by the laws of all the States, so far as we are aware, are bound, to the extent of their facilities, to furnish proper accommodation to all unobjectionable persons who in good faith apply for them. If the laws themselves make any unjust discrimination, amenable to the prohibitions of the 14th Amendment, Congress has full power to afford a remedy under that amendment and in accordance with it. When a man has emerged from slavery, and by the aid of beneficent legislation has shaken off the inseparable concomitants of that state, there must be some stage in the progress of his elevation when he takes the rank of a mere citizen, and ceases to be the special favorite of the laws....

Justice Harlan, dissenting.

The opinion in these cases proceeds, it seems to me, upon grounds entirely too narrow and artificial. I cannot resist the conclusion that the substance and spirit of the recent amendments of the Constitution have been sacrificed by a subtle and ingenious verbal criticism. Was it the purpose...simply to destroy the institution...and then remit the race, theretofore held in bondage, to the several States for such protection, in their civil rights, necessarily growing out of freedom, as those States, in their discretion, might choose to provide?...

But what was secured to colored citizens of the United States—as between them and their respective States—by the national grant to them of State citizenship? With what rights, privileges, or immunities did this grant invest them? There is one, if there be no other—exemption from race discrimination in respect of any civil right belonging to citizens of the white race in the same State. It is fundamental in American citizenship that, in respect of such rights, there shall be no discrimination by the State, or its officers, or by individuals or corporations exercising public functions or authority.

But if it were conceded that the power of Congress could not be brought into activity until the rights specified in the act of 1875 had been abridged or denied by some State law or State action, I maintain that the decision of the court is erroneous. In every material sense applicable to the practical enforcement of the 14th Amendment, railroad corporations, keepers of inns, and managers of places of public amusement are agents or instrumentalities of the State, because they are charged with duties to the public, and are amenable, in respect of their duties and functions, to governmental regulation. It seems to me a denial, by these instrumentalities of the State, to the citizen, because of his race, of that equality of civil rights secured to him by law, is a denial by the State, within the meaning of the 14th Amendment I agree that if one citizen chooses not to hold social intercourse with another, he is not and cannot be made amenable to the law; no legal right of a citizen is violated by the refusal of others to maintain merely social relations with him, even upon grounds of race. The rights which Congress, by the act of 1875, endeavored to secure and protect are legal, not social rights.

DOCUMENT ANALYSIS

1. On what basis did the Supreme Court rule that the Civil Rights Act of 1875 was unconstitutional?

2. What is the main point made in Justice Harlan's dissenting opinion?

Congressional Testimony
on the Actions of the Ku Klux Klan
(1872)

*In the post–Civil War South, some whites who opposed Reconstruction formed secret vigilante organizations such as the Ku Klux Klan. The Klan resorted to violence and terror—including murder—to intimidate former slaves from participating in politics. The Klan and similar organizations did not terrorize only African Americans, however, they also attacked whites who supported the Republican Party. Congress passed legislation in 1871 to go after the Klan, and held hearings in 1871 and 1872 on how the Klan operated in various states. This testimony from those hearings shows how the Klan accomplished its goals.**

The actual existence of the Klan in South Carolina in 1870 is shown by the testimony of W. K. Owens, already referred to, who was initiated before Christmas, 1870. He gives the oath, the signs, the pass-words; the fact that they are bound to obey all the orders of their chief; that if ordered to commit murder, the penalty for refusal is death; that they are bound to deny their membership, even as witnesses in court, and to clear each other by their testimony or as jurors; that it is organized all over the State; that he had recognized members in Columbia, Winnsborough, and Spartanburgh; also, members from North Carolina, thus showing the organization to be the same in both States. He speaks of murders committed in York County as communicated to him by his chief; of a raid upon which he went to arrest and murder the county treasurer of York, who escaped from them; gives the names of chiefs and members in the town of York; describes their disguises; states that it was part of their business to disarm negroes, and that their object was political—"to carry the negro for the democratic party"... (pp. 1363–1370.)

This testimony is so entirely in accordance with the acts committed by the Ku-Klux, with their declarations when committing them, and with the experience of the commu-

---

* From *Report of the Joint Select Committee to Inquire into The Condition of Affairs in the Late Insurrectionary States, Made to the Two Houses of Congress*, February 19, 1872 (Washington: Government Printing Office, 1872), pp. 30–32, accessible online at http://www.hti.umich.edu/.

nities in which they operate, that all who are conversant with these acts would ask for no further corroboration....

The order has sought to accomplish its purposes by coercing republicans publicly to renounce their political faith; by whippings, other indignities, and murder. In the county of Spartanburgh, forty-five persons had, during a few months after the election of 1870, published in the Spartan, the democratic newspaper, notices of such renunciation, one of which, as a specimen of the whole, is here given, (page 573):

[COMMUNICATED.]

MR. EDITOR: I desire to make this public announcement of my withdrawal from all affiliation with the republican party, with which I have heretofore acted. I am prompted to take this step from the conviction that the policy of said party, in encouraging fraud, bribery, and excessive taxation, is calculated to ruin the country; and that I did not vote at the last election, because I entertained my present opinion of the republicans, and have been so for the last twelve months.

Respectfully,

SAMUEL F. WHITE.

Mr. White is a respectable white man, a carpenter and millwright; fifty-four years of age, and a native of the county.

The value of public sentiment affected by such publications, as well as the sincerity of such political conversions, will be appreciated by learning from Mr. White's testimony the persuasive means that were used to obtain that card, (pp. 571, 572):

Question. Have you been visited at any time by the Ku-Klux?
Answer. Yes, sir.
Question. When?
Answer. It was the week of the court that was at Spartanburgh,...
Question. Of what month?
Answer. Of April last. It was on Wednesday night, I know.
Question. Go on and tell what they said and did.
Answer. They came there and surrounded the house in the night. I was asleep. They got around each door and demanded of me to make a light and to open the door. They were all around the house, some at one door and some at the other. I did not have much fire, and was slow getting it made up, when they commenced lamming at the back door. After I got up the light I walked to the front door and opened it, and the men there hollered to the others at the back door to stop lamming, and they stopped. They then ordered me to cross my hands; I did so. They asked for a rope; I told them there was none. I reckon one of them went up the stairs with a light to get a piece of rope—an old bed-cord or something, and they took a pillow-slip and slipped it over my head and led me into the yard. They asked me my principles, and I told them. They said, "That was what I thought you were."
Question. What did they say?

Answer. They asked if I was a Union man or a democrat. I told them I had always been a Union man. They said they thought so. They carried me off seventy-five or eighty yards from the house. They said, "Here is a limb," and they asked me whether I would rather be shot, hung, or whipped. I told them if it had to be one, I would have to take a whipping. They ordered me to run; I told them I did not wish to do that. Then they commenced on me.

Question. What did they do?

Answer. They whipped me.

Question. How?

Answer. They took little hickories and one thing or another.

Question. Was the whipping a severe one?

Answer. Yes, sir.

Question. How many strokes did they strike?

Answer. I suppose some thirty or forty.

Question. Did it bruise or cut your flesh?

Answer. Yes, sir.

Question. How many men were there?

Answer. I can't say as to that; I thought, from the number around the house, there were twenty or thirty.

Question. How were they dressed?

Answer. They were disguised.

Question. How were they disguised?

Answer. With horns and everything over their faces.

Question. Could you tell who any of them were?

Answer. No, sir.

Question. What time of night was it?

Answer. I think it was about 11 o'clock, as well as I can recollect.

Question. What was done after they were through whipping you?

Answer. They just untied my hands, got on their horses, and went out.

Question. Did they leave you there?

Answer. Yes, sir. He told me I must publish my principles.

Question. What did you understand by that?

Answer. I think they wanted me to alter my principles to a democrat.

Question. Did you make any such publication? Did you put anything of the kind in the paper.

Answer. Yes, sir. They told me I must do it against the next Wednesday.

Question. In what paper?

Answer. In "The Spartan" paper. They did not particularly mention it, but I put it in "The Spartan" paper; Mr. Trimmier's paper.

Question. What led you to do that?

Answer. They said if I did not publish it, they would come and see me again....

Question. Would you have published any card of this kind if these men had not required it?

Answer. No, sir.

Question. Do you know of others with whom that course has been taken in your part of the county—whipping?

Answer. I have heard of a good many. Dr. Winsmith was shot the same night, because they went off in that direction.

Other witnesses were examined to the same effect.

DOCUMENT ANALYSIS

1. What does Samuel White's testimony suggest about the effectiveness of the Ku Klux Klan's intimidation techniques? In what ways was White's experience less brutal than it might have been had he been an African American?

Henry Grady, "The New South" (1886)

In the aftermath of the Civil War, a number of leading Southern whites began to push for emulating the success of the North by industrializing their economy as quickly as possible. One of the leading advocates of this position was the editor of the Atlanta Journal-Constitution, *Henry W. Grady. In this speech given in New York in 1886, somewhat overstating the case, Grady insists that the South is already changing rapidly.**

But what is the sum of our work? We have found out that in the summing up the free negro counts more than he did as a slave. We have planted the school house on the hilltop and made it free to white and black. We have sowed towns and cities in the place of theories, and put business above politics. We have challenged your spinners in Massachusetts and your iron-makers in Pennsylvania. We have learned that the $400,000,000 annually received from our cotton crop will make us rich when the supplies that make it are home-raised. We have reduced the commercial rate of interest from 24 to 6 per cent., and are floating 4 per cent. bonds. We have learned that one northern immigrant is worth fifty foreigners; and have smoothed the path to southward, wiping out the place where Mason and Dixon's line used to be, and hung out latchstring to you and yours. We have reached the point that marks perfect harmony in every household, when the husband confesses that the pies which his wife cooks are as good as those his mother used to bake; and we admit that the sun shines as brightly and the moon as softly as it did before the war. We have established thrift in city and country. We have fallen in love with work. We have restored comfort to homes from which culture and elegance never departed. We have let economy take root and spread among us as rank as the crab-grass which sprung from Sherman's cavalry camps, until we are

* From Joel Chandler Harris, ed., *Life of Henry W. Grady, Including His Writings and Speeches* (New York: Cassell Publishing Company, 1890), pp. 83–93. Available online at http://itw.sewanee.edu/reconstruction/html/docs/Grady_New_South.html.

ready to lay odds on the Georgia Yankee as he manufactures relics of the battlefield in a one-story shanty and squeezes pure olive oil out of his cotton seed, against any down-easter that ever swapped wooden nutmegs for flannel sausage in the valleys of Vermont. Above all, we know that we have achieved in these "piping times of peace" a fuller inde-pendence for the South than that which our fathers sought to win in the forum by their eloquence or compel in the field by their swords.

It is a rare privilege, sir, to have had [a] part, however humble, in this work. Never was nobler duty confided to human hands than the uplifting and upbuilding of the prostrate and bleeding South—misguided, perhaps, but beautiful in her suffering, and honest, brave and generous always. In the record of her social, industrial and political illustration we await with confidence the verdict of the world.

But what of the negro? Have we solved the problem he presents or progressed in honor and equity toward solution? Let the record speak to the point. No section shows a more prosperous laboring population than the negroes of the South, none in fuller sympathy with the employing and land-owning class. He shares our school fund, has the fullest protection of our laws and the friendship of our people. Self-interest, as well as honor, demand that he should have this. Our future, our very existence depend upon our working out this problem in full and exact justice. We understand that when Lincoln signed the emancipation proclamation, your victory was assured, for he then committed you to the cause of human liberty, against which the arms of many cannot prevail—while those of our statesmen who trusted to make slavery the corner-stone of the Confederacy doomed us to defeat as far as they could, committing us to a cause that reason could not defend or the sword maintain in sight of advancing civilization....

But have we kept faith with you? In the fullest sense, yes. When Lee surren-dered...the South became, and has since been, loyal to this Union. We fought hard enough to know that we were whipped, and in perfect frankness accept as final the arbitrament of the sword to which we had appealed. The South found her jewel in the toad's head of defeat. The shackles that had held her in narrow limitations fell forever when the shackles of the negro slave were broken. Under the old regime the negroes were slaves to the South; the South was a slave to the system. The old plantation, with its simple police regulations and feudal habit, was the only type possible under slavery. Thus was gathered in the hands of a splendid and chivalric oligarchy the substance that should have been diffused among the people, as the rich blood, under certain artificial conditions, is gathered at the heart, filling that with affluent rapture but leaving the body chill and colorless.

The old South rested everything on slavery and agriculture, unconscious that these could neither give nor maintain healthy growth. The new South presents a perfect democracy, oligarchs leading in the popular movement—a social system compact and closely knitted, less splendid on the surface, but stronger at the core—a hundred farms for every plantation, fifty homes for every palace—and a diversified industry that meets the complex need of this complex age.

The new South is enamored of her new work. Her soul is stirred with the breath of a new life. The light of a grander day is falling fair on her face. She is thrilling with the con-sciousness of growing power and prosperity. As she stands upright, full-statured and equal among the people of the earth, breathing the keen air and looking out upon the expanded horizon, she understands that her emancipation came because through the inscrutable wisdom of God her honest purpose was crossed, and her brave armies were beaten.

DOCUMENT ANALYSIS

1. How does Grady describe the changes that have taken place in the South since the end of the Civil War?

2. What does Grady present as the status of the former slaves in the "New South"?

Chapter Study Questions

1. In his second inaugural address, Lincoln encouraged "malice toward none" in rebuilding the war-torn country. Why do you think that proved so difficult during the Reconstruction era? Who was to blame for the extent of the malice that pervaded much of the political debate for several years after the Civil War?

2. Why did many former slaves enter into sharecropping contracts following the Civil War? What was the alternative? To what extent did the Black Codes encourage such a labor arrangement, and why?

3. How did the Mississippi Black Codes in 1865, and the actions of the Ku Klux Klan throughout the South in subsequent years, seek to overturn the outcome of the Civil War?

4. Why did the *Civil Rights Cases* decision by the Supreme Court in 1883 not result in a massive public outcry in the North? Would the reaction have been as muted had the decision been made several years earlier? Explain.

5. Contrast Henry Grady's vision of the South with the reality of the sharecropper contract. In what ways, if any, were they compatible?

Seventeen

The West:
Exploiting an Empire

Westward expansion was an important part of America's development in the late nineteenth century. Spurred by cheap land and delivered by continent-spanning railroads, settlers from the East and abroad poured into the Great Plains to farm or ranch the prairie or otherwise make their fortunes. This expansion had dramatic effects on the Native Americans already living in the West, many of whom had been relocated there from their ancestral homelands further east.

Even after the Civil War, Native Americans still dominated much of the western United States. But by 1877, the buffalo had been decimated, and increasing numbers of settlers, ranchers, and railroaders encroached onto Indian land. Whites pressured Indians, often with blatant disregard for old treaties, onto reservations where they would be "reformed" under strict discipline. Native American groups who resisted were to be "killed off."

The reservation system devastated many Native American groups by destroying the patterns of tribal life, but the Dawes Act was even more insidious. Inspired in part by the national attention Helen Hunt Jackson's *A Century of Dishonor* (1881) drew to the Indians' plight, the act, passed in 1887, set the course for federal Native American policy for the next century. It stipulated that Native Americans acquire land individually, rather than tribally, in the hopes of simultaneously fostering a tradition of private land ownership and destroying the power of the Native American political organizations. In exchange, Native Americans would become citizens and would gain outright ownership of their land after twenty-five years. Native Americans lost approximately 60 percent of their lands in the twenty years after the passage of the Dawes Act.

Frederick Jackson Turner's piece has great historiographical significance; in it he argued that the frontier shaped and created the essential American character, a character defined by individualism and democratic values. Turner's thesis found a resonance in the 1890s, when America's own continental frontier was "closing" and the country was beginning to expand toward Asia and Latin America.

Seventeen.1

Helen Hunt Jackson, from *A Century of Dishonor* (1881)

Helen Hunt Jackson's A Century of Dishonor *brought national attention to the plight of Native Americans when it was published in 1881. Jackson, a Massachusetts native who had traveled to California, describes in particular the plight of the California Indians, who had seen 90 percent of their population die from war and disease in the years after the gold rush.**

There are within the limits of the United States between two hundred and fifty and three hundred thousand Indians, exclusive of those in Alaska. The names of the different tribes and bands, as entered in the statistical table so the Indian Office Reports, number nearly three hundred. One of the most careful estimates which have been made of their numbers and localities gives them as follows: "In Minnesota and States east of the Mississippi, about 32,500; in Nebraska, Kansas, and the Indian Territory, 70,650; in the Territories of Dakota, Montana, Wyoming, and Idaho, 65,000; in Nevada and the Territories of Colorado, New Mexico, Utah, and Arizona, 84,000; and on the Pacific slope, 48,000."

Of these, 130,000 are self-supporting on their own reservations, "receiving nothing from the Government except interest on their own moneys, or annuities granted them in consideration of the cession of their lands to the United States."

...Of the remainder, 84,000 are partially supported by the Government—the interest money due them and their annuities, as provided by treaty, being inadequate to their subsistence on the reservations where they are confined....

There are about 55,000 who never visit an agency, over whom the Government does not pretend to have either control or care. These 55,000 "subsist by hunting, fishing, on roots, nuts, berries, etc., and by begging and stealing"; and this also seems to dispose of the accusation that the Indian will not "work for a living." There remains a small portion, about 31,000, that are entirely subsisted by the Government.

* From Helen Hunt Jackson, *A Century of Dishonor* (New York, 1881).

There is not among these three hundred bands of Indians one which has not suffered cruelly at the hands either of the Government or of white settlers. The poorer, the more insignificant, the more helpless the band, the more certain the cruelty and outrage to which they have been subjected. This is especially true of the bands on the Pacific slope. These Indians found themselves of a sudden surrounded by and caught up in the great influx of gold-seeking settlers, as helpless creatures on a shore are caught up in a tidal wave. There was not time for the Government to make treaties; not even time for communities to make laws. The tale of the wrongs, the oppressions, the murders of the Pacific-slope Indians in the last thirty years would be a volume by itself, and is too monstrous to be believed.

It makes little difference, however, where one opens the record of the history of the Indians; every page and every year has its dark stain. The story of one tribe is the story of all, varied only by differences of time and place; but neither time nor place makes any difference in the main facts. Colorado is as greedy and unjust in 1880 as was Georgia in 1830, and Ohio in 1795; and the United States Government breaks promises now as deftly as then, and with an added ingenuity from long practice.

One of its strongest supports in so doing is the wide-spread sentiment among the people of dislike to the Indian, of impatience with his presence as a "barrier to civilization" and distrust of it as a possible danger. The old tales of the frontier life, with its horrors of Indian warfare, have gradually, by two or three generations' telling, produced in the average mind something like an hereditary instinct of questioning and unreasoning aversion which it is almost impossible to dislodge or soften....

President after president has appointed commission after commission to inquire into and report upon Indian affairs, and to make suggestions as to the best methods of managing them. The reports are filled with eloquent statements of wrongs done to the Indians, of perfidies on the part of the Government; they counsel, as earnestly as words can, a trial of the simple and unperplexing expedients of telling truth, keeping promises, making fair bargains, dealing justly in all ways and all things. These reports are bound up with the Government's Annual Reports, and that is the end of them....

The history of the Government connections with the Indians is a shameful record of broken treaties and unfulfilled promises. The history of the border white man's connection with the Indians is a sickening record of murder, outrage, robbery, and wrongs committed by the former, as the rule, and occasional savage outbreaks and unspeakably barbarous deeds of retaliation by the latter, as the exception.

Taught by the Government that they had rights entitled to respect, when those rights have been assailed by the rapacity of the white man, the arm which should have been raised to protect them has ever been ready to sustain the aggressor.

The testimony of some of the highest military officers of the United States is on record to the effect that, in our Indian wars, almost without exception, the first aggressions have been made by the white man....Every crime committed by a white man against an Indian is concealed and palliated. Every offense committed by an Indian against a white man is borne on the wings of the post or the telegraph to the remotest corner of the land, clothed with all the horrors which the reality or imagination can throw around it. Against such influences as these are the people of the United States need to be warned.

To assume that it would be easy, or by any one sudden stroke of legislative policy possible, to undo the mischief and hurt of the long past, set the Indian policy of the country right for the future, and make the Indians at once safe and happy, is the blunder of a hasty and uninformed judgment. The notion which seems to be growing more prevalent, that simply to make all Indians at once citizens of the United States would be a sovereign and instantaneous panacea for all their ills and all the Government's perplexities, is a very inconsiderate one. To administer complete citizenship of a sudden, all round, to all Indians, barbarous and civilized alike, would be as grotesque a blunder as to dose them all round with any one medicine, irrespective of the symptoms and needs of their diseases. It would kill more than it would cure. Nevertheless, it is true, as was well stated by one of the superintendents of Indian Affairs in 1857, that, "so long as they are not citizens of the United States, their rights of property must remain insecure against invasion. The doors of the federal tribunals being barred against them while wards and dependents, they can only partially exercise the rights of free government, or give to those who make, execute, and construe the few laws they are allowed to enact, dignity sufficient to make them respectable. While they continue individually to gather the crumbs that fall from the table of the United States, idleness, improvidence, and indebtedness will be the rule, and industry, thrift, and freedom from debt the exception. The utter absence of individual title to particular lands deprives every one among them of the chief incentive to labor and exertion—the very mainspring on which the prosperity of a people depends."

All judicious plans and measures for their safety and salvation must embody provisions for their becoming citizens as fast as they are fit, and must protect them till then in every right and particular in which our laws protect other "persons" who are not citizens....

However great perplexity and difficulty there may be in the details of any and every plan possible for doing at this late day anything like justice to the Indian, however, hard it may be for good statesmen and good men to agree upon the things that ought to be done, there certainly is, or ought to be, no perplexity whatever, on difficulty whatever, in agreeing upon certain things that ought not to be done, and which must cease to be done before the first steps can be taken toward righting the wrongs, curing the ills, and wiping out the disgrace to us of the present conditions of our Indians.

Cheating, robbing, breaking promises—these three are clearly things which must cease to be done. One more thing, also, and that is the refusal of the protection of the law to the Indian's rights of property, "of life, liberty, and the pursuit of happiness."

When these four things have ceased to be done, time, statesmanship, philanthropy, and Christianity can slowly and surely do the rest. Till these four things have ceased to be done, statesmanship and philanthropy alike must work in vain, and even Christianity can reap but small harvest.

DOCUMENT ANALYSIS

1. What examples does Jackson provide about the unpleasant history of the U.S. government in its dealings with Native Americans?

2. What assumptions does Jackson make about Native American character? Is Jackson convincing in arguing that individual property rights would help to bring "salvation" to the Indians?

Seventeen.2

Frederick Jackson Turner, "The Significance of the Frontier in American History" (1893)

Frederick Jackson Turner was one of a new group of professionally trained historians (he had been trained at Johns Hopkins). His essay argued the colonization of the American West formed the American character. His thesis was often used to describe the necessity of American expansion beyond the Pacific Ocean.

Up to our own day American history has been in a large degree the history of the colonization of the Great West. The existence of an area of free land, continuous recession, and the advance of American settlements westward, explain American development.

Behind institutions, behind constitutional forms and modifications lie the vital forces that call these organs into life and shape them to meet changing conditions. The peculiarity of American institutions is, the fact that they have been compelled to adapt themselves to the changes of an expanding people—to the changes involved in crossing a continent, this winning a wilderness, and in developing at each area of this progress out of the primitive economic and political conditions of the frontier into the complexity of city life....

Thus American development has exhibited not merely advance along a single line, but a return to primitive conditions on a continually advancing frontier line, and a new development for that area. American social development has been continually beginning over again on the frontier. This perennial rebirth, this fluidity of American life, this expansion westward with its new opportunities, its continuous touch with the simplicity of primitive society, furnish the forces dominating American character. The true point of view in the history of this nation is not the Atlantic coast, it is the West....

* From Frederick Jackson Turner, *The Frontier in American History* (New York: Henry Holt and Company, 1921).

The frontier is the line of most rapid and effective Americanization. The wilderness masters the colonist. It finds him a European in dress, industries, tools, modes of travel, and thought. It takes him from the railroad car and puts him in the birch canoe. It strips off the garments of civilization and arrays him in the hunting shirt and the moccasin. It puts him in the log cabin of the Cherokee and Iroquois and runs and Indian palisade around him. Before long he has gone to planting Indian corn and plowing with a sharp stick; he shouts the war cry and takes the scalp in orthodox Indian fashion. In short, at the frontier the environment is at first too strong for the man. He must accept the conditions which it furnishes, or perish, and so he fits himself into the Indian clearings and follows the Indian trails. Little by little he transforms the wilderness but the outcome is not the old Europe, not simply the development of Germanic germs, any more than the first phenomenon was a case of reversion to the Germanic mark. The fact is, that here is a new product that is American. At first, the frontier was the Atlantic coast. It was the frontier of Europe in a very real sense. Moving westward, the frontier became more and more American. As successive terminal moraines result from successive glaciations, so each frontier leaves its traces behind it, and when it becomes a settled area the region still partakes of the frontier characteristics. Thus the advance of the frontier has meant a steady movement away from the influence of Europe, a steady growth of independence on American lines. And to study this advance, the men who grew up under these conditions, and the political, economic, and social results of its, is to study the really American part of our history....

Since the days when the fleet of Columbus sailed into the waters of the New World, America has been another name for opportunity, and the people of the United States have taken their tone from the incessant expansion which has not only been open but has been forced upon them. He would be a rash prophet who should assert that the expansive character has now entirely ceased. Movement has been its dominant fact, and unless this training has no effect upon a people, the American energy will continually demand a wider field for its exercise. But never again will such gifts of free land offer themselves. For a moment, at the frontier, the bonds of custom are broken and unrestraint is triumphant. There is not *tabula rasa*. The stubborn American environment is there with its imperious summons to accept its conditions; the inherited ways of doing things are also there; and yet, in spite of environment, and in spite of custom, each frontier did indeed furnish a new field of opportunity, a gate of escape from the bondage of the past; and freshness and confidence, and scorn of older society, impatience of its restrains and its ideas, and indifference to its lessons, have accompanied the frontier. What the Mediterranean Sea was to the Greeks, breaking the bond of custom, offering new experiences, calling out new institutions and activities, that, and more, the ever retreating frontier has been to the United States directly, and to the nations of Europe more remotely. And now, four centuries from the discovery of America, at the end of a hundred years of life under the Constitution, the frontier has gone, and with its going has closed the first period in American history.

DOCUMENT ANALYSIS

1. What significance does Turner give to the frontier in shaping American history? Is he convincing in his analysis?

2. How does Turner's thesis compare to the notion of "manifest destiny"?

Chapter Study Questions

1. Compare Jackson's and Turner's descriptions of America at this time. What role does the frontier play in each description?
2. How would Native Americans view the validity of Turner's thesis on the significance of the frontier in American history?

Eighteen

The Industrial Society

R apid industrial expansion in the last quarter of the nineteenth century led to an explosion of economic growth, which in turn dramatically reshaped American society. By the end of the century the United States had become the foremost industrial power in the world and had transformed itself from an agrarian, homogeneous society into an urban, industrial, and heterogeneous power. The new America delivered prosperity and progress for some citizens, but many others never reaped the rewards of change. This chapter examines both sides of the transformation of American society.

During this period a group of businessmen rose to prominence—men like Andrew Carnegie, John D. Rockefeller, and J. Pierpont Morgan—and enormous money and power were concentrated in their hands. Using shrewd business techniques, including monopolies and trusts, they built up personal fortunes and corporations that dominated the national economy. In "The Gospel of Wealth," Andrew Carnegie, a steel magnate and the nation's most famous rags-to-riches story, provided a rationale for the accumulation and distribution of wealth.

The cult of success was quite strong in the late nineteenth century. Popular novels, such as those by Horatio Alger, told of earnest characters who rose to wealth and success by luck and pluck. The notion that everyone should seize the opportunity to strike it rich was championed in the popular lecture "Acres of Diamonds," by Rev. Russell Conwell, the founder of Temple University in Philadelphia. Unlike the more radical members of the Social Gospel movement at the turn of the twentieth century, Conwell believed wealth was ennobling and a duty and he delivered his lecture over 6,000 times to enthusiastic audiences.

The Knights of Labor was one of the earliest national attempts to unite workers together into one union. The Preamble to the Constitution of the Knights of Labor is included in this chapter. Peaking in the 1880s, the Knights of Labor brought skilled and unskilled workers together, often extended its membership to women and African

Americans, and sought broad social reforms to improve the lives of the middle class. In all of these ways, the Knights of Labor differed from a rival labor organization founded in the 1880s, the American Federation of Labor, or AFL. The AFL concentrated on skilled, white, male workers, and sought more limited goals: higher wages, shorter hours, and better working conditions. The AFL would prove far more adaptive to the American economic climate, while the Knights of Labor would falter and fade away.

In this era of industrialization, Asians were the focus of incredible nativistic hostility. Though it was thanks to Chinese workers that the transcontinental railroad was completed in 1869, native-born American workers felt threatened by their presence. Mobs attacked Chinese workers on the West Coast, and their immigration was cut off in the Chinese Exclusion Act of 1882.

Eighteen.1

Andrew Carnegie, from "The Gospel of Wealth" (1889)

Written in 1889 for The North American Review, *this piece justified the fortunes made by industrialists like Carnegie and provided a model for the distribution of their wealth. Carnegie believed laissez-faire economics were tied to social responsibility. Carnegie was born in Scotland and worked in the United States as a messenger for Western Union and a bobbin boy before, through shrewd salesmanship and investment, he became the head of Carnegie Steel Company, which, after it was sold to J. P. Morgan, became United States Steel.**

The problem of our age is the proper administration of wealth, that the ties of brother-hood may still bind together the rich and poor in harmonious relationship. The conditions of human life have not only been changed, but revolutionized, within the past few hundred years. In former days there was little difference between the dwelling, dress, food, and environment of the chief and those of his retainers....The contrast between the palace of the millionaire and the cottage of the laborer with us to-day measures the change which has come with civilization. This change, however, is not to be deplored, but welcomed as highly beneficial. It is well, say, essential, for the progress of the race that the houses of some should be homes for all that is highest and best in literature and the arts, and for all the refinements of civilization, rather than that none should be so. Much better this great irregularity than universal squalor. Without wealth there can be no Meccenas.

...to-day the world obtains commodities of excellent quality at prices which even the preceding generation would have deemed incredible. In the commercial world similar causes have produced similar results, and the race is benefited thereby. The poor enjoy what the rich could not before afford. What were the luxuries have become the neces-saries of life....

Objections to the foundations upon which society is based are not in order, because the condition of the race is better with these than it has been with any other which has

---

* From Andrew Carnegie, "Wealth," *North American Review*, 1889.

been tried....No evil, but good, has come to the race from the accumulation of wealth by those who have had the ability and energy to produce it....

We start, then, with a condition of affairs under which the best interests of the race are promoted, but which inevitably gives wealth to the few....What is the proper mode of administering wealth after the laws upon which civilization is founded have thrown it into the hands of the few?...

There are but three modes in which surplus wealth can be disposed of. It can be left to the families of the decedents; or it can be bequeathed for public purposes; or, finally, it can be administered by its possessors during their lives....

There remains, then, only one mode of suing great fortunes; but in this we have the true antidote for the temporary unequal distribution of wealth, the reconciliation of the rich and the poor—a reign of harmony, another ideal, differing, indeed, from that of the Communist in requiring only the further evolution of existing conditions, not the total overthrow of our civilization. It is founded upon the most intense Individualism.
...Under its sway we shall have an ideal State, in which the surplus wealth of the few will become, in the best sense, property of the many, because administering for the common good; and this wealth, passes through the hands of the few, can be made much more potent force for the elevation of our race than if distributed in small sums to the people themselves. Even the poorest can be made to see this, and to agree that great sums gathered by some of their fellow-citizens—spent for public purposes, from which masses reap the principal benefit, are more valuable to them than if scattered among themselves in trifling amounts through the course of many years.

If we consider the results which flow from the Cooper Institute, for instance..., and compare these with those who would have ensured for the good of the man form an equal sum distributed by Mr. Cooper in his lifetime in the form of wages, which the highest form of distributing, being work done and not for charity, we can estimate of the possibilities for the improvement of the race which lie embedded in the present law of the accumulation of wealth....

This, then, is held to be the duty of the man of wealth: To set an example of modest, unostentatious living, shunning display or extravagance; to provide moderately for the legitimate wants of those dependent upon him; and, after doing so, to consider all surplus revenues which come to him simply as trust funds, which he is called upon to administer, and strictly bound as a matter of duty to administer in the manner which, in his judgment, is best calculated to produce the most beneficial results for the community—the man of wealth thus becoming the mere trustee and agent for his poorer brethren, bringing to their service his superior wisdom, experience, and ability to administer, doing for them better than they would or could do for them selves....

In bestowing charity, the main consideration should be to help those who will help themselves; to provide part of the means by which those who desire to improve may do so; to give those who desire to rise the aids by which they may rise; to assist, but rarely or never to do all. Neither the individual nor the race is improved by alms giving. Those worthy of assistance, except in rare cases, seldom require assistance....

The rich man is thus almost restricted to following the examples of Peter Cooper, Enoch Pratt of Baltimore, Mr. Pratt of Brooklyn, Senator Stanford, and others, who know that the best means of benefiting the community is to place within its reach the ladders upon which the aspiring can rise—free libraries, parks, and means of recreation, by which men are helped in body and mind; works of art, certain to give pleasure and improve the general condition of the people; in this manner returning their surplus wealth to the mass of their fellows in the forms best calculated to do them lasting good.

Thus is the problem of rich and poor to be solved. The laws of accumulation will be left free, the laws of distribution free. Individualism will continue, but the millionaire will be but a trustee for the poor, intrusted for a season with a great part of the increased wealth of the community, but administering it for the community far better than if could or would have done for itself. The best minds will thus have reached a stage in the development of the race in which it is clearly seen that there is no mode of disposing of surplus wealth creditable to thoughtful and earnest men into whose hands it flows, save by using it year by year for the general good....

Such, in my opinion, is the true gospel concerning wealth, obedience to which is destined some day to solve the problem of the rich and the poor, and to bring "Peace on earth, among men good will."

Document Analysis

1. What does Andrew Carnegie assert to be the duty of the "man of wealth"? Does Carnegie's formula seem practical?

2. Does Carnegie's "Gospel of Wealth" promote or inhibit democratic opportunity?

Eighteen.2

Russell Conwell, from "Acres of Diamonds" (1915)

Russell H. Conwell (1843–1925) was, over the course of his interesting career, a journalist, a lawyer, an ordained minister, and the founder of Temple University in Philadelphia. Conwell's greatest renown, however, came from giving the same speech over 6,000 times. The speech was titled "Acres of Diamonds," and it built on a tale supposedly told to him in the Middle East when he took a tour of the world in the 1870s. A successful Persian farmer had supposedly been lured away from his home by the promise of distant riches, only to die alone and broke, and with "acres of diamonds" discovered on his own farm that he had abandoned. Conwell used the moral of this story to encourage everyone to take advantage of the opportunities around them in the United States to make themselves rich. *

I say you ought to be rich; you have no right to be poor. To live in Philadelphia and not be rich is a misfortune, and it is doubly a misfortune, because you could have been rich just as well as be poor. Philadelphia furnishes so many opportunities. You ought to be rich. But persons with certain religious prejudice will ask, "How can you spend your time advising the rising generation to give their time to getting money—dollars and cents—the commercial spirit?"

Yet I must say that you ought to spend time getting rich. You and I know there are some things more valuable than money; of course, we do. Ah, yes! By a heart made unspeakably sad by a grave on which the autumn leaves now fall, I know there are some things higher and grander and sublimer than money. Well does the man know, who has suffered, that there are some things sweeter and holier and more sacred than gold. Nevertheless, the man of common sense also knows that there is not any one of those things that is not greatly enhanced by the use of money. Money is power.

---

* From Russell H. Conwell, "Acres of Diamonds" (New York: Harper & Brothers, 1915). Accessible online at www.temple.edu/about/temples_founder/acres_text.html.

Love is the grandest thing on God's earth, but fortunate the lover who has plenty of money. Money is power: money has powers; and for a man to say, "I do not want money," is to say, "I do not wish to do any good to my fellowmen." It is absurd thus to talk. It is absurd to disconnect them. This is a wonderfully great life, and you ought to spend your time getting money, because of the power there is in money. And yet this religious prejudice is so great that some people think it is a great honor to be one of God's poor. I am looking in the faces of people who think just that way.

I heard a man once say in a prayer-meeting that he was thankful that he was one of God's poor, and then I silently wondered what his wife would say to that speech, as she took in washing to support the man while he sat and smoked on the veranda. I don't want to see any more of that kind of God's poor. Now, when a man could have been rich just as well, and he is now weak because he is poor, he has done some great wrong; he has been untruthful to himself; he has been unkind to his fellowmen. We ought to get rich if we can by honorable and Christian methods, and these are the only methods that sweep us quickly toward the goal of riches....

I think the best thing for me to do is to illustrate this, for if I say you ought to get rich, I ought, at least, to suggest how it is done. We get a prejudice against rich men because of the lies that are told about them. The lies that are told about Mr. Rockefeller because he has two hundred million dollars—so many believe them; yet how false is the representation of that man to the world. How little we can tell what is true nowadays when newspapers try to sell their papers entirely on some sensation! The way they lie about the rich men is something terrible, and I do not know that there is anything to illustrate this better than what the newspapers now say about the city of Philadelphia....

In our city especially, there are great opportunities for manufacturing, and the time has come when the line is drawn very sharply between the stockholders of the factory and their employees. Now, friends, there has also come a discouraging gloom upon this country and the laboring men are beginning to feel that they are being held down by a crust over their heads through which they find it impossible to break, and the aristocratic moneyowner himself is so far above that he will never descend to their assistance. That is the thought that is in the minds of our people. But, friends, never in the history of our country was there an opportunity so great for the poor man to get rich as there is now and in the city of Philadelphia. The very fact that they get discouraged is what prevents them from getting rich. That is all there is to it. The road is open, and let us keep it open between the poor and the rich.

I know that the labor unions have two great problems to contend with, and there is only one way to solve them. The labor unions are doing as much to prevent its solving as are capitalists today, and there are positively two sides to it. The labor union has two difficulties; the first one is that it began to make a labor scale for all classes on a par, and they scale down a man that can earn five dollars a day to two and a half a day, in order to level up to him an imbecile that cannot earn fifty cents a day. That is one of the most dangerous and discouraging things for the working man. He cannot get the results of his work if he do better work or higher work or work longer; that is a dangerous thing, and in order to get every laboring man free and every American equal to every other American, let the laboring man ask what he is worth and get it—not let any capitalist say to him: "You shall work for me for half of what you are worth"; nor let any labor organization say: "You shall work for the capitalist for half your worth."

Be a man, be independent, and then shall the laboring man find the roar ever open from poverty to wealth.

The other difficulty that the labor union has to consider, and this problem they have to solve themselves, is the kind of orators who come and talk to them about the oppressive rich. I can in my dreams recite the oration I have heard again and again under such circumstances. My life has been with the laboring man. I am a laboring man myself. I have often, in their assemblies, heard the speech of the man who has been invited to address the labor union. The man gets up before the assembled company of honest laboring men and he begins by saying: "Oh, ye honest, industrious laboring men, who have furnished all the capital of the world, who have built all the palaces and constructed all the railroads and covered the ocean with her steamships. Oh, you laboring men! You are nothing but slaves; you are ground down in the dust by the capitalist who is gloating over you as he enjoys his beautiful estates and as he has his banks filled with gold, and every dollar he owns is coined out of the heart's blood of the honest laboring man." Now, that is a lie, and you know it is a lie; and yet that is the kind of speech that they are hearing all the time, representing the capitalists as wicked and the laboring man so enslaved.

Why, how wrong it is! Let the man who loves his flag and believes in American principles endeavor with all his soul to bring the capitalists and the laboring man together until they stand side by side, and arm in arm, and work for the common good of humanity....

DOCUMENT ANALYSIS

1. How does Conwell respond to those who view poverty as a sign of moral or religious superiority?

2. What criticisms does Conwell make of labor unions of his era? How does his attitude toward labor unions compare to his remarks about the oil millionaire John D. Rockefeller?

Eighteen.3

Terence V. Powderly, Preamble to the Constitution of the Knights of Labor (1878)

The Knights of Labor began as a secret organization, dedicated to bringing all workers together into one umbrella national union. This is the Preamble to the organization's constitution, written by Terence Powderly, who later served as the head of the Knights during its peak. It shows how the Knights of Labor had a broader social agenda than its rival, the American Federation of Labor (AFL). The AFL pushed for higher wages, shorter hours, and better working conditions, and tended to avoid broader social reforms. *

The recent alarming development and aggression of aggregated wealth, which, unless checked, will invariably lead to the pauperization and hope less degradation of the toiling masses, render it imperative, if we desire to enjoy the blessings of life, that a check should be placed upon its power and upon unjust accumulation, and a system adopted which will secure to the laborer the fruits of his toil; and as this much-desired object can only be accomplished by the thorough unification of labor, and the united efforts of those who obey the divine injunction that "In the sweat of thy brow shalt thou eat bread," we have formed the ***** with a view of securing the organization and direction, by co-operative effort, of the power of the industrial classes; and we submit to the world the object sought to be accomplished by our organization, calling upon all who believe in securing "the greatest good to the greatest number" to aid and assist us:—

I. To bring within the folds of organization every department of productive industry, making knowledge a standpoint for action, and industrial and moral worth, not wealth, the true standard of individual and national greatness.

II. To secure to the toilers a proper share of the wealth that they create; more of the leisure that rightfully belongs to them; more societary advantages; more of the benefits, privileges, and emoluments of the world; in a word, all those rights and privileges nec-

* From Terence V. Powderly, *Thirty Years of Labor, 1859–1889* (Philadelphia: T.V. Powderly, 1890).

essary to make them capable of enjoying, appreciating, defending, and perpetuating the blessing of good government.

III. To arrive at the true condition of the producing masses in their educational, moral, and financial condition, by demanding from the various governments the establishment of bureaus of Labor Statistics.

IV. The establishment of co-operative institutions, productive and distributive.

V. The reserving of the public lands—the heritage of the people—for the actual settler;—not another acre for railroads or speculators.

VI. The abrogation of all laws that do not bear equally upon capital and labor, the removal of unjust technicalities, delays, and discriminations in the administration of justice, and the adopting of measures providing for the health and safety of those engaged in mining, manufacturing, or building pursuits.

VII. The enactment of laws to compel chartered corporations to pay their employees weekly, in full, for labor performed during the preceding week, in the lawful money of the country.

VIII. The enactment of laws giving mechanics and laborers a first lien on their work for their full wages.

IX. The abolishment of the contract system on national, state, and municipal work.

X. The substitution of arbitration for strikes, whenever and wherever employers and employees are willing to meet on equitable grounds.

XI. The prohibition of the employment of children in workshops, mines, and factories before attaining their fourteenth year.

XII. To abolish the system of letting out by contract the labor of convicts in our prisons and reformatory institutions.

XIII. To secure for both sexes equal pay for equal work.

XIV. The reduction of the hours of labor to eight per day, so that the laborers may have more time for social enjoyment and intellectual improvement, and be enabled to reap the advantages conferred by the labor-saving machinery which their brains have created.

XV. To prevail upon governments to establish a purely national circulating medium, based upon the faith and resources of the nation, and issued directly to the people, without the intervention of any system of banking corporations, which money shall be a legal tender in payment of all debts, public or private.

DOCUMENT ANALYSIS

1. What are the key goals set forth by the Knights of Labor in this preamble to their constitution? Which of these goals seem the least radical today?

Eighteen.4

Chinese Exclusion Act
(1882)

A major influx of Chinese immigrants in the 1850s, 1860s, and 1870s created a backlash, especially in the western United States. Drawn to the United States to work building railroads, mining ore, or serving as domestic servants, the Chinese immigrants were overwhelmingly male, lived in their own tight-knit communities, dressed distinctively, and observed their own cultural traditions—all of which made whites suspicious. Moreover, the Chinese were known as reliable workers who usually accepted lower wages than their non-Chinese counterparts. Resentment over their role in depressing wages, distrust of their culture, and fear of additional Chinese arrivals led politicians, labor leaders, and journalists in western states to pressure the federal government. Congress responded in 1882, enacting the Chinese Exclusion Act. It was the first immigration law that singled out a specific ethnic group for exclusion.*

A n Act to execute certain treaty stipulations relating to Chinese.

Whereas in the opinion of the Government of the United States the coming of Chinese laborers to this country endangers the good order of certain localities within the territory thereof: Therefore,

Be it enacted by the Senate and House of Representatives of the United States of America in Congress assembled, That from and after the expiration of ninety days next after the passage of this act, and until the expiration of ten years next after the passage of this act, the coming of Chinese laborers to the United States be, and the same is hereby, suspended; and during such suspension it shall not be lawful for any Chinese laborer to come, or having so come after the expiration of said ninety days to remain within the United States.

* From 47 Congress, Session I, 1882, Chapter 26, accessible online at http://www.ourdocuments.gov/doc.php?doc=47.

SEC. 2. That the master of any vessel who shall knowingly bring within the United States on such vessel, and land or permit to be landed, any Chinese laborer, from any foreign port or place, shall be deemed guilty of a misdemeanor, and on conviction thereof shall be punished by a fine of not more than five hundred dollars for each and every such Chinese laborer so brought, and maybe also imprisoned for a term not exceeding one year.

SEC. 3. That the two foregoing sections shall not apply to Chinese laborers who were in the United States on the seventeenth day of November, eighteen hundred and eighty,...

SEC. 4. That for the purpose of properly identifying Chinese laborers who were in the United States on the seventeenth day of November eighteen hundred and eighty, or who shall have come into the same before the expiration of ninety days next after the passage of this act, and in order to furnish them with the proper evidence of their right to go from and come to the United States of their free will and accord, as provided by the treaty between the United States and China dated November seventeenth, eighteen hundred and eighty, the collector of customs of the district from which any such Chinese laborer shall depart from the United States shall, in person or by deputy, go on board each vessel having on board any such Chinese laborers and cleared or about to sail from his district for a foreign port, and on such vessel make a list of all such Chinese laborers, which shall be entered in registry-books to be kept for that purpose, in which shall be stated the name, age, occupation, last place of residence, physical marks of peculiarities, and all facts necessary for the identification of each of such Chinese laborers, which books shall be safely kept in the custom-house; and every such Chinese laborer so departing from the United States shall be entitled to, and shall receive, free of any charge or cost upon application therefor, from the collector or his deputy, at the time such list is taken, a certificate, signed by the collector or his deputy and attested by his seal of office, in such form as the Secretary of the Treasury shall prescribe, which certificate shall contain a statement of the name, age, occupation, last place of residence, persona description, and facts of identification of the Chinese laborer to whom the certificate is issued, corresponding with the said list and registry in all particulars....

SEC. 6. That in order to the faithful execution of articles one and two of the treaty in this act before mentioned, every Chinese person other than a laborer who may be entitled by said treaty and this act to come within the United States, and who shall be about to come to the United States, shall be identified as so entitled by the Chinese Government in each case, such identity to be evidenced by a certificate issued under the authority of said government, which certificate shall be in the English language or (if not in the English language) accompanied by a translation into English, stating such right to come, and which certificate shall state the name, title or official rank, if any, the age, height, and all physical peculiarities, former and present occupation or profession, and place of residence in China of the person to whom the certificate is issued and that such person is entitled, conformably to the treaty in this act mentioned to come within the United States. Such certificate shall be prima-facie evidence of the fact set forth therein, and shall be produced to the collector of customs, or his deputy, of the port in the district in the United States at which the person named therein shall arrive.

SEC. 7. That any person who shall knowingly and falsely alter or substitute any name for the name written in such certificate or forge any such certificate, or knowingly utter any forged or fraudulent certificate, or falsely personate any person named in any such certificate, shall be deemed guilty of a misdemeanor; and upon conviction thereof shall be fined in a sum not exceeding one thousand dollars, and imprisoned in a penitentiary for a term of not more than five years....

SEC. 12. That no Chinese person shall be permitted to enter the United States by land without producing to the proper officer of customs the certificate in this act required of Chinese persons seeking to land from a vessel....

SEC. 13. That this act shall not apply to diplomatic and other officers of the Chinese Government traveling upon the business of that government, whose credentials shall be taken as equivalent to the certificate in this act mentioned, and shall exempt them and their body and household servants from the provisions of this act as to other Chinese persons.

SEC. 14. That hereafter no State court or court of the United States shall admit Chinese to citizenship; and all laws in conflict with this act are hereby repealed.

SEC. 15. That the words "Chinese laborers", wherever used in this act shall be construed to mean both skilled and unskilled laborers and Chinese employed in mining.

Approved, May 6, 1882.

DOCUMENT ANALYSIS

1. The Chinese Exclusion Act opens with a rationale for why this legislation was deemed necessary. What was it?
2. What does the act specify about Chinese becoming U.S. citizens in the future?

Chapter Study Questions

1. Why do Carnegie and Conwell celebrate the pursuit of wealth as noble? Are they persuasive?

2. What could have motivated the passage of the Chinese Exclusion Act, or any such act which specifically targeted an immigrant group?

3. Do you find anything in the Preamble to the Constitution of the Knights of Labor which would indicate it would be unable to survive as the AFL did?

Nineteen

Toward an Urban Society, 1877–1900

I n the years between the end of Reconstruction and the turn of the century, America's move toward industrialization and urbanization was not easy. Immigrants and African Americans faced discrimination and racism; "nationalism" grew increasingly important to some native-born Americans; and people sought various ways to address the inherent problems which arose during this transitional period.

Edward Bellamy's best-selling *Looking Backward: 2000–1887* described a utopia in the year 2000, where, under the direction of the national government, all people lived in prosperity and had an equal share in a new society. Although his utopia was similar in many ways to socialism, Bellamy called his utopian system "nationalism"—appealing to the new nationalism of industrializing and imperialistic America. Bellamy's book was a huge success; its publisher, Houghton Mifflin, proudly proclaimed, "Of only one other book have 300,000 copies been printed within two years of its publication." (*Uncle Tom's Cabin* was the other.) *Looking Backward* furthermore inspired the formation of over 150 Nationalist Clubs throughout the country, their purpose being to turn Bellamy's ideas into reality.

While the South slowly recovered from the Civil War much of its population remained marginalized, none more so than former slaves who lived under the yoke of overt prejudice, poverty, and institutionalized segregation. Already shaped by slavery, relations between whites and African Americans deteriorated further in the years following the Civil War. Lynchings were commonplace, while Jim Crow laws legislating segregation blanketed the South. In 1896, the Supreme Court declared in *Plessy v. Ferguson* that "separate but equal" facilities for the races did not violate the Fourteenth Amendment's clause mandating equal protection under the law for all citizens.

The African American community had divergent responses to these developments. Booker T. Washington, a former slave and the founder of the Tuskegee Institute in Alabama, argued that African Americans would only make their way to freedom and success through hard work and self-help. In his Atlanta Exposition address, reprinted here,

Washington declared his loyalty to the Southern economic system and his acceptance of the status of African Americans. His speech was well received by its white audience.

W. E. B. Du Bois was a Massachusetts-raised African American who had received his Ph.D. from Harvard University and was one of the founders of the National Association for the Advancement of Colored People (NAACP). Du Bois argued that African Americans needed to fight to win equal justice, that an educated black elite (the "talented tenth") should lead blacks (in the United States and in Africa) to freedom, and that Booker T. Washington's accommodation strategy set back the African American cause.

Between 1860 and 1920, more than 25 million hopeful immigrants arrived in the United States, drawn by the promise of opportunity, the growing American economy's need for cheap labor, and economic instability in Europe and Asia. Along with many rural Americans they flocked to cities like New York, Chicago, Pittsburgh, and St. Louis. These immigrants arriving on American shores provided a stark contrast to those who had preceded them in the earlier part of the century: The "old" immigration, prior to 1890, was from northern and western Europe—places like England, Germany, Sweden, and Ireland; the "new" immigrants came from eastern and southern Europe—places like Russia, Poland, Italy, and Greece—as well as other lands including China and Mexico. These new immigrants, often unskilled workers and in many cases temporary, settled in urban neighborhoods and profoundly transformed the American city.

Asian immigrants, mostly Chinese men working on the railroad, were concentrated on the West Coast and had already faced the kind of discrimination which had led to the passage of the Chinese Exclusion Act. But increasingly, Asians, like Lee Chew in this chapter, made their way to East Coast urban hubs. But all immigrants were at risk for attack, as a wave of nativism swept the United States in the 1880s driven by anti-Catholicism and fear of job loss to newer, cheaper workers. The American Protective Association gained widespread popularity for its anti-Catholic, anti-immigrant stance. Included here is the secret oath of this organization.

Cities were transformed in the late nineteenth century as new transportation technologies—subways, trolleys, and cable cars—expanded the urban environment. New transportation fostered the growth of new residential areas outside the confines of the city proper. With the growth of such suburbs, rich and poor no longer lived side by side. While the rich and the emergent middle class escaped the cities, the poor—overwhelmingly new immigrants and African Americans—were sequestered in neighborhoods filled with crime, substandard services, and disease. The development of these essentially new cities led to a new urban culture and new political systems while the cities' concentrations of poverty inspired new attempts to reform the desperate conditions.

In poor sections of cities like New York, Chicago, and Philadelphia, thousands of families packed into overcrowded tenements. Sanitation was virtually nonexistent, and manure and mud filled city streets while disease—smallpox, diphtheria, and yellow fever—ran rampant. Included here are two descriptions of city life in New York City, one by a New York City Health Commissioner and the other by one of the founders of the Children's Aid Society. These pieces describe not only the horrors of urban life, but also some of the motivations and biases of the reformers, in city government and private charities, who tried to improve the urban environment.

Edward Bellamy, from *Looking Backward* (1888)

Bellamy's Looking Backward *is the story of Julian West, a wealthy young Bostonian who enters a hypnotic sleep in 1887 and awakes 113 years later. In the society to which he awakens, the squalor of Boston's slums has been replaced by "a great city," made up of "miles of broad streets, shaded by trees and lined with fine buildings." The injustice of the nineteenth century's industrial system has given way to a socialist utopia, while its business monopolies evolved into one great trust, taken over by the nation. "Credit cards" gave each citizen an equal share of the goods created by the new society. The collective society eradicated crime, poverty, war, and advertising—all without violence. Less appealing or arduous tasks are filled voluntarily because people filling them work shorter hours and under good conditions. The key to Bellamy's book was its inclusion of most of the reform ideas of his generation and the presentation of a society based on such ideas in a nonthreatening form. The following excerpt describes Julian West before he falls into his sleep and later, having the future described to him by Dr. Leete, his affable guide.**

I myself was rich and also educated, and possessed, therefore, all the elements of happiness enjoyed by the most fortunate in that age. Living in luxury, and occupied only with the pursuit of the pleasures and refinements of life, I derived the means of my support from the labor of others, rendering no sort of service in return. My parents and grand-parents lived in the same way, and I expected that my descendants, if I had any, would enjoy a like easy existence.

...This mystery of use without consumption, of warmth without combustion, seems like magic, but was merely an ingenious application of the art now happily lost but carried to a great perfection by your ancestors, of shifting the burden of one's support on the shoulders of others. The man who had accomplished this, and it was the end all

---

* From E. Bellamy, *Looking Backward* (New York: Modern Library, 1951).

sought, was said to live on the income of his investments....I shall only stop now to say that interest on investments was a species of tax in perpetuity upon the product of those engaged in industry which a person possessing or inheriting money was able to levy....

* * * * *

"I would give a great deal for just one glimpse of the Boston of your day," replied Dr. Leete. "No doubt, as you imply, the cities of that period were rather shabby affairs. If you had the taste to make them splendid, which I would not be so rude as to question, the general poverty resulting from your extraordinary industrial system would not have given you the means. Moreover, the excessive individualism which then prevailed was inconsistent with much public spirit. What little wealth you had seems almost wholly to have been lavished in private luxury. Nowadays, on the contrary, there is no destination of the surplus wealth so popular as the adornment of the city, which all enjoy in equal degree."...

* * * * *

"As no such thing as the labor question is known nowadays," replied Dr. Leete, "and there is no way in which it could arise, I suppose we may claim to have solved it....The solution came as the result of a process of industrial evolution which could not have terminated otherwise. All that society had to do was to recognize and cooperate with that evolution, when its tendency had become unmistakable."...

"Meanwhile, without being in the smallest degree checked by the clamor against it, the absorption of business by ever larger monopolies continued. In the United States there was not, after the beginning of the last quarter of the century, any opportunity whatever for individual enterprise in any important field of industry, unless backed by great capital. During the last decade of the century, such small businesses as still remained were fast-failing survivals of a past epoch....The railroads had gone on combining till a few great syndicates controlled every rail in the land. In manufactories, every important staple was controlled by a syndicate. These syndicates, pools, trusts, or whatever their name, fixed prices and crushed all competition except when combinations as vast as themselves arose. Then a struggle, resulting in still greater consolidation, ensued.

"...The movement toward the conduct of business by larger and larger aggregations of capital, the tendency toward monopolies, which had been so desperately and vainly resisted, was recognized at last, in its true significance, as a process which only needed to complete its logical evolution to open a golden future to humanity.

"Early in the last century the evolution was completed by the final consolidation of the entire capital of the nation. The industry and commerce of the country, ceasing to be conducted by a set of irresponsible corporations and syndicates of private persons at their caprice and for their profit, were intrusted to a single syndicate representing the people, to be conducted in the common interest for the common profit. The nation, that is to say, organized as the one great business corporation in which all other corporations were absorbed...."

DOCUMENT ANALYSIS

1. In Bellamy's utopian society, what has happened to the often haphazard, cut-throat business competition and consolidation of the late nineteenth century?

2. What has happened to individualism in Bellamy's utopian society of the future?

Nineteen.2

From *Plessy v. Ferguson*
(1896)

This infamous court decision upheld the constitutionality of segregation in public accommoda-
tions. The case was brought by Homer A. Plessy, a young mixed-race carpenter from
Louisiana, who challenged a Louisiana law that segregated trains for "the comfort of passen-
gers." Segregation was not common during the Reconstruction and post-Reconstruction periods
of the 1870s and 1880s, but laws like that challenged by Plessy *in Louisiana were passed after*
a Supreme Court ruling in 1883 ruled that private individuals could not be punished for
racial discrimination. *

This case turns upon the constitutionality of an act of the general assembly of the state of Louisiana, passed in 1890, providing for separate railway carriages for the white and colored races....

The constitutionality of this act is attacked upon the ground that it conflicts both with the 13th Amendment of the Constitution, abolishing slavery, and the 14th Amendment, which prohibits certain restrictive legislation on the part of the states.

1. That it does not conflict with the 13th Amendment, which abolished slavery and involuntary servitude, except as a punishment for crime, is too clear for argument....Indeed, we do not understand that the 13th Amendment is strenuously relied upon by the plaintiff....

The object of the [14th] amendment was undoubtedly to enforce the absolute equality of the two races before the law, but in the nature of things it could not have been intended to abolish distinctions based upon color, or to enforce social, as distinguished from political, equality, or a commingling of the two races upon terms unsatisfactory to either. Laws permitting, and even requiring their separation in places where they are liable to be brought into contact do not necessarily imply the inferiority of either race to

---

* From *Plessy v. Ferguson*, Supreme Court, 163, 537 (1896).

the other, and have been generally, if not universally, recognized as within the competency of the state legislatures in the exercise of their police power....

We consider the underlying fallacy of the plaintiff's argument to consist in the assumption that the enforced separation of the two races stamps the colored race with a badge of inferiority. If this be so, it is not by reason of anything found in the act, but solely because the colored race chooses to put that construction upon it....

The argument also assumes that social prejudice may be overcome by legislation, and that equal rights cannot be secured to the Negro except by an enforced commingling of the two races. We cannot accept this proposition. If the two races are to meet on terms of social equality, it must be the result of natural affinities, a mutual appreciation of each other's merits and a voluntary consent of individuals....Legislation is powerless to eradicate racial instincts or abolish distinctions based upon physical differences and the attempt to do so can only result in accentuating the difficulties of the present situation. If the civil and political right of both races be equal, one cannot be inferior to the other civilly or politically. If one race be inferior to the other socially, the Constitution of the United States cannot put them upon the same plane.

DOCUMENT ANALYSIS

1. In its ruling in *Plessy v. Ferguson*, why did the Supreme Court find that segregated trains in Louisiana did not violate the Fourteenth Amendment? Is the court's argument convincing? Explain.

2. How do you think the ruling in this case provided a green light to local and state governments to enact far more segregation laws?

Nineteen.3

Booker T. Washington, Atlanta Exposition Address (1895)

Booker T. Washington, the dominant black leader of the late nineteenth century, believed that blacks needed to accommodate themselves to white prejudices, at least temporarily, and concentrate on self-improvement. Because of these beliefs, he was considered by whites to be a moderate, "reasonable" black leader. But while in public he minimized the importance of civil and political rights, behind the scenes he lobbied against discriminatory measures and financed test cases in the courts. Washington was born a slave and taught himself to read; eventually he worked his way through the Hampton Institute. In 1881, he became the head of the Tuskegee Institute. This document, drawn from a speech delivered by Washington at the Cotton State Exposition of Industry and the Arts is famous for its presentation of the "Atlanta compromise" approach to race relations. The exhibition, held in Atlanta in 1895, was designed to encourage diversification of the Southern economy. The publishers and bankers who organized it invited Washington to address the mostly white gathering almost as an afterthought. Nevertheless, his speech received overwhelming approval, garnering favorable responses from such diverse sources as the editor of the Atlanta Constitution *and President Grover Cleveland.**

. . . Ignorant and inexperienced, it is not strange that in the first years of our new life we began at the top instead of at the bottom; that a seat in Congress or the state legislature was more sought than real estate or industrial skill; that the political convention or stump speaking had more attractions than starting a dairy farm or truck garden.

A ship lost at sea for many days suddenly sighted a friendly vessel. From the mast of the unfortunate vessel was seen a signal, "Water, water; we die of thirst!" The answer from the friendly vessel at once came back, "Cast down your bucket where you

* From Booker T. Washington's Atlanta Exposition Address (1895), reprinted in R. Twornbly, *Blacks in White America Since 1865* (New York: David McKay, 1971).

are."...The captain of the distressed vessel, at last heeding the injunction, cast down his bucket, and it came up full of fresh, sparkling water....To those of my race who underestimate the importance of cultivating friendly relations with the southern white man, who is their next-door neighbor, I would say: "Cast down your bucket where you are"— cast it down in making friends in every manly way of the people of all races by whom we are surrounded.

Cast it down in agriculture, mechanics, in commerce, in domestic service, and in the professions....Our greatest danger is that in the great leap from slavery to freedom we may overlook the fact that the masses of us are to live by the productions of our hands, and fail to keep in mind that we shall prosper in proportion as we learn to dignify and glorify common labour, and put brains and skill into the common occupations of life....No race can prosper till it learns that there is as much dignity in tilling a field as in writing a poem. It is at the bottom of life we must begin, and not at the top.

To those of the white race who look to the incoming of those of foreign birth and strange tongue and habits for the prosperity of the South, were I permitted I would repeat what I say to my own race, "Cast down your bucket where you are." Cast it down among the eight millions of Negroes whose habits you know, whose fidelity and love you have tested in days when to have proved treacherous meant the ruin of your firesides. Cast down your bucket among these people who have, without strikes and labour wars, tilled your fields, cleared your forests, built your railroads and cities, and brought forth treasures from the bowels of the earth....Casting down your bucket among my people...you will find that they will buy your surplus land, make blossom the waste places in your fields, and run your factories. While doing this, you can be sure in the future, as in the past, that you and your families will be surrounded by the most patient, faithful, law-abiding, and unresentful people that the world has seen....In all things that are purely social we can be as separate as the fingers, yet one as the hand in all things essential to mutual progress....

The wisest among my race understand that the agitation of questions of social equality is the extremest folly, and that progress in the enjoyment of all the privileges that will come to us must be the result of severe and constant struggle rather than of artificial forcing. No race that has anything to contribute to the markets of the world is long in any degree ostracized. It is important and right that all privileges of the law be ours, but it is vastly more important that we be prepared for the exercise of these privileges. The opportunity to earn a dollar in a factory just now is worth infinitely more than the opportunity to spend a dollar in an opera-house.

DOCUMENT ANALYSIS

1. What does Booker T. Washington mean by his advice "cast down your bucket where you are"? Do you think this is sound advice?

2. How does Washington appeal to white Southerners in this speech? What do you think white Southerners would have found most appealing about Washington's argument presented here?

Nineteen.4

W. E. B. Du Bois, from "Of Mr. Booker T. Washington and Others" (1903)

W. E. B. Du Bois was a Massachusetts native who received his Ph.D. from Harvard University in 1895 and made a career as a teacher at Atlanta University. He believed that if blacks prepared themselves only to be farmers, mechanics, and domestics, as Booker T. Washington advised, they would remain forever in such occupations. Du Bois was one of the founders of the Niagara Movement and was a founding member of the National Association for the Advancement of Colored People (NAACP) and agitated for political rights and higher education for blacks. This document is from "Of Mr. Booker T. Washington and Others," one of the essays in his The Souls of Black Folk *(1903). In it, Du Bois argues that Washington's approach contributed to the loss of political rights, the erection of caste barriers, and the diversion of funds from academic education for talented blacks.* *

Easily the most striking thing in the history of the American Negro since 1876 is the ascendancy of Mr. Booker T. Washington....His programme of industrial education, conciliation of the South, and submission and silence as to civil and political rights was not wholly original....But Mr. Washington first indissolubly linked these things; he...changed it from a by-path into a veritable Way of Life....

Mr. Washington represents in Negro thought the old attitude of adjustment and submission; but adjustment at such a peculiar time as to make his programme unique. This is an age of unusual economic development, and Mr. Washington's programme naturally takes an economic cast, becoming a gospel of Work and Money to such an extent as apparently almost completely to overshadow the higher aims of life....Mr. Washington's programme practically accepts the alleged inferiority of the Negro races...In the history of nearly all other races and peoples the doctrine preached at such

---

* From W. E. B. Du Bois, "Of Mr. Booker T. Washington and Others" (1903), reprinted in W. E. B. Du Bois, *The Souls of Black Folk* (New York: New American Library, 1969).

crises has been that manly self-respect is worth more than lands and houses, and that a people who voluntarily surrender such respect, or cease striving for it, are not worth civilizing.

...Mr. Washington distinctly asks that black people give up, at least for the present, three things,—

First, political power.

Second, insistence on civil rights.

Third, higher education of Negro youth,

...The question then comes: Is it possible, and probable, that nine millions of men can make effective progress in economic lines if they are deprived of political rights, made a servile caste, and allowed only the most meagre chance for developing their exceptional men? If history and reason give any distinct answer to these questions, it is an emphatic No....

...while it is a great truth to say that the Negro must strive and strive mightily to help himself, it is equally true that unless his striving be not simply seconded, but rather aroused and encouraged, by the initiative of the richer and wiser environing group, he cannot hope for great success.

...So far as Mr. Washington preaches Thrift, Patience, and Industrial Training for the masses, we must hold up his hands and strive with him, rejoicing in his honors and glorying in the strength of this Joshua called of God and of man to lead the headless host. But so far as Mr. Washington apologizes for injustice, North or South, does not rightly value the privilege and duty of voting, belittles the emasculating effects of caste distinctions, and opposes the higher training and ambition of our brighter minds,—so far as he, the South, or the Nation, does this, we must unceasingly and firmly oppose them.

DOCUMENT ANALYSIS

1. What does Du Bois find appealing and unappealing in Booker T. Washington's message to African Americans in this era?

Lee Chew, from *Life of a Chinese Immigrant* (1903)

The next selection is from a biography of a Chinese immigrant commissioned by the reformist journal The Independent. *Note that Chew arrived in the United States before the Chinese Exclusion Act of 1882, and was therefore dictating this as a middle-aged man. Chew was involved in many of the jobs associated with Chinese immigrants during this period—mining, laundry, and railroad construction.** *

The village where I was born is situated in the province of Canton, on one of the banks of the Si-Kiang River. It is called a village, altho it is really as big as a city, for there are about 5,000 men in it over eighteen years of age—women and children and even youths are not counted in our villages....

...I heard about the American foreign devils, that they were false, having made a treaty by which it was agreed that they could freely come to China, and the Chinese as freely go to their country. After this treaty was made China opened its doors to them and then they broke the treaty that they had asked for by shutting the Chinese out or their country....

The man had gone away from our village a poor boy. Now he returned with unlimited wealth, which he had obtained in the country of the American wizards. After many amazing adventures he had become a merchant in a city called Mott Street, so it was said....

Having made his wealth among the barbarians this man had faithfully returned to pour it out among his tribesmen, and he is living in our village now very happy, and a pillar of strength to the poor.

The wealth of this man filled my mind with the idea that I, too, would like to go to the country of the wizards and gain some of their wealth, and after a long time my father consented, and gave me his blessing, and my mother took leave of me with tears,

* From *The Independent*, 54 (2818), February 19, 1903, 417–423.

while my grandfather laid his hand upon my head and told me to remember and live up to the admonitions of the Sages, to avoid gambling, bad women and men of evil minds, and so to govern my conduct that when I died my ancestors might rejoice to welcome me as a guest on high.

My father gave me $100, and I went to Hong Kong with five other boys from our place and we got steerage passage on a steamer, paying $50 each....

...Of the great power of these people I saw many signs. The engines that moved the ship were wonderful monsters, strong enough to lift mountains. When I got to San Francisco, which was before the passage of the Exclusion act, I was half starved, because I was afraid to eat the provisions of the barbarians, but a few days' living in the Chinese quarter made me happy again....

The Chinese laundryman does not learn his trade in China; there are no laundries in China....All the Chinese laundrymen here were taught in the first place by American women just as I was taught.

When I went to work for that American family I could not speak a word of English, and I did not know anything about house work. The family consisted of husband, wife and two children. They were very good to me and paid me $3.50 a week, of which I could save $3....

In six months I had learned how to do the work of our house quite well, and I was getting $5 a week and board, and putting away about $4.25 a week. I had also learned some English, and by going to a Sunday school I learned more English and something about Jesus, who was a great Sage, and whose precepts are like those of Kong-foo-tsze.

It was twenty years ago when I came to this country, and I worked for two years as a servant, getting at least $35 a month. I sent money home to comfort my parents....

When I first opened a laundry it was in company with a partner, who had been in the business for some years. We went to a town about 500 miles inland, where a railroad was building. We got a board shanty and worked for the men employed by the railroads....

We were three years with the railroad, and then went to the mines, where we made plenty of money in gold dust, but had a hard time, for many of the miners were wild men who carried revolvers and after drinking would come into our place to shoot and steal shirts, for which we had to pay. One of these men hit his head hard against a flat iron and all the miners came and broke our laundry, chasing us out of town. They were going to hang us. We lost all our property and $365 in money, which a member of the mob must have found.

Luckily most of our money was in the hands of the Chinese bankers in San Francisco. I drew $500 and went east to Chicago, where I had a laundry for three years, during which I increased my capital to $2,500. After that I was four years in Detroit. I went home to China in 1897, but returned in 1898, and began a laundry business in Buffalo.

The ordinary laundry shop is generally divided into three rooms. In front is the room where the customers are received, behind that a bedroom and in the back the work shop, which is also the dining room and kitchen. The stove and cooking utensils are the same as those of the Americans....

I have found out, during my residence in this country, that much of the Chinese prejudice against Americans is unfounded, and I no longer put faith in the wild tales that were told about them in our village, tho some of the Chinese, who have been here twenty years and who are learned men, still believe that there is no marriage in this country, that the land is infested with demons and that all the people are given over to general wickedness.

I know better. Americans are not all bad, nor are they wicked wizards. Still, they have their faults, and their treatment of us is outrageous....

The reason why so many Chinese go into the laundry business in this country is because it requires little capital and is one of the few opportunities that are open....

There is no reason for the prejudice against the Chinese. The cheap labor cry was always a falsehood. Their labor was never cheap, and is not cheap now. It has always commanded and highest market price. But the trouble is that the Chinese are such excellent and faithful workers that bosses will have no others when they can get them. If you look at men working on the street you will find an overseer for every four or five of them. That watching is not necessary for Chinese. They work as well when left to themselves as they do when some one is looking at them....

DOCUMENT ANALYSIS

1. What led Lee Chew to immigrate to the United States? How were Americans perceived by the Chinese in this era?

2. How was Chew able to afford opening a laundry? What does his sacrifice suggest about how immigrants became successful?

Nineteen.6

The Secret Oath
of the American Protective Association
(1893)

The American Protective Association (APA) was one of the largest and most powerful anti-immigrant and anti-Catholic organizations of the late nineteenth century, claiming more than a million members by 1896. Taking its cue and beliefs from anti-Catholic biases perpetuated in Europe since the Inquisition and the Protestant Reformation, it arose, in part, as a nativist response to the large numbers of immigrants from Catholic countries and spread rumors that Catholics intended to slaughter non-Catholics and that Catholic elected officials discriminated against non-Catholic job applicants and citizens.*

I do most solemnly promise and swear that I will always, to the utmost of my ability, labor, plead, and wage a continuous warfare against ignorance and fanaticism; that I will use my utmost power to strike the shackles and chains of blind obedience to the Roman Catholic church from the hampered and bound consciences of a priest-ridden and church-oppressed people; that I will never allow anyone, a member of the Roman Catholic Church, to become a member of this order, I knowing him to be such; that I will use my influence to promote the interest of all Protestants everywhere in the world that I may be; that I will not employ a Roman Catholic in any capacity, if I can procure the services of a Protestant.

I furthermore promise and swear that I will not aid in building or maintaining, by my resources, any Roman Catholic church or institution of their sect or creed whatsoever, but will do all in my power to retard and break down the power of the Pope, in this country or any other; that I will not enter into any controversy with a Roman Catholic upon the subject of this order, nor will I enter into any agreement with a Roman Catholic to strike or create a disturbance whereby the Catholic employees may undermine and substitute their Protestant co-workers; that in all grievances I will seek only

* From *Documents of American Catholic History*, ed. T. Ellis (Wilmington, DE: Michael Glazier, Inc., 1956), 500–501. A Bruce Publishing Company.

Protestants, and counsel with them to the exclusion of all Roman Catholics, and will not make known to them anything of any nature matured at such conferences.

I furthermore promise and swear that I will not countenance the nomination, in any caucus or convention, of a Roman Catholic for any office in the gift of the American people, and that I will not vote for, or counsel others to vote for, any Roman Catholic, but will vote only for a Protestant, so far as may lie in my power (should there be two Roman Catholics in opposite tickets, I will erase the name on the ticker I vote); that I will at all times endeavor to place the political positions of this government in the hands of Protestants, to the entire exclusion of the Roman Catholic Church, of the members thereof, and the mandate of the Pope.

To all of which I do most solemnly promise and swear, so help me God.

Amen.

DOCUMENT ANALYSIS

1. According to the Secret Oath of the APA, what about the Catholic faith seemed to scare the APA the most? Explain.

Nineteen.7

George Waring,
Sanitary Conditions in New York
(1897)

The following is an analysis of conditions in New York City by a New York City sanitation commissioner. Writing in 1897, twenty years after Charles Loring Brace, George Waring argues that improved sanitary conditions were made possible by the breakdown of the boss system in New York. *

Before 1895 the streets were almost universally in a filthy state. In wet weather they were covered with slime, and in dry weather the air was filled with dust. Artificial sprinkling in summer converted the dust into mud, and the drying winds changed the mud to powder. Rubbish of all kinds, garbage, and ashes lay neglected in the streets, and in the hot weather the city stank with the emanations of putrefying organic matter. It was not always possible to see the pavement, because of the dirt that covered it. One expert, a former contractor of street-cleaning, told me that West Broadway could not be cleaned, because it was so coated with grease from wagon-axles; it was really coated with slimy mud. The sewer inlets were clogged with refuse. Dirty paper was prevalent everywhere, and black rottenness was seen and smelled on every hand.

The practice of standing unharnessed trucks and wagons in the public streets was well-nigh universal in all except the main thoroughfares and the better residence districts. The Board of Health made an enumeration of vehicles so standing on Sunday, counting twenty-five thousand on a portion of one side of the city; they reached the conclusion that there were in all more than sixty thousand. These trucks not only restricted traffic and made complete street-cleaning practically impossible, but they were harbors of vice and crime. Thieves and highwaymen made them their dens, toughs caroused in them, both sexes resorted to them, and they were used for the vilest purposes, until they became, both figuratively and literally, a stench in the nostrils of the people. In the crowded districts they were a veritable nocturnal hell. Against all this the poor people were powerless

---

* From George W. Waring, Jr., *Street Cleaning* (New York: Doubleday and McClure, 1897), 13–31.

to get relief. The highest city officials, after feeble attempts at removal, declared that New York was so peculiarly constructed (having no alleys through which the rear of the lots could be reached) that its commerce could not be carried on unless this privilege were given to its truckmen; in short, the removal of the trucks was "an impossibility"...

The condition of the streets, of the force, and of the stock was the fault of no man and of no set of men. It was the fault of the system. The department was throttled by partisan control—so throttled it could neither do good work, command its own respect and that of the pubic, not maintain its material in good order. It was run as an adjunct of a political organization. In that capacity it was a marked success. It paid fat tribute; it fed thousands of voters, and it gave power and influence to hundreds of political leaders. It had this appointed function, and it performed it well....

New York is now thoroughly clean in every part, the empty vehicles are gone...."Clean streets" means much more than the casual observer is apt to think. It has justly been said that "cleanliness is catching," and clean streets are leading to clean hallways and stair cases and cleaner living-rooms....

Few realize the many minor ways in which the work of the department has benefited the people at large. For example, there is far less injury from dust to clothing, to furniture, and to goods in shops; mud is not tracked from the streets on to the sidewalks, and thence into the houses; boots require far less cleaning; the wearing of overshoes has been largely abandoned; wet feet and bedraggled skirts are mainly things of the past; and children now make free use of a playground of streets which were formerly impossible to them. "Scratches," a skin disease of horses due to mud and slush, used to entail very serious cost on truckmen and liverymen. It is now almost unknown. Horses used to "pick up a nail" with alarming frequency, and this caused great loss of service, and, like scratches made the bill of the veterinary surgeon a serious matter. There are practically no nails now to be found in the streets.

The great, the almost inestimable, beneficial effect of the work of the department is showing the large reduction of the death-rate and in the less keenly realized but still more important reduction in the sick-rate. As compared with the average death-rate of 26.78 of 1882–94, that of 1895 was 23.10, that of 1896 was 21.52, and that of the first half of 1897 was 19.63. If this latter figure is maintained throughout the year, there will have been fifteen thousand fewer deaths than there would have been had the average rate of the thirteen previous years prevailed. The report of the Board of Health for 1896, basing its calculations on diarrheal diseases July, August, and September, in the filthiest wards, in the most crowded wards, and in the remainder of the city, shows a very marked reduction in all, and the largest reduction in the first two classes.

Document Analysis

1. What sanitary improvements does Waring claim to have occurred in New York? What picture does he paint of the city streets prior to these sanitary improvements?

Chapter Study Questions

1. Why do you think Bellamy's *Looking Backward* was so extraordinarily popular, particularly among the middle class?

2. Why would Booker T. Washington find Du Bois elitist and impractical? In what ways were Washington and Du Bois speaking to different audiences within the black community?

3. How did the Supreme Court's ruling in *Plessy v. Ferguson* reinforce the racial separation advocated by Booker T. Washington? How well did this segregation serve African Americans over the decades that followed?

4. Based on the descriptions in the documents in this chapter, what was life like in New York and Chicago in the late nineteenth and early twentieth centuries? What would attract you to life there, and what would make you want to stay away?

5. The Chinese Exclusion Act and the Secret Oath of the American Protective Association reflect the anti-immigration reaction that grew in the late nineteenth century. How does this compare to the debate over immigration in the early twenty-first century?

6. Was Lee Chew's experience unusual for an immigrant?

Twenty

Political Realignments in the 1890s

F arming life on the frontier was incredibly uncertain and difficult. Your text shows that increasingly, after depressions in the 1880s and 1890s, farmers in the West and in the South organized into political groups to improve their social and economic status. They formed farmer's alliances, cooperatives, and public schools. In 1892 the Populist party was formed as an independent third party fielding a candidate in the presidential election. In general, Populists were isolated farmers who were disenchanted and disengaged from traditional party politics and social structures. The platform of the Populist party, included here, reflects this in its calls for a reform of the nation's political and social systems, including government takeover of the railroads, banks, and telephone and telegraph systems. Although the Populist presidential candidate, James B. Weaver, gained only 8.5 percent of the popular vote, Populists had sufficiently strong support in rural areas in the South and the West to elect a number of governors from the party.

A leading critic of the Populists was William Allen White, the young editor of the *Emporia Gazette* in Kansas. Populists had gained political power in Kansas and several other states in the early 1890s, and White viewed them as radical demagogues who were harming his state. When William Jennings Bryan became the Democratic-Populist fusion candidate for president in 1896, White wrote a blistering editorial, "What's the Matter with Kansas?"

The new vibrant cities of the late 1800s had tremendous attraction for young people, drawn by the bright lights, mansions and skyscrapers, fine clothing and furnishings, entertainment, and seemingly endless possibilities. Theodore Dreiser explores the draw of the new city and the compromises a young woman is willing to make in order to succeed in his novel *Sister Carrie*, first published in 1900. Carrie is a young woman from a small farm town who moves to Chicago with high hopes, only to realize how difficult the city can be. She will gradually loosen her morals in order to find comfort, run off with a wealthy married man, and become a successful actress.

The Omaha Platform of the Populist Party (1892)

*This is a selection from the Populist Party platform, drafted at their national convention in Omaha, Nebraska, where the party nominated James B. Weaver for president. The Populists, mostly small farmers in the South and West, attempted to broaden their base in their platform, trying to appeal in particular to urban workers.**

Preamble

The conditions which surround us best justify our cooperation; we meet in the midst of a nation brought to the verge of moral, political, and material ruin. Corruption dominates the ballot-box, the Legislatures, the Congress, and touches even the ermine of the bench. The people are demoralized; most of the States have been compelled to isolate the voters at the polling places to prevent universal intimidation and bribery. The newspapers are largely subsidized or muzzled, public opinion silenced, business prostrated, homes covered with mortgages, labor impoverished, and the land concentrating in the hands of capitalists. The urban workmen are denied the right to organize for self-protection, imported pauperized labor beats down their wages, a hireling standing army, unrecognized by our laws, is established to shoot them down, and they are rapidly degenerating into European conditions. The fruits of the toil of millions are boldly stolen to build up colossal fortunes for a few, unprecedented in the history of mankind and the possessors of these, in turn, despise the Republic and endanger liberty. From the same prolific womb of governmental injustice we breed the two great classes—tramps and millionaires....

Assembled on the anniversary of the birthday of the nation, and filled with the spirit of the grand general and chief who established our independence, we seek to restore the government of the Republic to the hands of the "plain people," with which class it orig-

* From the Omaha Platform, Edward McPherson, *A Handbook of Politics for 1892* (Da Capo Press).

inated. We assert our purposes to be identical with the purposes of the National Constitution; to form a more perfect union and establish justice, insure domestic tranquillity, provide for the common defense, promote the general welfare, and secure the blessings of liberty for ourselves and our posterity....

Platform

We declare, therefore—

First.—That the union of the labor forces of the United States this day consummated shall be permanent and perpetual; may its spirit enter into all hearts for the salvation of the Republic and the uplifting of mankind.

Second.—Wealth belongs to him who creates it, and every dollar taken from industry without an equivalent is robbery. "If any will not work, neither shall he eat." The interests of rural and civil labor are the same; their enemies are identical.

Third.—We believe that the time has come when the railroad corporations will either own the people or the people must own the railroads....

FINANCE.—We demand a national currency, safe, sound, and flexible issued by the general government only, a full legal tender for all debts, public and private....

1. We demand free and unlimited coinage of silver and gold at the present legal ratio of 16 to 1.

2. We demand that the amount of circulating medium be speedily increased to not less than $50 per capita.

3. We demand a graduated income tax.

4. We believe that the money of the country should be kept as much as possible in the hands of the people, and hence we demand that all State and national revenues shall be limited to the necessary expenses of the government, economically and honestly administered.

5. We demand that postal savings banks be established by the government for the safe deposit of the earnings of the people and to facilitate exchange.

TRANSPORTATION.—Transportation being a means of exchange and a public necessity, the government should own and operate the railroads in the interest of the people. The telegraph and telephone, like the post-office system, being a necessity for the transmission of news, should be owned and operated by the government in the interest of the people.

LAND.—The land, including all the natural sources of wealth, is the heritage of the people, and should not be monopolized for speculative purposes, and alien ownership of land should be prohibited. All land now held by railroads and other corporations in excess of their actual needs, and all lands now owned by aliens should be reclaimed by the government and held for actual settlers only.

Expressions of Sentiments

1. RESOLVED, That we demand a free ballot, and a fair count of all elections, and pledge ourselves to secure it to every legal voter without Federal intervention, through the adoption by the States of the unperverted Australian or secret ballot system.

2. RESOLVED, That the revenue derived from a graduated income tax should be applied to the reduction of the burden of taxation now levied upon the domestic industries of this country.

3. RESOLVED, That we pledge our support to fair and liberal pensions to ex-Union soldiers and sailors.

4. RESOLVED, That we condemn the fallacy of protecting American labor under the present system, which opens our ports to the pauper and criminal classes of the world and crowds out our wage-earners; and we denounce the present ineffective laws against contract labor, and demand the further restriction of undesirable emigration.

5. RESOLVED, That we cordially sympathize with the efforts of organized working-men to shorten the hours of labor, and demand a rigid enforcement of the existing eight-hour law on Government work, and ask that a penalty clause be added to the said law.

6. RESOLVED, That we regard the maintenance of a large standing army of mercenaries, known as the Pinkerton system, as a menace to our liberties, and we demand its abolition....

7. RESOLVED, That we commend to the favorable consideration of the people and the reform press the legislative system known as the initiative and referendum.

8. RESOLVED, That we favor a constitutional provision limiting the office of President and Vice-President to one term, and providing for the election of Senators of the United States by a direct vote of the people.

9. RESOLVED, That we oppose any subsidy or national aid to any private corporation for any purpose.

DOCUMENT ANALYSIS

1. Which planks of the Omaha Platform are aimed at rural voters, and which are aimed at urban voters? Why do you think urban voters were suspicious of the Populists?

2. How radical would the Omaha Platform be considered today? Explain.

Twenty.2

William Allen White,
"What's the Matter with Kansas?"
(1896)

As the Populist Party won victories in several states in the 1890s, some observers were not impressed. William Allen White, editor of the Emporia Gazette *newspaper, viewed the rise of Populism in his native Kansas with deep suspicion. White was still more horrified when the Democrats and Populists united behind William Jennings Bryan's presidential candidacy in 1896, and he feared that Bryan might actually win the election. White wrote a scathing editorial in the* Gazette, *titled "What's the Matter with Kansas?" in which he mocks Kansas Populist politicians as well as Bryan's candidacy. Republicans had it reprinted by the thousands and distributed throughout the Midwest.* *

Today the Kansas Department of Agriculture sent out a statement which indicates that Kansas has gained less than two thousand people in the past year. There are about two hundred and twenty-five thousand families in the state, and there were about ten thousand babies born in Kansas, and yet so many people have left the state that the natural increase is cut down to less than two thousand net.

This has been going on for eight years.

If there had been a high brick wall around the state eight years ago, and not a soul had been admitted or permitted to leave, Kansas would be a half million souls better off than she is today. And yet the nation has increased in population. In five years ten million people have been added to the national population, yet instead of gaining a share of this—say, half a million—Kansas has apparently been a plague spot and, in the very garden of the world, has lost population by ten-thousands every year.

Not only has she lost population, but she has lost money. Every moneyed man in the state who could get out without loss has gone. Every month in every community sees someone who has a little money pack up and leave the state. This has been going on for

* From William Allen White, "What's the Matter with Kansas," *Emporia Gazette*, August 15, 1896, available online at www.emporia.com/waw/kansas.html.

eight years. Money has been drained out all the time. In towns where ten years ago there were three or four or half a dozen money-lending concerns, stimulating industry by furnishing capital, there is now none, or one or two that are looking after the interests and principal already outstanding....

Yet the nation has grown rich; other states have increased in population and wealth—other neighboring states. Missouri has gained over two million, while Kansas has been losing half a million. Nebraska has gained in wealth and population while Kansas has gone downhill. Colorado has gained every way, while Kansas has lost every way since 1888....

What's the matter with Kansas?

We all know; yet here we are at it again. We have an old mossback Jacksonian who snorts and howls because there is a bathtub in the state house; we are running that old jay for Governor. We have another shabby, wild-eyed, rattle-brained fanatic who has said openly in a dozen speeches that "the rights of the user are paramount to the rights of the owner"; we are running him for Chief Justice, so that capital will come tumbling over itself to get into the state. We have raked the old ash heap of failure in the state and found an old human hoop-skirt who has failed as a businessman, who has failed as an editor, who has failed as a preacher, and we are going to run him for Congressman-at-Large. He will help the looks of the Kansas delegation at Washington. Then we have discovered a kid without a law practice and have decided to run him for Attorney General. Then, for fear some hint that the state had become respectable might percolate through the civilized portions of the nation, we have decided to send three or four harpies out lecturing, telling the people that Kansas is raising hell and letting the corn go to weeds.

Oh, this is a state to be proud of! We are a people who can hold up our heads! What we need is not more money, but less capital, fewer white shirts and brains, fewer men with business judgment, and more of those fellows who boast that they are "just ordinary clodhoppers but they know more in a minute about finance than John Sherman"; we need more men who are "posted," who can bellow about the crime of '73, who hate prosperity and who think, because a man believes in national honor, he is a tool of Wall Street....

We don't need population, we don't need wealth, we don't need well-dressed men on the streets, we don't need standing in the nation, we don't need cities on the fertile prairies; you bet we don't! What we are after is the money power. Because we have become poorer and ornerier all and meaner than a spavined, distempered mule, we, the people of Kansas, propose to kick; we don't care to build up, we wish to tear down.

"There are two ideas of government," said our noble Bryan at Chicago. "There are those who believe that if you just legislate to make the well-to-do prosperous, this prosperity will leak through on those below. The Democratic idea has been that if you legislate to make the masses prosperous their prosperity will find its way up through every class which rests upon them."

That's the stuff! Give the prosperous man the dickens! Legislate the thriftless man into ease, whack the stuffings out of the creditors and tell debtors who borrowed the money five years ago when money "per capita" was greater than it is now, that the contraction of currency gives him a right to repudiate.

Whoop it up for the ragged trousers; put the lazy, greasy fizzle, who can't pay his debts, on an altar, and bow down and worship him. Let the state ideal be high. What we need is not the respect of our fellow men, but the chance to get something for nothing.

Oh, yes, Kansas is a great state. Here are people fleeing from it by the score every day, capital going out of the state by the hundreds of dollars; and every industry but farming paralyzed, and that crippled, because its products have to go across the ocean before they can find a laboring man at work who can afford to buy them. Let's don't stop this year. Let's drive all the decent, self-respecting men out of the state. Let's keep the old clod-hoppers who know it all. Let's encourage the man who is "posted." He can talk, and what we need is not mill hands to eat our meat, nor factory hands to eat our wheat, nor cities to oppress the farmer by consuming his butter and eggs and chickens and produce. What Kansas needs is men who can talk, who have large leisure to argue the currency question while their wives wait at home for that nickel's worth of bluing.

What's the matter with Kansas?

Nothing under the shining sun. She is losing wealth, population and standing. She has got her statesmen, and the money power is afraid of her. Kansas is all right. She has started in to raise hell, as Mrs. Lease advised, and she seems to have an over-production. But that doesn't matter. Kansas never did believe in diversified crops....

DOCUMENT ANALYSIS

1. What does William Allen White believe to be "the matter with Kansas" in 1896? How does White characterize many of the Kansas politicians of his day?

2. What seems to be White's chief criticism of Bryan in this editorial, and how is it tied to White's dislike of the Populists?

Theodore Dreiser, from *Sister Carrie* (1900)

Theodore Dreiser's novel Sister Carrie *was published in 1900, although, because of controversy, it wasn't widely distributed until several years later. Dreiser's story of a young woman, Carrie Meeber, shows her economic and social rise coinciding with her moral decline. Dreiser depicts the powerful allure of the city to Carrie, even though she comes to learn that not everything is actually as glamorous as it seems. In this excerpt from early in the novel, Carrie has recently arrived in Chicago, and is looking for a job, despite her limited qualifications.* *

"Mr. McManus," called the man at the desk, "this young woman wants to see you."

The short gentleman turned about towards Carrie, and she arose and came forward.

"What can I do for you, miss?" he inquired, surveying her curiously.

"I want to know if I can get a position," she inquired.

"As what?" he asked.

"Not as anything in particular," she faltered.

"Have you ever had any experience in the wholesale dry goods business?" he questioned.

"No, sir," she replied.

"Are you a stenographer or typewriter?"

"No, sir."

"Well, we haven't anything here," he said. "We employ only experienced help."

She began to step backward toward the door, when something about her plaintive face attracted him.

"Have you ever worked at anything before?" he inquired.

"No, sir," she said.

---

* From Theodore Dreiser, *Sister Carrie* (1900).

"Well, now, it's hardly possible that you would get anything to do in a wholesale house of this kind. Have you tried the department stores?"

She acknowledged that she had not.

"Well, if I were you," he said, looking at her rather genially, "I would try the department stores. They often need young women as clerks."...

At that time the department store was in its earliest form of successful operation, and there were not many. The first three in the United States, established about 1884, were in Chicago. Carrie was familiar with the names of several through the advertisements in the "Daily News," and now proceeded to seek them. The words of Mr. McManus had somehow managed to restore her courage, which had fallen low, and she dared to hope that this new line would offer her something. Some time she spent in wandering up and down, thinking to encounter the buildings by chance....At last she inquired of a police officer, and was directed to proceed "two blocks up," where she would find "The Fair."

The nature of these vast retail combinations, should they ever permanently disappear, will form an interesting chapter in the commercial history of our nation. Such a flowering out of a modest trade principle the world had never witnessed up to that time. They were along the line of the most effective retail organisation, with hundreds of stores coördinated into one and laid out upon the most imposing and economic basis. They were handsome, bustling, successful affairs, with a host of clerks and a swarm of patrons. Carrie passed along the busy aisles, much affected by the remarkable displays of trinkets, dress goods, stationery, and jewelry. Each separate counter was a show place of dazzling interest and attraction. She could not help feeling the claim of each trinket and valuable upon her personally, and yet she did not stop. There was nothing there which she could not have used—nothing which she did not long to own. The dainty slippers and stockings, the delicately frilled skirts and petticoats, the laces, ribbons, hair-combs, purses, all touched her with individual desire, and she felt keenly the fact that not any of these things were in the range of her purchase. She was a work-seeker, an outcast without employment, one whom the average employee could tell at a glance was poor and in need of a situation....

Not only did Carrie feel the drag of desire for all which was new and pleasing in apparel for women, but she noticed too, with a touch at the heart, the fine ladies who elbowed and ignored her, brushing past in utter disregard of her presence, themselves eagerly enlisted in the materials which the store contained. Carrie was not familiar with the appearance of her more fortunate sisters of the city. Neither had she before known the nature and appearance of the shop girls with whom she now compared poorly. They were pretty in the main, some even handsome, with an air of independence and indifference which added, in the case of the more favoured, a certain piquancy. Their clothes were neat, in many instances fine, and wherever she encountered the eye of one it was only to recognise in it a keen analysis of her own position—her individual shortcomings of dress and that shadow of *manner* which she thought must hang about her and make clear to all who and what she was. A flame of envy lighted in her heart. She realised in a dim way how much the city held—wealth, fashion, ease—every adornment for women, and she longed for dress and beauty with a whole heart.

DOCUMENT ANALYSIS

1. How does Dreiser describe Carrie's attitude as she is walking through the aisles of the department store? How might her reaction reflect Dreiser's sense of the power of these new establishments?

2. What economic class issues seem to be at work in these department stores?

Chapter Study Questions

1. Given his opinions in the "What's the Matter with Kansas?" editorial, what planks would William Allen White be most likely to criticize in the Populists' Omaha Platform?

2. What does Carrie Meeber's attempt to find work in Chicago suggest to you about how prepared Americans were for the explosion of cities at this time? What job opportunities were available to women like Carrie in this era?

Twenty-one

Toward Empire

As its economy steadily grew and it filled in the continent in the decades after the Civil War, America began to turn its expansionist energies abroad. Business groups sought a foreign policy that would support their interests, while many Americans believed that it was America's manifest destiny to spread American civilization over the globe. Leading political figures were concerned that unless the United States expanded, European powers would continue to dominate around the world. This chapter is an overview of the different ideologies and critiques of American imperialism.

The Spanish-American War marked the emergence of the United States as a world power. In this "splendid little war," the United States fought for the liberation of Cuba from what was seen as tyrannical Spanish rule. American victory brought on a national debate about the morality of additional expansion and involvement elsewhere, particularly in the Philippines. Some Americans considered it the duty of America as a Christian nation to dominate the world and spread "civilization" throughout. Josiah Strong, one of the voices in this chapter, was a Congregationalist minister and one of the foremost advocates of missionary expansionism.

Other Americans, like Indiana Senator Albert Beveridge, also believed in an expansionist foreign policy but for different reasons. Beveridge, in particular, believed that the United States needed to expand in order to dominate world markets because, in his words, "the trade of the world must and should be ours." American industries were producing more goods than the American market could absorb and the overseas market was necessary, in his eyes, to support the American economy. In this selection from Beveridge's famous "The March of the Flag," the senator argued for keeping the Philippines. On the other hand, many people, particularly intellectuals, opposed this so-called American imperialism. William Graham Sumner, a sociologist at Yale known as a leading advocate of social Darwinism, argued that acquiring colonies was anti-American and that it could do great harm to American society.

The final decision about the Philippines rested with President William McKinley. The document included here explains his reasons for keeping the Philippines—which he did, a decision that led to the war and the expansion of the American empire into the South Pacific. The struggle in the Philippines proved bloody and costly: over 100,000 Americans served there, of whom 4,000 were wounded while 20,000 Filipinos were killed and perhaps 200,000 died of disease and starvation.

Twenty-one.1

Josiah Strong, from *Our Country* (1885)

Strong, like others, believed the Anglo-Saxon people were superior to non-Christian, non-white peoples, and that it was the responsibility of the United States to spread its way of life. Our Country is the articulation of so-called missionary expansionism. *

Every race which has deeply impressed itself on the human family has been the representative of some great idea—one or more—which had given direction to the nation's life and form to its civilization. Among the Egyptians this seminal idea was life, among the Persians it was light, among the Hebrews it was purity, among the Greeks it was beauty, among the Romans it was law. The Anglo-Saxon is the representative of two great ideas, which are closely related. One of them is that of civil liberty. Nearly all of the civil liberty in the world is enjoyed by Anglo-Saxons: the English, the British colonists, and the people of the United States.... The noblest races have always been lovers of liberty. That love ran strong in early German blood, and has profoundly influenced the institutions of all the branches of the great German family; but it was left for the Anglo-Saxon branch fully to recognize the right of the individual to himself, and formally to declare it the foundation stone of government.

The other great idea of which the Anglo-Saxon is the exponent is that of a pure spiritual Christianity. It was no accident that great reformation of the sixteenth century originated among a Teutonic, rather than a Latin people. It was the fire of liberty burning in the Saxon heart that flamed up against the absolutism of the Pope....

It is not necessary to argue to those for whom I write that the two great needs of mankind, that all men may be lifted up into the light of the highest Christian civilization, are, first, a pure, spiritual Christianity, and, second, civil liberty. Without controversy, these are the forces which, in the past, have contributed most to the elevation of

* From Josiah Strong, *Our Country: Its Possible Future and Its Present Crisis* (New York: Baker & Taylor, 1885), 159–161, 165, 170, 178–180.

the human race, and they must continue to be, in the future, the most efficient minis-ters to its progress. It follows, then, that the Anglo-Saxon, as the great representative of these two ideas, the depositary [*sic*] of these two greatest blessings, sustains peculiar relations to the world's future, is divinely commissioned to be, in a peculiar sense, his brother's keeper....

There can be no reasonable doubt that North America is to be the great home of the Anglo-Saxon, the principal seat of his power, the center of his life and influence. Not only does it constitute seven-elevenths of his possessions, but this empire is unsevered, while the remaining four-elevenths are fragmentary and scattered over the earth. Australia will have a great population; but its disadvantages, as compared with North America, are too manifest to need mention. Our continent has room and resources and climate, it lies in the pathway of the nations, it belongs to the zone of power, and already, among Anglo-Saxons, do we lead in population and wealth.

Mr. Darwin is not only disposed to see, in the superior vigor of our people, an illustra-tion of his favorite theory of natural selection, but even intimates that the world's history thus far has been simply preparatory for our future, and tributary to it. He says: "There is apparently much truth in the belief that the wonderful progress of the United States, as well as the character of the people, are the results of natural selection; for the more ener-getic, restless, and courageous men from all parts of Europe have emigrated during the last ten or twelve generations to that great country, and have there succeeded best...."

...The time is coming when the pressure of population on the means of subsistence will be felt there as it is now felt in Europe and Asia. Then will the world enter upon a new stage of its history—the final competition of races, for which the Anglo-Saxon is being schooled. Long before the thousands millions are here, the mighty centrifugal tendency, inherent in this stock and strengthened in the United States, will assert itself. Then this race of unequaled energy, with all the majesty of numbers and the might of wealth behind it—the representative, let us hope, of the largest liberty, the purest Christianity, the highest civilization—having developed peculiarly aggressive traits cal-culated to impress its institutions upon mankind, will spread itself over the earth. If I read not amiss, this powerful race will move down upon Mexico, down upon Central and South America, out upon the islands of the sea, over upon Africa and beyond. And can anyone doubt that the result of this competition of races will be the "survival of the fittest"?...

In my own mind, there is no doubt that the Anglo-Saxon is to exercise the com-manding influence in the world's future; but the exact nature of that influence is, as yet, undetermined. How far his civilization will be materialistic and atheistic, and how long it will take thoroughly to Christianize and sweeten it, how rapidly he will hasten the coming of the kingdom wherein dwelleth righteousness, or how many ages he may retard it, is still uncertain; but it is now being swiftly determined....

Notwithstanding the great perils which threaten it, I cannot think our civilization will perish; but I believe it is fully in the hand of the Christians of the United States, during the next fifteen or twenty years, to hasten or retard the coming of Christ's kingdom in the world by hundreds, and perhaps thousands, of years. We of this generation and nation occupy the Gibraltar of the ages which command the world's future.

DOCUMENT ANALYSIS

1. According to Josiah Strong, why must the United States become a world power? Do you find Strong's argument persuasive? Explain.

Twenty-one.2

Albert Beveridge, "The March of the Flag" (1898)

Albert Beveridge, a Republican senator from Indiana, was one of the leading spokesmen for a strongly expansionist foreign policy. In this address, which was widely read during the period, Beveridge merged prevalent opinions about America's civilizing mission with its economic destiny.*

It is a noble land that God has given us; a land that can feed and clothe the world; a land whose coastlines would enclose half the countries of Europe; a land set like a sentinel between the imperial oceans of the globe, a greater England with a nobler destiny.

It is a mighty people that He has planted on this soil; a people sprung from the most masterful blood of history; a people perpetually revitalized by the virile, man-producing working folk of all the earth; a people imperial by virtue of their power, by right of their institutions, by authority of their Heaven-directed purposes—the propagandists and not the misers of liberty.

It is a glorious history our God has bestowed upon His chosen people; a history heroic with faith in our mission and our future; a history of statesmen who flung the boundaries of the Republic out into unexplored lands and savage wilderness; a history of soldiers who carried the flag across blazing deserts and through the ranks of hostile mountains, even to the gates of sunset; a history of a multiplying people who overran a continent in half a century; a history of prophets who saw the consequences of evils inherited from the past and of martyrs who died to save us from them; a history divinely logical, in the process of whose tremendous seasoning we find ourselves today.

Therefore, in this campaign, the question is larger than a party question. It is an American question. It is a world question. Shall the American people continue their march toward the commercial supremacy of the world? Shall free institutions broaden

* From "The March of the Flag," printed in the *Indianapolis Journal*, September 17, 1898. From Albert J. Beveridge, *The Meaning of Times* (Indianapolis: Bobbs-Merrill, 1908), 47–49, 56–57.

their blessed reign as the children of liberty wax in strength, until the empire of our principles is established over the hearts of all mankind?

Have we no mission to perform, no duty to discharge to our fellowman? Has God endowed us with gifts beyond our deserts and marked us as the people of His peculiar favor, merely to rot in our own selfishness, as men and nations must, who take cowardice for their companion and self for their deity—as China has, as India has, as Egypt has?

Shall we be as the man who had one talent and hid it, or as he who had ten talents and use them until they grew to riches? And shall we reap the reward that waits on our discharge of our high duty; shall we occupy new markets for what our farmers raise, our factories make, our merchants sell—aye, and, please God, new markets for what our ships shall carry?

Hawaii is ours, Puerto Rico is to be ours; at the prayer of her people Cuba finally will be ours; in the islands of the East, even to the gates of Asia, coaling stations are to be ours at the very least; the flag of a liberal government is to float over the Philippines, and may it be the banner that Taylor unfurled in Texas and Frémont carried to the coast.

The Opposition tells us that we ought not to govern a people without their consent. I answer, The rule of liberty that all just government derives its authority from the consent of the governed, applies only to those who are capable of self-government. We govern the Indians without their consent, we govern our territories without their consent, we govern our children without their consent. How do they know that our government would be without their consent? Would not the people of the Philippines prefer the just, human, civilizing government of this Republic to the savage, bloody rule of pillage and extortion from which we have rescued them?

And, regardless of this formula of words made only for enlightened, self-governing people, do we owe no duty to the world? Shall we turn these peoples back to the reeking hands from which we have taken them? Shall we abandon them, with Germany, England, Japan, hungering for them? Shall we save them from those nations, to give them a self-rule of tragedy?…Then, like man and not like children, let us on to our tasks, our mission, and our destiny.

Wonderfully has God guided us. Yonder at Bunker Hill and Yorktown His providence was above us. At New Orleans and on ensanguined seas His hand sustained us. Abraham Lincoln was His minister and His was the altar of freedom the Nation's soldiers set up on a hundred battle-fields. His power directed Dewey in the East and delivered the Spanish fleet into our hands, as He delivered the elder Armada into the hands of our English sires two centuries ago. The American people can not use a dishonest medium of exchange; it is ours to set the world its example of right and honor. We can not fly from our world duties; it is ours to execute the purpose of a fate that has driven us to be greater than our small intentions. We can not retreat from any soil where Providence has unfurled our banner; it is ours to save that soil for liberty and civilization.

DOCUMENT ANALYSIS

1. How does Beveridge characterize America's proper role in the world?

2. How does Beveridge answer opponents of American expansionism?

Twenty-one.3

William Graham Sumner, from "On Empire and the Philippines" (1898)

"On Empire and the Philippines," the essay from which this extract comes, was written in 1898 and was published in Sumner's War and Other Essays. *Known as a social Darwinist, Sumner was also an ardent anti-imperialist. After entering Yale as a student in 1859, Sumner studied abroad after graduation, and returned to teach at his alma mater until his death in 1910.**

There is not a civilized nation that does not talk about its civilizing mission just as grandly as we do. The English, who really have more to boast of it in this respect than anybody else, talk least about it, but the Phariseeism with which they correct and instruct other people has made them hated all over the globe. The French believe themselves the guardians of the highest and purest culture, and that the eyes of all mankind are fixed on Paris, whence they expect oracles of thought and taste. The Germans regard themselves as charged with a mission, especially to us Americans, to save us from egoism and materialism. The Russians, in their books and newspapers, talk about the civilizing mission of Russian in language that might be translated from some of the finest paragraphs of our imperialistic newspapers.

The first principle of Mohammedanism is that we Christians are dogs and infidels, fit only to be enslaved or butchered by Moslems. It is a corollary that wherever Mohammedanism extends it carries, in the belief of its votaries, the highest blessings, and that the whole human race would be enormously elevated if Mohammedanism should supplant Christianity everywhere.

To come, last, to Spain, the Spaniards have, for centuries, considered themselves the most zealous and self-sacrificing Christians, especially charged by the Almighty, on this account, to spread the true religion and civilization over the globe. They think themselves free and noble, leaders in refinement and the sentiments of personal honor, and

* From William Graham Sumner, *War and Other Essays* (Ayer Co. Publications, Inc., 1911).

they despise us as sordid money-grabbers and heretics. I could bring you passages from peninsular authors of the first rank about the grand role of Spain and Portugal in spreading freedom and truth.

Now each nation laughs at all the others when it observes these manifestations of national vanity. You may rely upon it that they are all ridiculous by virtue of these pretensions, including ourselves. The point is that each of them repudiated the standards of the others, and the outlying nations, which are to be civilized, hate all the standards of civilized men.

We assume that what we like and practice, and what we think better, must come as a welcome blessing to Spanish-Americans and Filipinos. This is grossly and obviously untrue. They hate our ways. They are hostile to our ideas. Our religion, language, institutions, and manners offend them. They like their own ways, and if we appear amongst them as rulers, there will be social discord in all the great departments of social interest. The most important thing which we shall inherit from the Spaniards will be the task of suppressing rebellions.

If the United States takes out of the hands of Spain her mission, on the ground that Spain is not executing it well, and if this nation in its turn attempts to be schoolmistress to others, it will shrivel up into the same vanity and self-conceit of which Spain now presents an example. To read our current literature one would think that we were already well on the way to it.

Now, the great reason why all these enterprises which begin by saying to somebody else, "We know what is good for you better than you know yourself and we are going to make you do it," are false and wrong is that they violate liberty; or, to turn the same statement into other words, the reason why liberty, of which we Americans talk so much, is a good thing is that it means leaving people to live out their own lives in their own way, while we do the same.

If we believe in liberty, as an American principle, why do we not stand by it? Why are we going to throw it away to enter upon a Spanish policy of dominion and regulation?

DOCUMENT ANALYSIS

1. On what grounds does Sumner base his opposition to American imperialism? Is his argument convincing?

Twenty-one.4

William McKinley, "Decision on the Philippines" (1900)

In this speech to a group of ministers, the president outlined his rationale for deciding to annex the Philippines, paying the Spanish (under duress) $20 million for the privilege. It was a difficult decision, and a decision that determined the path of American foreign policy for much of the next century. *

When next I realized that the Philippines had dropped into our laps, I confess I did not know what to do with them. I sought counsel from all sides—Democrats as well as Republicans—but got little help. I thought first we would take only Manila; then Luzon; then other islands, perhaps, also.

I walked the floor of the White House night after night until midnight; and I am not ashamed to tell you, gentlemen, that I went down on my knees and prayed to Almighty God for light and guidance more than one night. And one night late it came to me this way—I don't know how it was, but it came:

(1) That we could not give them back to Spain—that would be cowardly and dishonorable;

(2) That we could not turn them over to France or Germany, our commercial rivals in the Orient—that would be bad business and discreditable;

(3) That we could not leave them to themselves—they were unfit for self-government, and they would soon have anarchy and misrule worse then Spain's was; and

(4) That there was nothing left for us to do but to take them all, and to educate the Filipinos, and uplift and civilize and Christianize them and by God's grace do the very best we could by them, as our fellow men for whom Christ also died.

* This document is a report of an interview with McKinley at the White House, November 21, 1899, written by one of the interviewers and confirmed by others present. Published in *The Christian Advocate*, January 22, 1903, it is here cited from C. S. Olcott, *The Life of William McKinley* (1916), vol. 2, 110–111.

And then I went to bed and went to sleep, and slept soundly, and the next morning I sent for the chief engineer of the War Department (our map-maker), and I told him to put the Philippines on the map of the United States (pointing to a large map on the wall of his office), and there they are and there they will stay while I am President!

DOCUMENT ANALYSIS

1. How does President McKinley justify his decision to retain control of the Philippines after the Spanish-American War?

2. How might President McKinley's audience (expansionist Methodist ministers and missionaries) have influenced this speech?

Chapter Study Questions

1. What racial assumptions do the authors in this chapter share? Where do they differ? How do the arguments of Strong, Beveridge, and Sumner rely upon the doctrine of social Darwinism?

2. In what ways did this new American expansionism of the late nineteenth and early twentieth centuries represent a turning away from the nation's early ideals? In what ways was this expansionism a necessary response to a changing world?

3. Upon what did McKinley base his decision?

Twenty-two

The Progressive Era

One of the many forces propelling the progressive reform movement was a group of journalists known as "muckrakers." The muckrakers investigated corruption in business and government, and wrote powerful magazine articles and books exposing the truth about such topics as how local political bosses cheated the taxpayers, how food and drug companies failed to properly ensure the safety of their products, and how monopolies extended their reach through ruthless practices and the bribery of public officials. One of the earliest muckrakers was Ida M. Tarbell, who provided a carefully researched and hard-hitting account of John D. Rockefeller's rise to power in *The History of the Standard Oil Company*. An excerpt from Tarbell's book is included in this chapter.

Immigration and urban growth coincided with and often encouraged the development of new systems of political organization in the United States. Most significant among these developments was the machine system, another focus of progressive reform. Machine bosses promised services (turkeys at Christmas, money in a time of need, shoes for children, and the like) in exchange for votes and controlled the infrastructure of the city. Bosses accepted bribes from, among others, prostitutes and saloon owners; appointed their friends and family members to city jobs; and siphoned off as much as they could from city coffers for themselves and their blocs. But although they were corrupt, bosses weren't simply thieves. They also provided some valuable social services to their constituents in an era when government did little to help the poor. One of the documents in this chapter, a selection of conversations with a ward boss, reveals the motivations and perceptions of boss politics.

Leading the fight against Jim Crow and lynching in the South was another progressive, Ida B. Wells-Barnett, a journalist and newspaper editor in Memphis, Tennessee. After three successful grocery-store owners were lynched in 1892, Wells-Barnett began to campaign against lynching and to write about the culture of the South. Her accounts of lynching and racism in the South gained her a national audience. Like W. E. B. Du Bois, she disagreed with Booker T. Washington and was among the first women to join the NAACP. Later in life, she broke with the NAACP, considering it too timid, and supported the controversial Marcus Garvey and his calls for black pride, if not his back-to-Africa movement.

One of the most well-known women of the era was Jane Addams. Addams was active on a number of social and political issues, but was best known for her pioneering work in the settlement house movement. Addams had taken an old mansion, Hull House, in Chicago and opened its doors to the public in 1889 to offer assistance to neighborhood immigrants. A free health clinic, English classes, a soup kitchen, day care, art classes, and a lecture series were among the services provided by Hull House, which also ventured into the public arena by investigating social problems. The last document in the chapter is an excerpt from Addams's 1910 autobiography, *Twenty Years at Hull House*.

Twenty-two.1

Ida M. Tarbell,
from *The History of the Standard Oil Company*
(1904)

Ida M. Tarbell's lengthy study, The History of the Standard Oil Company, *first began appearing as a series of articles in* McClure's *Magazine in 1902, then was published as a full-length book in 1904. Although Tarbell gave credit to the shrewd business sense of John D. Rockefeller, much of the book detailed the ruthlessness with which Rockefeller and his oil company steamrolled over competitors to form one of the most powerful monopolies the world had ever known. Tarbell didn't like being labeled a "muckraker," but her work epitomizes the effort of Progressive-era journalists in their effort to expose business and government abuses to the public.* *

The pushing of the business, the buying and the selling, fell to Rockefeller. From the start his effect was tremendous. He had the frugal man's hatred of waste and disorder, of middlemen and unnecessary manipulation, and he began a vigorous elimination of these from his business. The residuum that other refineries let run into the ground, he sold. Old iron found its way to the junk shop. He bought his oil directly from the wells. He made his own barrels. He watched and saved and contrived. The ability with which he made the smallest bargain furnishes topics to Cleveland story-tellers to-day. Low-voiced, soft-footed, humble, knowing every point in every man's business, he never tired until he got his wares at the lowest possible figure. "John always got the best of the bargain," old men tell you in Cleveland to-day, and they wince though they laugh in telling it. "Smooth," "a savy fellow," is their description of him. To drive a good bargain was the joy of his life. "The only time I ever saw John Rockefeller enthusiastic," a man told the writer once, "was when a report came in from the creek that his buyer had secured a cargo of oil at a figure much below the market price. He bounded from his chair with a shout of joy, danced up and down, hugged me, threw up his hat, acted so like a madman that I have never forgotten it."...

* From Ida M. Tarbell, *The History of the Standard Oil Company* (New York: McClure, Phillips, and Co., 1904), pp. 43–46, 49–51, 98–99, 101–102, available online at http://www.history.rochester.edu/fuels/tarbell.

These qualities told. The firm grew as rapidly as the oil business of the town, and started a second refinery—William A. Rockefeller and Company. They took in a partner, H. M. Flagler, and opened a house in New York for selling oil. Of all these concerns John D. Rockefeller was the head. Finally, in June, 1870, five years after he became an active partner in the refining business, Mr. Rockefeller combined all his companies into one—the Standard Oil Company. The capital of the new concern was $1,000,000....

Then its chief competitors began to suspect something. John Rockefeller might get his oil cheaper now and then, they said, but he could not do it often. He might make close contracts for which they had neither the patience nor the stomach. He might have an unusual mechanical and practical genius in his partner. But these things could not explain all. They believed they bought, on the whole, almost as cheaply as he, and they knew they made as good oil and with as great, or nearly as great, economy. He could sell at no better price than they. Where was his advantage? There was but one place where it could be, and that was in transportation. He must be getting better rates from the railroads than they were....

Now in 1870 the Standard Oil Company had a daily capacity of about 1,500 barrels of crude. The refinery was the largest in the town, though it had some close competitors. Nevertheless on the strength of its large capacity it received the special favour. It was a plausible way to get around the theory generally held then, as now, though not so definitely crystallised into law, that the railroad being a common carrier had no right to discriminate between its patrons. It remained to be seen whether the practice would be accepted by Mr. Rockefeller's competitors without a contest, or, if contested, would be supported by the law.

What the Standard's rebate on Eastern shipments was in 1870 it is impossible to say. Mr. Alexander says he was never able to get a rate lower than $1.33 a barrel by rail, and that it was commonly believed in Cleveland that the Standard had a rate of ninety cents....

It would seem from the above as if the one man in the Cleveland oil trade in 1870 who ought to have been satisfied was Mr. Rockefeller. His was the largest firm in the largest refining centre of the country; that is, of the 10,000 to 12,000 daily capacity divided among the twenty-five or twenty-six refiners of Cleveland he controlled 1,500 barrels....

Not only did Mr. Rockefeller control the largest firm in this most prosperous centre of a prosperous business, he controlled one of amazing efficiency. The combination, in 1870, of the various companies with which he was connected had brought together a group of remarkable men....

It must have been evident to every business man who came in contact with the young Standard Oil Company that it would go far. The firm itself must have known it would go far. Indeed nothing could have stopped the Standard Oil Company in 1870—the oil business being what it was—but an entire change in the nature of the members of the firm, and they were not the kind of material which changes.

With such a set of associates, with his organisation complete from his buyers on the creek to his exporting agent in New York, with the transportation advantages which none of his competitors had had the daring or the persuasive power to get, certainly Mr. Rockefeller should have been satisfied in 1870. But Mr. Rockefeller was far from satisfied. He was a brooding, cautious, secretive man, seeing all the possible dangers as well as all the possible opportunities in things, and he studied, as a player at chess, all the possible combinations which might imperil his supremacy. These twenty-five Cleveland rivals of his—how could he at once and forever put them out of the game? He and his partners had somehow conceived a great idea—the advantages of combination. What might they not do if they could buy out and absorb the big refineries now competing with them in Cleveland? The possibilities of the idea grew as they discussed it....

Now the Oil Regions learned for the first time of the sudden and phenomenal expansion of the company. Where there had been at the beginning of 1872 twenty-six refining firms in Cleveland, there were but six left. In three months before and during the Oil War the Standard had absorbed twenty plants. It was generally charged by the Cleveland refiners that Mr. Rockefeller had used the South Improvement scheme to persuade or compel his rivals to sell to him. "Why," cried the oil men, "the Standard Oil Company has done already in Cleveland what the South Improvement Company set out to do for the whole country, and it has done it by the same means."

If Mr. Rockefeller had been an ordinary man the outburst of popular contempt and suspicion which suddenly poured on his head would have thwarted and crushed him. But he was no ordinary man. 'He had the powerful imagination to see what might be done with the oil business if it could be centered in his hands—the intelligence to analyse the problem into its elements and to find the key to control. He had the essential element of all great achievement, a steadfastness to a purpose once conceived which nothing can crush....

Mr. Rockefeller...believed that the "good of all" was in a combination which would control the business as the South Improvement Company proposed to control it. Such a combination would end at once all the abuses the business suffered. As rebates and special rates were essential to this control, he favoured them. Of course Mr. Rockefeller must have known that the railroad was a common carrier, and that the common law forbade discrimination. But he knew that the railroads had not obeyed the laws governing them, that they had regularly granted special rates and rebates to those who had large amounts of freight. That is, you were able to bargain with the railroads as you did with a man carrying on a strictly private business depending in no way on a public franchise. Moreover, Mr. Rockefeller probably believed that, in spite of the agreements, if he did not get—rebates somebody else would; that they were for the wariest, the shrewdest, the most persistent. If somebody was to get rebates, why not he? This point of view was no uncommon one. Many men held It and felt a sort of scorn, as practical men always do for theorists, when it was contended that the shipper was as wrong in taking rates as the railroads in granting them.

Thus, on one hand there was an exaggerated sense of personal independence, on the other a firm belief in combination; on one hand a determination to root out the vicious system of rebates practised by the railway, on the other a determination to keep it alive and profit by it. Those theories which the body of oil men held as vital and fundamental Mr. Rockefeller and his associates either did not comprehend or were deaf to. This lack of comprehension by many men of what seems to other men to be the most obvious principles of justice is not rare. Many men who are widely known as good, share it. Mr. Rockefeller was "good." There was no more faithful Baptist in Cleveland than he. Every enterprise of that church he had supported liberally from his youth. He gave to its poor. He visited its sick. He wept with its suffering. More over, he gave unostentatiously to many outside charities of whose worthiness he was satisfied. He was simple and frugal in his habits. He never went to the theatre, never drank wine. He gave much time to the training of his children, seeking to develop in them his own habits of economy and of charity. Yet he was willing to strain every nerve to obtain for himself special and unjust privileges from the railroads which were bound to ruin every man in the oil business—not sharing them with him. He was willing to array himself against the combined better sentiment of a whole industry, to oppose a popular movement aimed at righting an injustice, so revolting to one's sense of fair play as that of railroad discriminations. Religious emotion and sentiments of charity, propriety and self-denial seem to have taken the place in him of notions of justice and regard for the rights of others.

Unhampered, then, by any ethical consideration, undismayed by the clamour of the Oil Regions, believing firmly as ever that relief for the disorders in the oil business lay in combining and controlling the entire refining interest, this man of vast patience and foresight took up his work. That work now was to carry out some kind of a scheme which would limit the output of refined oil.

Document Analysis

1. According to this excerpt from Tarbell's book, what accounted for John D. Rockefeller's early success in the oil industry?

2. How does Tarbell differentiate between Rockefeller's personal life and behavior on one hand, and his business dealings on the other?

Twenty-two.2

William L. Riordon,
from *Plunkitt of Tammany Hall*
(1905)

This is an excerpt from William L. Riordon's Plunkitt of Tammany Hall, *a collection of conversations Riordon allegedly had with George Washington Plunkitt, a Tammany ward boss. Plunkitt's transportation and general-contracting business thrived through his connections with Tammany bosses. Plunkitt distinguished between "honest graft," which he argued was the oil that kept the machine running, and "dishonest graft."* *

"Everybody is talkin' these days about Tammany men growin' rich on graft, but nobody thinks of drawin' the distinction between honest graft and dishonest graft. There's all the difference in the world between the two. Yes, many of our men have grown rich in politics. I have myself. I've made a big fortune out of the game, and I'm gettin' richer every day, but I've not gone in for dishonest graft—blackmailin' gamblers, saloon-keepers, disorderly people, etc.—and neither has any of the men who have made big fortunes in politics.

"There's an honest graft, and I'm an example of how it works. I might sum up the whole thing by sayin': 'I seen my opportunities and I took 'em.'

"Just let me explain my examples. My party's in power in the city, and it's goin' to undertake a lot of public improvements. Well, I'm tipped off, say, that they're going to lay out a new park at a certain place.

"I see my opportunity and I take it. I go to that place and I buy up all the land I can in the neighborhood. Then the board of this or that makes its plan public, and there is a rush to get my land, which nobody cared particular for before.

"Ain't it perfectly honest to charge a good price and make a profit on my investment and foresight? Of course it is. Well, that's honest graft....

"...It's just like lookin' ahead in Wall Street or in the coffee or cotton market.

* From W. Riordon, *Plunkitt of Tammany Hall* (New York: McClure, Phillips & Co., 1905).

"...Now, let me tell you that most politicians who are accused of robbin' the city get rich the same way.

"They didn't steal a dollar from the city treasury. They just seen their opportunities and took them. That is why, when a reform administration comes in and spends a half million dollars in tryin' to find the public robberies they talk about in the campaign, they don't find them.

"The books are always all right. The money in the city treasury is all right. Everything is all right. All they can show is that the Tammany heads of departments looked after their friends, within the law, and gave them what opportunities they could to make honest graft....

"I've been readin' a book by Lincoln Steffens on *The Shame of the Cities*. Steffens means well but, like all reformers, he don't know how to make distinctions. He can't see no difference between honest graft and dishonest graft and, consequent, he gets things all mixed up. There's the biggest kind of a difference between political looters and politicians who make a fortune out of politics by keepin' their eyes wide open. The looter goes in for himself alone without considerin' his organization or his city. The politician looks after his own interests, the organization's interests, and the city's interests all at the same time...."

DOCUMENT ANALYSIS

1. What is the distinction Plunkitt makes between "honest graft" and "dishonest graft"? Do you think he really believes this explanation? Explain.

2. What is Plunkitt's attitude toward the reformer Lincoln Steffens, who attacked the political boss system of this era?

Twenty-two.3

Ida B. Wells-Barnett, from *A Red Record* (1895)

In the South, lynching was considered to be proper punishment for African American men accused of raping white women. However, as Wells-Barnett's research into lynching revealed, many victims of lynching committed no transgression but being black and financially independent. Wells-Barnett wrote editorials for her Memphis paper, the Free Speech, *criticizing the myth of Southern white female purity and even suggested that white women might be sexually attracted to black men. Soon after these editorials, the offices of* Free Speech *were burned and threats were made against Wells-Barnett's life. She did not return to the South for thirty years. The following selection from Wells-Barnett's autobiography,* A Red Record, *describes her early editorials and her work against lynching.**

A word as to the charge itself. In considering the third reason assigned by the Southern white people for the butchery of blacks, the question must be asked, what the white man means when he charges the black man with rape. Does he mean the crime which the statutes of the states describe as such? Not by any means. With the Southern white man, any misalliance existing between a white woman and a colored man is a sufficient foundation for the charge of rape. The southern white man says that it is impossible for a voluntary alliance to exist between a white woman and a colored man, and therefore, the fact of an alliance is a proof of force. In numerous instances where colored men have been lynched on the charge of rape, it was positively known at the time of lynching, and indisputably proven after the victim's death, that the relationship sustained between the man and the woman was voluntary and clandestine, and that in no court of law could even the charge of assault have been successfully maintained.

It was for the assertion of this fact, in the defense of her own race, that the writer hereof became an exile; her property destroyed and her return to her home forbidden

* From Ida Wells-Barnett, *A Red Record* (Chicago: Donohue & Henneberry, 1895), 8–15.

under penalty of death, for writing the following editorial which was printed in her paper, the *Free Speech*, in Memphis, Tenn., May 21, 1892:

"Eight Negroes lynched since last issue of the *Free Speech*: one at Little Rock, Ark., last Saturday morning where the citizens broke (?) into the penitentiary and got their man; three near Anniston, Ala., one near New Orleans; and three at Clarksville, Ga.; the last three for killing a white man, and five on the same old racket—the new alarm about raping white women. The same programme of hanging, then shooting bullets into the lifeless bodies was carried out to the letter. Nobody in this section of the country believes in the old threadbare lie that Negro men rape white women. If Southern white men are not careful, they will overreach themselves and public sentiment will have a reaction; a conclusion will then be reached which will be very damaging to the moral reputation of their women."

But threats cannot suppress the truth, and while the Negro suffers the soul deformity, resultant from two and a half centuries of slavery, he is no more guilty of this vilest of all vile charges than the white man who would blacken his name.

During all the years of slavery, no such charge was ever made, not even during the dark days of the rebellion....While the master was away fighting to forge the fetters upon the slave, he left his wife and children with no protectors save the Negroes themselves....

Likewise during the period of alleged "insurrection," and alarming "race riots," it never occurred to the white man that his wife and children were in danger of assault. Nor in the Reconstruction era, when the hue and cry was against "Negro Domination," was there ever a thought that the domination would ever contaminate a fireside or strike toward the virtue of womanhood....

It is not the purpose of this defense to say one word against the white women of the South. Such need not be said, but it is their misfortune that the...white men of that section...to justify their own barbarism...assume a chivalry which they do not possess. True chivalry respects all womanhood, and no one who reads the record, as it is written in the faces of the million mulattos in the South, will for a minute conceive that the southern white man had a very chivalrous regard for the honor due the women of his race, or respect for the womanhood which circumstances placed in his power....Virtue knows no color line, and the chivalry which depends on complexion of skin and texture of hair can command no honest respect.

When emancipation came to the Negroes...from every nook and corner of the North, brave young white women...left their cultured homes, their happy associations and their lives of ease, and with heroic determination went to the South to carry light and truth to the benighted blacks....They became the social outlaws in the South. The peculiar sensitiveness of the southern white men for women, never shed its protecting influence about them. No friendly word from their own race cheered them in their work; no hospitable doors gave them the companionship like that from which they had come. No chivalrous white man doffed his hat in honor or respect. They were "Nigger teachers"—unpardonable offenders in the social ethics of the South, and were insulted, persecuted and ostracized, not by Negroes, but by the white manhood which boasts of its chivalry toward women.

And yet these northern women worked on, year after year....Threading their way through dense forests, working in schoolhouses, in the cabin and in the church, thrown at all times and in all places among the unfortunate and lowly Negroes, whom they had come to find and to serve, these northern women, thousands and thousands of them, have spent more than a quarter of a century in giving the colored people their splendid lessons for home and heart and soul. Without protection, save that which innocence gives to every good woman, they went about their work, fearing no assault and suffering none. Their chivalrous protectors were hundreds of miles away in their northern homes, and yet they never feared any "great dark-faced mobs."...They never complained of assaults, and no mob was ever called into existence to avenge crimes against them. Before the world adjudges the Negro a moral monster, a vicious assailant of womanhood and a menace to the sacred precincts of home, the colored people ask the consideration of the silent record of gratitude, respect, protection and devotion of the millions of the race in the South, to the thousands of northern white women who have served as teachers and missionaries since the war....

These pages are written in no spirit of vindictiveness....We plead not for the colored people alone, but for all victims of the terrible injustice which puts men and women to death without form of law. During the year 1894, there were 132 persons executed in the United States by due form of law, while in the same year, 197 persons were put to death by mobs, who gave the victims no opportunity to make a lawful defense. No comment need be made upon a condition of public sentiment responsible for such alarming results.

DOCUMENT ANALYSIS

1. According to Wells-Barnett, what caused many of the lynchings of black men in the late nineteenth-century South?

Twenty-two.4

Jane Addams, from *Twenty Years at Hull House* (1910)

Jane Addams established Hull House, a settlement house to help the immigrant poor in Chicago, in the late 1880s. Addams was a leading spokesperson for the settlement house move- ment for the next several decades, and she sought to use the settlement houses not only to assist the indigent, but to champion Progressive reform, on the local, state, and national levels. In this brief excerpt from Addams's autobiography, Twenty Years at Hull House, *Addams quotes from her 1892 speech in which she makes it clear that in addition to helping the needy, the settlement houses could provide useful work for disengaged upper class youth.* *

We have in America a fast-growing number of cultivated young people who have no recognized outlet for their active faculties. They hear constantly of the great social maladjustment, but no way is provided for them to change it, and their uselessness hangs about them heavily....These young people have had advantages of college, of European travel, and of economic study, but they are sustaining this shock of inaction. They have pet phrases, and they tell you that the things that make us all alike are stronger than the things that make us different. They say that all men are united by needs and sympathies far more permanent and radical than anything that temporarily divides them and sets them in opposition to each other. If they affect art, they say that the decay in artistic expression is due to the decay in ethics, that art when shut away from the human interests and from the great mass of humanity is self-destructive. They tell their elders with all the bitterness of youth that if they expect success from them in busi- ness or politics or in whatever lines their ambition for them has run, they must let them consult all of humanity; that they must let them find out what the people want and how they want it. It is only the stronger young people, however, who formulate this.

* From Jane Addams, *Twenty Years at Hull House* (New York: Phillips Publishing Company, 1910), pp. 91–100, available online at http://wps.ablongman.com/wps/media/objects/1676/1716309/documents/ doc_d22d08.html.

Many of them dissipate their energies in so-called enjoyment. Others not content with that, go on studying and go back to college for their second degrees; not that they are especially fond of study, but because they want something definite to do, and their powers have been trained in the direction of mental accumulation. Many are buried beneath this mental accumulation with lowered vitality and discontent....

The Settlement...is an experimental effort to aid the solution of the social and industrial problems which are engendered by the modern conditions of life in a great city. It insists that these problems are not confined to any one portion of a city. It is an attempt to relieve, at the same time, the overaccumulation at one end of society and the destitution at the other, but it assumes that this overaccumulation and destitution is most sorely felt in the things that pertain to social and educational advantages. From its very nature it can stand for no political or social propaganda. It must, in a sense, give the warm welcome of an inn to all such propaganda, if perchance one of them be found an angel. The one thing to be dreaded in the Settlement is that it lose its flexibility, its power of quick adaptation, its readiness to change its methods as its environment may demand. It must be open to conviction and must have a deep and abiding sense of tolerance. It must be hospitable and ready for experiment. It should demand from its residents a scientific patience in the accumulation of facts and the steady holding of their sympathies as one of the best instruments for that accumulation. It must be grounded in a philosophy whose foundation is on the solidarity of the human race, a philosophy which will not waver when the race happens to be represented by a drunken woman or an idiot boy. Its residents must be emptied of all conceit of opinion and all self-assertion, and ready to arouse and interpret the public opinion of their neighborhood. They must be content to live quietly side by side with their neighbors, until they grow into a sense of relationship and mutual interests. Their neighbors are held apart by differences of race and language which the residents can more easily overcome. They are bound to see the needs of their neighborhood as a whole, to furnish data for legislation, and to use their influence to secure it. In short, residents are pledged to devote themselves to the duties of good citizenship and to the arousing of the social energies which too largely lie dormant in every neighborhood given over to industrialism. They are bound to regard the entire life of their city as organic, to make an effort to unify it, and to protest against its over-differentiation.

It is always easy to make all philosophy point one particular moral and all history adorn one particular tale, but I may be forgiven the reminder that the best speculative philosophy sets forth the solidarity of the human race; that the highest moralists have taught that without the advance and improvement of the whole, no man can hope for any lasting improvement in his own moral or material individual condition; and that the subjective necessity for Social Settlements is therefore identical with that necessity, which urges us on toward social and individual salvation.

DOCUMENT ANALYSIS

1. How does Addams see the settlement house as filling a need on both the higher and lower ends of society?

2. Does Addams see the settlement house as promoting a particular ideological point of view? Explain.

Chapter Study Questions

1. How did the work of Jane Addams at Hull House and Ida Tarbell's exposé of Standard Oil reflect the underlying spirit of the Progressive era?

2. How did the Tammany Hall machine function? Why might progressives have targeted such machines?

3. Why would Ida B. Wells-Barnett have disagreed with Booker T. Washington and agreed with Du Bois? Do you find anything in the excerpt which would lead you to that conclusion?

Twenty-three

From Roosevelt to Wilson in the Age of Progressivism

E arlier chapters have illustrated the contributions of progressive reformers on the state and local levels. This chapter focuses on progressivism and the changes it wrought on the national political system. The Progressive movement established the framework for American liberalism and changed the relationship between government and society, making government the agent of change aimed at improving Americans' quality of life. Using terms like "regulate," "bring order," and "make more efficient," the progressive agenda focused on solutions for problems created by the new economic order and urban growth.

The presidency of Theodore Roosevelt catapulted the Progressive movement onto the national political scene. Roosevelt's strong support for the movement brought it popularity and publicity—never more so than in 1912 when, after losing the Republican nomination to William Taft, the current president, Roosevelt walked out of the Republican convention and established the Progressive party. In the presidential campaign that followed, two of the candidates—Roosevelt, who had been president from 1902 to 1908, and Woodrow Wilson, a former president of Princeton University and governor of New Jersey—ran on strongly progressive platforms.

Wilson and Roosevelt debated how to deal with the most pressing problem of the new century, economic concentration of wealth and industrial power. Selections in this chapter contrast Roosevelt's and Wilson's visions for the role of federal government and the appropriate use of its power.

At the 1912 Progressive party convention in Chicago, which nominated Roosevelt, Jane Addams seconded his nomination while a banner reading "Votes for Women" hung in the auditorium. Women's groups had been actively campaigning for suffrage since the Seneca Falls convention of 1848, but had gained the vote only in a few western states. By the early 1900s, women's rights groups became increasingly more militant and successful, as new leadership connected the vote to the reform movement. If women were to protect themselves against industrial overwork, rape, and prostitution, and continue "urban housekeeping"—cleaning up cities and closing down saloons—and if newly arrived immigrants could vote, certainly women deserved the right to vote. The selection in this chapter describes the rationale for women suffrage, which was only granted with the passage of the Nineteenth Amendment in 1920, after militant protests during World War I.

Twenty-three.1

Theodore Roosevelt,
from *The New Nationalism*
(1910)

In this speech, delivered at Osawatomie, Kansas, in 1910, Roosevelt outlined the ideas which would become the basis of his 1912 presidential campaign. He expounded on his vision of a "new nationalism," which recognized the inevitability of economic concentration and called on government to regulate the new economic structures and to become the "steward of public welfare." *

Practical equality of opportunity for all citizens, when we achieve it, will have two great results. First, every man will have a fair chance to make of himself all that in him lies; to reach the highest point to which his capacities, unassisted by special privilege of his own and unhampered by the special privilege of others, can carry him, and to get for himself and his family substantially what he has earned. Second, equality of opportunity means that the commonwealth will get from every citizen the highest service of which he is capable. No man who carries the burden of special privileges of another can give to the commonwealth that service to which it is fairly entitled....

Now, this means that our government, national and state, must be freed from the sinister influence or control of special interests. Exactly as the special interests of cotton and slavery threatened our political integrity before the Civil War, so now the great special business interests too often control and corrupt the men and methods of government for their own profit. We must drive the special interest out of politics. That is one of our tasks today....

The true friend of property, the true conservative, is he who insists that property shall be the servant and not the master of the commonwealth; who insists that the creature of man's making shall be the servant and not the master of the man who made it. The citizens of the United States must effectively control the mighty commercial forces which they have themselves called into being....

* From Theodore Roosevelt, *The New Nationalism*, 1910.

It has become entirely clear that we must have government supervision of the capitalization, not only of the public service corporations, including, particularly, railways, but of all corporations doing an interstate business. I do not wish to see the nation forced into the ownership of the railways if it can be possibly avoided, and the only alternative is thoroughgoing and effective regulation, which shall be based on a full knowledge of all the facts, including a physical valuation of property....

Combinations in industry are the result of an imperative economic law which cannot be repealed by political legislation. The effort at prohibiting all combination has substantially failed. The way out lies, not in attempting to prevent such combinations, but in completely controlling them in the interest of the public welfare.

DOCUMENT ANALYSIS

1. What does Theodore Roosevelt want the federal government to do in order to address problems created by business monopolies?

Twenty-three.2

Woodrow Wilson, from *The New Freedom* (1913)

This excerpt is from Woodrow Wilson's book published after the campaign, The New Freedom: A Call for the Emancipation of the Generous Energies of a People. *Wilson believed federal power should be controlled and limited.* *

The doctrine that monopoly is inevitable and that the only course open to the people of the United States is to submit to and regulate it found a champion during the campaign of 1912 in the new party or branch of the Republican party, founded under the leadership of Mr. Roosevelt, with the conspicuous aid,—I mention him with no satirical intention, but merely to set the facts down accurately,—of Mr. George W. Perkins, organizer of the Steel Trust and the Harvester Trust, and with the support of patriotic, conscientious and high-minded men and women of the land. The fact that its acceptance of monopoly was a feature of the new party platform from which the attention of the generous and just was diverted by the charm of a social program of great attractiveness to all concerned for the amelioration of the lot of those who suffer wrong and privation, and the further fact that, even so, the platform was repudiated by the majority of the nation, render it no less necessary to reflect on the party in the country's history. It may be useful, in order to relieve the minds of many from an error of no small magnitude, to consider now, the heat of a presidential contest being past, exactly what it was that Mr. Roosevelt proposed.

Mr. Roosevelt attached to his platform some very splendid suggestions as to noble enterprises which we ought to undertake for the uplift of the human race;...If you have read the trust plank in that platform as often as I have read it, you have found it very long, but very tolerant. It did not anywhere condemn monopoly, except in words; its essential meaning was that the trusts have been bad and must be made to be good. You

---

* From Woodrow Wilson, *The New Freedom: A Call for the Emancipation of the Generous Energies of a People*, 1913.

111

know that Mr. Roosevelt long ago classified trusts for us as good and bad, and he said that he was afraid only of the bad ones. Now he does not desire that there should be any more of the bad ones, but proposes that they should all be made good by discipline, directly applied by a commission of executive appointment. All he explicitly complains of is lack of publicity and lack of fairness; not the exercise of power, for throughout that plank the power of the great corporations is accepted as the inevitable consequence of the modern organization of industry. All that it is proposed to do is to take them under control and deregulation.

The fundamental part of such a program is that the trusts shall be recognized as a permanent part of our economic order, and that the government shall try to make trusts the ministers, the instruments, through which the life of this country shall be justly and happily developed on its industrial side....

Shall we try to get the grip of monopoly away from our lives, or shall we not? Shall we withhold our hand and say monopoly is inevitable, that all we can do is to regulate it? Shall we say that all we can do is to put government in competition with monopoly and try its strength against it? Shall we admit that the creature of our own hands is stronger that we are? We have been dreading all along the time when the combined power of high finance would be greater than the power of government.

DOCUMENT ANALYSIS

1. According to this document, what is Woodrow Wilson's attitude toward monopoly?

2. Why did Wilson mention George W. Perkins's involvement with the Progressive party? What was Wilson implying by doing so?

Twenty-three.3

National American Woman Suffrage Association, Mother's Day Letter (1912)

The National American Woman Suffrage Association (NAWSA) was formed in 1890 from the merger of two organizations, founded by Elizabeth Cady Stanton and Susan B. Anthony respectively in 1869. Under the leadership of Carrie Chapman Catt, membership in the organization rose to two million. Catt's organization was relatively mainstream, especially in contrast to the militant National Woman's Party, which adopted radical tactics including hunger strikes, demonstrations, and pickets. *

Dear Sir:

"Mother's Day" is becoming more and more observed in the churches of our land, and many clergymen on that day are delivering special sermons, calling attention to the Mother's influence in the Home....

In view of the fact that in the moral and social reform work of the churches, the Mothers and Women of the churches are seeking to correct serious evils that exist in our cities as a menace to the morals of their children outside the home, and in view of the fact that churchwomen are finding that much of their effort is ineffective and of no value, because they are denied the weapon of Christian warfare, the ballot...we ask of you, will you not in justice to the Mothers of your church choose for your topic on "Mother's Day" some subject bearing on "The need of the Mother's influence in the State?"

Women are recognized as the most religious, the most moral and the most sober portion of the American people. Why deny them a voice in public affairs when we give it for the asking to every ignorant foreigner who comes to our shores?

The women have always been the mainstay and chief supporters of the churches, and

---

* From "Report of the Church Work Committee," *Proceedings of the Forty-Fourth Annual Convention of the National American Woman Suffrage Association* (New York: National American Woman Suffrage Association, 1912), 55–57.

in their struggle for their civil liberty. Should not their clergymen or Christian brothers sympathize with them and "Remember those in bonds as bound with them" and help them in their struggle? On behalf of the church work committee representing Christian Mothers in every State in the Union, I would be pleased to know if you will be one to raise your voice on "Mother's Day" in favor of the extension of the Mother's influence in our land "to help those women that labored with you in the Gospel?"

DOCUMENT ANALYSIS

1. In what ways does this letter seek to use the observance of Mother's Day to promote the political goal of women's suffrage? Is the argument made in the letter convincing? Explain.

Chapter Study Questions

1. Why would both strict capitalists and socialists find Theodore Roosevelt's New Nationalism unappealing? How would they react to Woodrow Wilson's New Freedom? Based upon their ideas of New Nationalism and New Freedom, respectively, how would Roosevelt and Wilson differ in how they would deal with the clout of Standard Oil described by Tarbell in Chapter 22?

2. Compare the visions of the role of the federal government in Roosevelt's New Nationalism and Wilson's New Freedom. Which approach most accurately reflected the economic realities of the late nineteenth and early twentieth centuries? Which most accurately anticipated the future?

3. In its Mother's Day letter, how did the NAWSA view women as different from men? Do you think that differentiation is accurate? Discuss how this view relates to the actual work being done by Ida Tarbell (from Chapter 22).

Twenty-four

The Nation at War

Following President McKinley's assassination by an anarchist in 1901, Vice President Theodore Roosevelt, former governor of New York, became the new president. Formerly Assistant Secretary of the Navy, Roosevelt had been a fervid supporter of the Spanish-American War, even joining a group known as the Rough Riders, who fought on horseback in Cuba. As president, Roosevelt asserted the power of the United States to obtain what it wanted, including the right to build a canal in Panama. In December 2004, Roosevelt announced an extension of the Monroe Doctrine, alerting nations of Latin America that the United States would intervene if they had domestic disorder.

When war broke out in 1914, Americans thought that Europe had gone mad. As your text shows, President Wilson, who had been elected because of his domestic policies, found himself forced to develop a foreign policy—one that would keep the United States out of the conflict. Wilson believed he could accomplish this if the United States remained completely neutral. In the 1916 presidential campaign he ran on a platform that promised "Peace, Prosperity, and Progress," but just one year later, after peace negotiations failed and the Germans resumed unrestricted submarine warfare, Wilson asked the Congress for a declaration of war against Germany.

Some Americans, including Wilson, considered the war an extension of the progressive reform movement. The president promised the war would "make the world safe for democracy" and insisted that it was a moral crusade. Helping Wilson was the Committee on Public Information headed by George Creel, which through speeches, pamphlets, posters, and movies exhorted Americans to support the war effort. This patriotic hysteria was often militantly racist, anti-German, and anti-immigrant. The Boy Scouts pamphlet included in this chapter was written in part by the Committee on Public Information and depicts some of the zeal and militancy of the war effort.

The Creel Committee and the passage of the Espionage and Sedition Acts helped create a domestic environment in which dissent was associated with treason. Socialists, labor activists, pacifists, and all those who questioned the war could be subject to imprisonment. Eugene Debs, the former Socialist presidential candidate, was sentenced to ten years in prison for his opposition to the war. Socialist newspapers were banned; union organizers and pacifists were attacked by mobs or hanged in effigy. Debs' speech to the court at his sentencing in 1918 is included in this chapter. The government, and large numbers of the American public, demanded unquestioning patriotism. The selection included here from the memoirs of Secretary of War Newton Baker describes his concerns about the treatment of German Americans.

While patriotism ran high, the United States entered the war in 1917 unprepared for military action. The American doughboy quickly learned that Sherman had been right: war was indeed hell. In the selection from Eugene Kennedy's diary, a soldier describes the horrors of life on the front lines in France.

Long before the war ended, Wilson began to plan the peace—a peace that he hoped would lead to a better society. In his Fourteen Points, Wilson presented a plan that would make the world "fit and safe to live in." He presented his points at the Paris peace conference, but the resulting Versailles Treaty, calling for extensive German war reparations and a German declaration of war guilt, ran counter to Wilson's plan. Wilson hoped to improve upon the Versailles Treaty through his League of Nations, an organization founded to negotiate international disputes. The League was rejected by Congress in 1920 and Wilson ended his presidency an enfeebled, partially paralyzed man.

Twenty-four.1

The Roosevelt Corollary
to the Monroe Doctrine
(1904)

In a message to Congress in 1904, President Theodore Roosevelt announced a bold extension of the long-standing Monroe Doctrine of the United States. The Monroe Doctrine of 1823 had been a warning to foreign powers to leave Latin American countries alone, but the Roosevelt Corollary went further. With the United States now an emerging world power, Roosevelt stated that the United States would intervene if domestic unrest in any country in the Western Hemisphere required the intervention of some "civilized" nation. *

It is not true that the United States feels any land hunger or entertains any projects as regards the other nations of the Western Hemisphere save such as are for their welfare. All that this country desires is to see the neighboring countries stable, orderly, and prosperous. Any country whose people conduct themselves well can count upon our hearty friendship. If a nation shows that it knows how to act with reasonable efficiency and decency in social and political matters, if it keeps order and pays its obligations, it need fear no interference from the United States. Chronic wrongdoing, or an impotence which results in a general loosening of the ties of civilized society, may in America, as elsewhere, ultimately require intervention by some civilized nation, and in the Western Hemisphere the adherence of the United States to the Monroe Doctrine may force the United States, however reluctantly, in flagrant cases of such wrongdoing or impotence, to the exercise of an international police power. If every country washed by the Caribbean Sea would show the progress in stable and just civilization which with the aid of the Platt Amendment Cuba has shown since our troops left the island, and which so many of the republics in both Americas are constantly and brilliantly showing, all question of interference by this Nation with their affairs would be at an end. Our interests and those of our Southern neighbors are in reality identical. They have great natural

* From Theodore Roosevelt, *Annual Message to Congress*, December 6, 1904, accessible online at http://www.ourdocuments.gov).

riches, and if within their borders the reign of law and justice obtains, prosperity is sure to come to them. While they thus obey the primary laws of civilized society they may rest assured that they will be treated by us in a spirit of cordial and helpful sympathy. We would interfere with them only in the last resort, and then only if it became evident that their inability or unwillingness to do justice at home and abroad had violated the rights of the United States or had invited foreign aggression to the detriment of the entire body of American nations. It is a mere truism to say that every nation, whether in America or anywhere else, which desires to maintain its freedom, its independence, must ultimately realize that the right of such independence can not be separated from the responsibility of making good use of it.

DOCUMENT ANALYSIS

1. How does Roosevelt justify the necessity of his new corollary to the Monroe Doctrine? Is his argument compelling?

2. How would citizens of Latin American countries likely react to the Roosevelt Corollary?

Twenty-four.2

Boy Scouts of America, from "Boy Scouts Support the War Effort" (1917)

This is a selection from a pamphlet published by the Boy Scouts of America. The pamphlet encourages vigilantism and loyalty checks, among other "patriotic" measures. Many Americans became formal or informal loyalty enforcers during World War I and many individuals were sent to prison for published or unpublished criticisms of the war efforts or Wilson's policies. The Boy Scouts played an important role on the home front, which included planting vegetable gardens and recycling. *

To the Members of the Boy Scouts of America!

Attention, Scouts! We are again called upon to do active service for our country! Every one of the 285,661 Scouts and 76,957 Scout Officials has been summoned by President Woodrow Wilson, Commander-in-Chief of the Army and Navy, to serve as a dispatch bearer from the Government at Washington to the American people all over the country. The prompt, enthusiastic, and hearty response of every one of us has been pledged by our [Scout] President, Mr. Livingstone. Our splendid record of accomplishments in war activities promises full success in this new job.

This patriotic service will be rendered under the slogan: "EVERY SCOUT TO BOOST AMERICA" AS A GOVERNMENT DISPATCH BEARER. The World War is for liberty and democracy.

America has long been recognized as the leader among nations standing for liberty and democracy. American entered the war as a sacred duty to uphold the principles of liberty and democracy.

As a democracy, our country faces great danger—not so much from submarines, battleships and armies, because, thanks to our allies, our enemies have apparently little chance of reaching our shores.

* From a pamphlet entitled Committee on Public Information, Boy Scouts of America, 1917.

Our danger is from within. Our enemies have representatives everywhere; they tell lies; they misrepresent the truth; they deceive our own people; they are a real menace to our country.

Already we have seen how poor Russia has been made to suffer because her people do not know the truth. Representatives of the enemy have been very effective in their deceitful efforts to make trouble for the Government.

Fortunately here in America our people are better educated—they want the truth. Our President recognized the justice and wisdom of this demand when in the early stages of the war he created the Committee on Public Information. He knew that the Government would need the confidence, enthusiasm and willing service of every man and woman, every boy and girl in the nation. He knew that the only possible way to create a genuine feeling of partnership between the people and its representatives in Washington was to take the people into his confidence by full, frank statements concerning the reasons for our entering the war, the various steps taken during the war and the ultimate aims of the war.

Neither the President as Commander-in-Chief, nor our army and navy by land and sea, can alone win the war. At this moment the best defense that America has is an enlightened and loyal citizenship. Therefore, we as scouts are going to have the opportunity of rendering real patriotic service under our slogan.

"EVERY SCOUT TO BOOST AMERICA" AS A GOVERNMENT DISPATCH BEARER.

Here is where our service begins. We are to help spread the facts about America and America's part in the World War. We are to fight lies with truth.

We are to help create public opinion "just as effective in helping to bring victory as ships and guns," to stir patriotism, the great force behind the ships and guns. Isn't that a challenge for every loyal Scout?

"EVERY SCOUT TO BOOST AMERICA" AS A GOVERNMENT DISPATCH BEARER: HOW?

As Mr. George Creel, the Chairman of the Committee on Public Information, says in his letter, scouts are to serve as direct special representatives of the Committee on Public Information to keep the people informed about the War and its causes and progress. The Committee has already prepared a number of special pamphlets and other will be prepared. It places upon the members of the Boy Scouts of America the responsibility of putting the information in these pamphlets in homes of the American people. Every Scout will be furnished a credential card by his Scoutmaster. Under the direction of our leaders, the Boy Scouts of America are to serve as an intelligence division of the citizens' army, always prepared and alert to respond to any call which may come from the President of the United States and the Committee on Public Information at Washington.

...Each Scoutmaster is to be furnished with a complete set of all of the government publications, in order that all of the members of his troop may be completely informed. Each scout and scout official is expected to seize every opportunity to serve the Committee on Public Information by making available authoritative information. It is up to the Boy Scouts to see that as many people as possible have an intelligent under-

standing of any and all facts incident to our present national crisis and the World War....
    PAMPHLETS NOW READY FOR CIRCULATION
    Note:—A set will be sent to every Scoutmaster. You will need to know what is in these pamphlets so as to act as a serviceable bureau of information and be able to give each person the particular intelligence he seeks.

DOCUMENT ANALYSIS

1. According to this pamphlet, how are the Boy Scouts to help the federal government promote the war effort?
2. What does the pamphlet mean when it refers to "our danger is from within"?

Twenty-four.3

Newton D. Baker,
"The Treatment of German-Americans"
(1918)

This selection is taken from the wartime writings of the secretary of war. In this piece, Baker expressed concern about the treatment of German-Americans and argued that the government was not responsible for nativist actions. *

The spirit of the country seems unusually good, but there is a growing frenzy of suspicion and hostility toward disloyalty. I am afraid we are going to have a good many instances of people roughly treated on very slight evidence of disloyalty. Already a number of men and some women have been "tarred and feathered," and a portion of the press is urging with great vehemence more strenuous efforts at detection and punishment. This usually takes the form of advocating "drum-head courts-martial" and "being stood up against a wall and shot," which are perhaps none too bad for real traitors, but are very suggestive of summary discipline to arouse mob spirit, which unhappily does not take time to weigh evidence.

In Cleveland a few days ago a foreign-looking man got into a street car and, taking a seat, noticed pasted in the window next to him a Liberty Loan poster, which he immediately tore down, tore into small bits, and stamped under his feet. The people in the car surged around him with the demand that he be lynched, when a Secret Service man showed his badge and placed him under arrest, taking him in a car to the police station, where he was searched and found to have two Liberty Bonds in his pocket and to be a non-English Pole. When an interpreter was procured, it was discovered that the circular which he had destroyed had had on it a picture of the German Emperor, which had so infuriated the fellow that he destroyed the circular to show his vehement hatred of the common enemy. As he was unable to speak a single word of English, he would undoubtedly have been hanged but for the intervention and entirely accidental presence of the Secret Service agent.

* From Frederick Palmer, *Newton D. Baker*, vol. 2 (Dodd, Mead & Company, 1931), 162–163.

I am afraid the grave danger in this sort of thing, apart from its injustice, is that the German Government will adopt retaliatory measures. While the Government of the United States is not only responsible for these things, but very zealously trying to prevent them, the German Government draws no fine distinctions.

DOCUMENT ANALYSIS

1. What evidence does Baker provide that wartime super-patriotism can be dangerous?

Twenty-four.4

Eugene Kennedy,
A "Doughboy" Describes the Fighting Front
(1918)

This selection from the diary of Eugene Kennedy describes life on the front lines in Europe. American soldiers were often poorly equipped and ill-fed, as this doughboy reports. *

Thursday, September 12, 1918

Hiked through dark woods. No light allowed, guided by holding on the pack of the man ahead. Stumbled through underbrush for about half mile into an open field where we waited in soaking rain until about 10:00 P.M. We then started on our hike to the St. Mihiel front, arriving on the crest of a hill at 1:00 A.M. I saw a sight which I shall never forget. It was the zero hour and in one instant the entire front as far as the eye could reach in either direction was a sheet of flame while the heavy artillery made the earth quake. The barrage was so intense that for a time we could not make out whether the Americans or Germans were putting it over. After timing the interval between flash and report we knew that the heaviest artillery was less than a mile away and consequently it was ours. We waded through pools and mud across open lots into a woods on a hill and had to pitch tents in mud. Blankets all wet and we are soaked to the skin. Have carried full pack from 10:00 P.M. to 2:00 A.M., without a rest....Despite the cannonading I slept until 8:00 A.M. and awoke to find every discharge of 14-inch artillery shaking our tent like a leaf. Remarkable how we could sleep. No breakfast....The doughboys had gone over the top at 5:00 A.M. and the French were shelling the back areas toward Metz....Firing is incessant, so is rain. See an air battle just before turning in.

Friday, September 13, 1918

Called at 3:00 A.M. Struck tents and started to hike at 5:00 A.M. with full packs and a pick.

* From the diary of Eugene Kennedy. Courtesy of Eugene Kennedy Collection, Hoover Institution on War, Revolution, and Peace, Stanford University.

Put on gas mask at alert position and hiked about five miles to St. Jean, where we unslung full packs and went on about four miles further with short packs and picks. Passed several batteries and saw many dead horses who gave out at start of push. Our doughboys are still shoving and "Jerry" is dropping so many shells on road into no man's land that we stayed back in field and made no effort to repair shell-torn road. Plenty of German prisoners being brought back....Guns booming all the time....

Thursday, October 17, 1918

Struck tents at 8:00 A.M. and moved about four miles to Chatel. Pitched tents on a side hill so steep that we had to cut steps to ascend. Worked like hell to shovel out a spot to pitch tent on. Just across the valley in front of us about two hundred yards distant, there had occurred an explosion due to a mine planted by the "Bosche" [Germans] and set with a time fuse. It had blown two men (French), two horses, and the wagon into fragments....Arriving on the scene we found Quinn ransacking the wagon. It was full of grub. We each loaded a burlap bag with cans of condensed milk, peas, lobster, salmon, and bread. I started back...when suddenly another mine exploded, the biggest I ever saw. Rocks and dirt flew sky high. Quinn was hit in the knee and had to go to hospital....At 6:00 P.M. each of our four platoons left camp in units to go up front and throw three foot and one artillery bridge across the Aire River. On way to river we were heavily shelled and gassed....We put a bridge across 75-foot span....Third platoon men had to get into water and swim or stand in water to their necks. The toughest job we had so far....

Monday, October 21, 1918

Fragment from shell struck mess-kit on my back....Equipment, both American and German, thrown everywhere, especially Hun helmets and belts of machine gunners....Went scouting...for narrow-gauge rails to replace the ones "Jerry" spoiled before evacuating. Negro engineers working on railroad same as at St. Mihiel, that's all they are good for....

Friday, November 1, 1918

Started out at 4:00 A.M. The drive is on. Fritz is coming back at us. Machine guns cracking, flares and Verry lights, artillery from both sides. A real war and we are walking right into the zone, ducking shells all the way. The artillery is nerve racking and we don't know from which angle "Jerry" will fire next. Halted behind shelter of railroad track just outside of Grand Pre after being forced back off main road by shell fire. Trees splintered like toothpicks. Machine gunners on top of railroad bank...."Jerry" drove Ewell and me into a two-by-four shell hole, snipers' bullets close.

Sunday, November 3, 1918

Many dead Germans along the road. One heap on a manure pile....Devastation everywhere. Our barrage has rooted up the entire territory like a ploughed field. Dead horses galore, many of them have a hind quarter cut off—the Huns need food. Dead men here and there. The sight I enjoy better than a dead German is to see heaps of them. Rain again. Couldn't keep rain out of our faces and it was pouring hard. Got up at midnight and drove stakes to secure shelter-half over us, pulled our wet blankets out of mud and made the bed all over again. Slept like a log with all my equipment in the open. One hundred forty-two planes sighted in evening.

Sunday, November 10, 1918

First day off in over two months....Took a bath and we were issued new underwear but the cooties [lice] got there first....The papers show a picture of the Kaiser entitled "William the Lost," and stating that he had abdicated. Had a good dinner. Rumor at night that armistice was signed. Some fellows discharged their arms in the courtyard, but most of us were too well pleased with dry bunk to get up.

DOCUMENT ANALYSIS

1. How would you describe Kennedy's experience as a doughboy on the front during World War I? What difficulties did he encounter?

Twenty-four.5

Eugene V. Debs, Statement to the Court (1918)

Eugene V. Debs, a labor organizer from Terre Haute, Indiana, first became well known nationwide in 1894. That year, as head of the newly formed American Railway Union, Debs organized a secondary strike in support of the Pullman strikers, for which he was arrested and sent to prison. By 1901, Debs had become head of the Socialist Party in the United States, and ran as its candidate for President four times, garnering nearly six percent of the national vote in 1912. Like most Socialists, Debs strongly opposed U.S. involvement in World War I, and he was sent to prison for giving a speech in Canton, Ohio, in 1918 advocating defiance of the draft. At his sentencing, he made this impassioned statement.*

Your Honor, years ago I recognized my kinship with all living beings, and I made up my mind that I was not one bit better than the meanest on earth. I said then, and I say now, that while there is a lower class, I am in it, and while there is a criminal element I am of it, and while there is a soul in prison, I am not free.

I listened to all that was said in this court in support and justification of this prosecution, but my mind remains unchanged. I look upon the Espionage Law as a despotic enactment in flagrant conflict with democratic principles and with the spirit of free institutions...

Your Honor, I have stated in this court that I am opposed to the social system in which we live; that I believe in a fundamental change—but if possible by peaceable and orderly means...

Standing here this morning, I recall my boyhood. At fourteen I went to work in a railroad shop; at sixteen I was firing a freight engine on a railroad. I remember all the

* From Eugene V. Debs, Statement to the Court, in James Andrews and David Zarefsky, eds., *American Voices: Significant Speeches in American History* (New York: Longman, 1989), accessible online at http://www.wfu.edu/~zulick/341/Debs1918.html.

hardships and privations of that earlier day, and from that time until now my heart has been with the working class. I could have been in Congress long ago. I have preferred to go to prison…

I am thinking this morning of the men in the mills and the factories; of the men in the mines and on the railroads. I am thinking of the women who for a paltry wage are compelled to work out their barren lives; of the little children who in this system are robbed of their childhood and in their tender years are seized in the remorseless grasp of Mammon and forced into the industrial dungeons, there to feed the monster machines while they themselves are being starved and stunted, body and soul. I see them dwarfed and diseased and their little lives broken and blasted because in this high noon of Christian civilization money is still so much more important than the flesh and blood of childhood. In very truth gold is god today and rules with pitiless sway in the affairs of men.

In this country—the most favored beneath the bending skies—we have vast areas of the richest and most fertile soil, material resources in inexhaustible abundance, the most marvelous productive machinery on earth, and millions of eager workers ready to apply their labor to that machinery to produce in abundance for every man, woman, and child—and if there are still vast numbers of our people who are the victims of poverty and whose lives are an unceasing struggle all the way from youth to old age, until at last death comes to their rescue and lulls these hapless victims to dreamless sleep, it is not the fault of the Almighty: it cannot be charged to nature, but it is due entirely to the outgrown social system in which we live that ought to be abolished not only in the interest of the toiling masses but in the higher interest of all humanity…

I believe, Your Honor, in common with all Socialists, that this nation ought to own and control its own industries. I believe, as all Socialists do, that all things that are jointly needed and used ought to be jointly owned—that industry, the basis of our social life, instead of being the private property of a few and operated for their enrichment, ought to be the common property of all, democratically administered in the interest of all…

I am opposing a social order in which it is possible for one man who does absolutely nothing that is useful to amass a fortune of hundreds of millions of dollars, while millions of men and women who work all the days of their lives secure barely enough for a wretched existence.

This order of things cannot always endure. I have registered my protest against it. I recognize the feebleness of my effort, but, fortunately, I am not alone. There are multiplied thousands of others who, like myself, have come to realize that before we may truly enjoy the blessings of civilized life, we must reorganize society upon a mutual and cooperative basis; and to this end we have organized a great economic and political movement that spreads over the face of all the earth.…

Your Honor, I ask no mercy and I plead for no immunity. I realize that finally the right must prevail. I never so clearly comprehended as now the great struggle between the powers of greed and exploitation on the one hand and upon the other the rising hosts of industrial freedom and social justice.

I can see the dawn of the better day for humanity. The people are awakening. In due time they will and must come to their own.

When the mariner, sailing over tropic seas, looks for relief from his weary watch, he turns his eyes toward the southern cross, burning luridly above the tempest-vexed ocean. As the midnight approaches, the southern cross begins to bend, the whirling worlds change their places, and with starry finger-points the Almighty marks the passage of time upon the dial of the universe, and though no bell may beat the glad tidings, the lookout knows that the midnight is passing and that relief and rest are close at hand. Let the people everywhere take heart of hope, for the cross is bending, the midnight is passing, and joy cometh with the morning.

I am now prepared to receive your sentence.

DOCUMENT ANALYSIS

1. How does Debs view the Espionage Act?
2. Although sentenced to prison for speaking out against the involvement of the United States in World War I, what struggle does Debs spend most of his time discussing in his statement to the court? How do you think he sees the war as tied to that other struggle?

Woodrow Wilson, The Fourteen Points (1918)

Included here are Wilson's Fourteen Points, presented as a speech to Congress on January 8, 1918, designed to make the world safe for all people and formulate the agenda for postwar peace negotiations. *

It will be our wish and purpose that the processes of peace, when they are begun, shall be absolutely open and that they shall involve and permit henceforth no secret understandings of any kind. The day of conquest and aggrandizement is gone by; so is also the day of secret covenants entered into in the interest of particular governments and likely at some unlooked-for moment to upset the peace of the world....

We entered this war because violations of right had occurred which touched us to the quick and made the life of our own people impossible unless they were corrected and the world secure once for all against their recurrence.

What we demand in this war, therefore, is nothing peculiar to ourselves. It is that the world be made fit and safe to live in; and particularly that it be made safe for every peace-loving nation which, like our own, wishes to live its own life, determine its own institutions, be assured of justice and fair dealing by the other peoples of the world as against force and selfish aggressions.

All the peoples of the world are in effect partners in this interest, and for our own part we see very clearly that unless justice be done to others it will not be done to us. The program of the world's peace, therefore, is our program; and that program, the only possible program, as we see it, is this:

1. Open covenants of peace, openly arrived at, after which there shall be no private international understandings of any kind but diplomacy shall proceed always frankly and in the public view.

* From Woodrow Wilson, *Message to Congress*, January 8, 1918.

2. Absolute freedom of navigation upon the seas, outside territorial waters, alike in peace and in war, except as the seas may be closed in whole or in part by international action for the enforcement of international covenants.

3. The removal, so far as possible, of all economic barriers and the establishment of an equality of trade conditions among all the nations consenting to the peace and associating themselves for its maintenance.

4. Adequate guarantees given and taken that national armaments will be reduced to the lowest points consistent with domestic safety.

5. A free, open-minded, and absolutely impartial adjustment of all colonial claims, based upon a strict observance of the principle that in determining all such questions of sovereignty the interests of the populations concerned must have equal weight with the equitable claims of the government whose title is to be determined.

6. The evacuation of all Russian territory and such a settlement of all questions affecting Russia as will secure the best and freest cooperation of the other nations of the world in obtaining for her an unhampered and unembarrassed opportunity for the independent determination of her own political development and national policy and assure her of a sincere welcome into the society of free nations under institutions of her own choosing; and, more than a welcome, assistance also of every kind that she may need and may herself desire. The treatment accorded Russian by her sister nations in the months to come will be the acid test of their good will, of their comprehension of her needs as distinguished from their own interests, and of their intelligent and unselfish sympathy.

7. Belgium, the whole world will agree, must be evacuated and restored, without any attempt to limit the sovereignty which she enjoys in common with all other free nations. No other single act will serve as this will serve to restore confidence among the nations in the laws which they have themselves set and determined for the government of their relations with one another. Without this healing act the whole structure and validity of international law is forever impaired.

8. All French territory should be freed and the invaded portions restored, and the wrong done to France by Prussia in 1871 in the matter of Alsace-Lorraine, which has unsettled the peace of the world for nearly fifty years, should be righted, in order that peace may once more be made secure in the interest of all.

9. A readjustment of the frontiers of Italy should be affected along clearly recognizable lines of nationality.

10. The peoples of Austria-Hungary, whose place among the nations we wish to see safeguarded and assured, should be accorded the freest opportunity of autonomous development.

11. Rumania, Serbia, and Montenegro should be evacuated; occupied territories restored; Serbia accorded free and secure access to the sea; and the relations of the several Balkan states to one another determined by friendly counsel along historically established lines of allegiance and nationality; and international guarantees of the polit-

ical and economic independence and territorial integrity of the several Balkan states should be entered into.

12. The Turkish portions of the present Ottoman Empire should be assured a secure sovereignty, but the other nationalities which are now under Turkish rule should be assured an undoubted security of life and an absolutely unmolested opportunity of autonomous development, and the Dardanelles should be permanently opened as a free passage to the ships and commerce of all nations under international guarantees.

13. An independent Polish state should be erected which should include the territories inhabited by indisputably Polish populations, which should be assured a free and secure access to the sea, and whose political and economic independence and territorial integrity should be guaranteed by international covenant.

14. A general association of nations must be formed under specific covenants for the purpose of affording mutual guarantees of political independence and territorial integrity to great and small states alike.

In regard to these essential rectifications of wrong and assertions of right we feel ourselves to be intimate partners of all the governments and peoples associated together against the imperialists. We cannot be separated in interest or divided in purpose. We stand together until the end....

An evident principle runs through the whole program I have outlined. It is the principle of justice to all peoples and nationalities, and their right to live on equal terms of liberty and safety with one another, whether they be strong or weak.

Unless this principle be made its foundation no part of the structure of international justice can stand. The people of the United States could act upon no other principle; and to the vindication of this principle they are ready to devote their lives, their honor, and everything that they possess. The moral climax of this the culminating and final war for human liberty has come, and they are ready to put their own strength, their own highest purpose, their own integrity and devotion to the test.

DOCUMENT ANALYSIS

1. What are some of the highlights of Wilson's Fourteen Points? Which ones seem the most realistic, and which the most idealistic?

2. At the conclusion, Wilson refers to World War I as "the culminating and final war for human liberty." How has this been disproved?

Chapter Study Questions

1. In what way did the Roosevelt Corollary change the Monroe Doctrine? How did the Corollary change American foreign policy? Is the Corollary still influencing American foreign policy today?

2. To what extent are the Boy Scout pamphlet, the incidents described by Newton Baker, and the prosecution of Debs for opposing the war all tied together? Why does wartime typically lead to a zeal for loyalty and a suspicion of free expression?

3. In what ways are both Debs and Wilson promoting an idealistic future in their respective speeches? Which do you find more appealing, and why?

4. How does Kennedy's gritty experience as a doughboy compare to the idealistic, patriotic fervor of the Boy Scout pamphlet or Wilson's Fourteen Points?

Twenty-five

Transition to Modern America

In the turbulent year of 1919—a year of deadly influenza, postwar jitters, unprecedented strikes, and race riots—a series of mail bombs were sent by anarchists to political and business leaders. One of those bombs was carried by an anarchist to the home of U.S. Attorney General A. Mitchell Palmer in Washington, D.C. The bomb went off before the anarchist got away, and he was blown to pieces, while Palmer and his family were greatly shaken by the experience. Palmer hoped to win the Democratic nomination for President in 1920 to succeed Woodrow Wilson, and he became an outspoken crusader against what he considered a "Red menace" threatening the United States. On New Year's Day, 1920, Palmer organized a series of hundreds of simultaneous raids on the offices and homes of known radicals, seeking to prove a Bolshevik-like conspiracy was at work. No such conspiracy was found, however. Palmer's popularity cooled, and the Red Scare largely fizzled out.

The 1920s were a decade of growing middle-class affluence and cultural conflict. As technology like the automobile, electricity, and running water became available to more Americans and improved their daily lives, the new society of the 1920s was becoming increasingly intolerant, xenophobic, and racist. The youth, freedom, and consumerism trumpeted by advertising and mass culture and most visibly represented by the automobile and city life often strained against America's rural roots and deep-seated fears of rapid change. The Ku Klux Klan expanded (most notably in urban areas) while the passage of Prohibition indicated that many believed that morality could be legislated.

In the early 1920s, Congress, bowing to nativist pressure, moved to restrict or even bar immigration. The 1924 Comprehensive Immigration Law, included here, banned all immigration from Asia (Chinese immigration had already been banned in 1882 and Japanese immigration in 1908) and limited immigration from southern and eastern Europe. To a great extent, Mexican and African American workers filled the labor shortages caused by these immigration restrictions.

One of the heroes of the 1920s was Yankee baseball star Babe Ruth, a bad boy who swatted more home runs than any slugger in history by day, and indulged all the pleasures of life by night. But perhaps the greatest American hero of this decade was the aviation pioneer Charles Lindbergh, a much more sober and industrious man, who made the first solo flight across the Atlantic in May 1927. When he returned to the United States, he was greeted with wild enthusiasm, including a ticker tape parade in New York, and a presidential welcome in Washington. An excerpt from President Calvin Coolidge's speech welcoming Lindbergh home from Paris is one of the documents in this chapter.

The 1920s are often referred to as the "Jazz Age," referring to the growing popularity of jazz music in this era. With roots in African American traditions, jazz evolved in the early twentieth century, and it emphasized freedom, improvisation, and a sensual rhythm. And it was in the 1920s that black intellectuals and artists flocked to New York City to learn and draw inspiration from one another, forming what came to be called the Harlem Renaissance. In Harlem and elsewhere, African Americans debated the merits of Marcus Garvey and his message of black pride and separateness. Garvey scorned the attempt by blacks to integrate into white society, arguing that whites would never offer full equality, and, regardless, African Americans should emphasize their own cultural roots and traditions and focus on Africa and self-help. The fourth document in this chapter provides excerpts of a speech given by Garvey in 1923, in which he explains the aims of his Universal Negro Improvement Association.

Women gained the vote just as World War I ended and entered the 1920s with their legal rights expanding and their social role changing. Increasingly, women attended college and worked outside the home; divorce laws were liberalized. Most famously, the 1920s saw the advent of the so-called New Woman and the flapper—a liberated woman who embraced sex, short skirts, and smoking. Yet simultaneously the 1920s saw a reemphasis of the importance of women's fulfillment in the home and marriage—rather than in the workplace. Women were still clustered in "women's jobs" and the number of women in professions dropped.

Twenty-five.1

A. Mitchell Palmer, "The Case Against the Reds" (1920)

U.S. Attorney General A. Mitchell Palmer coordinated a series of raids on the offices and homes of known radicals in early 1920, based on his suspicion that a widespread conspiracy was at work to overthrow the government. Many Americans lauded Palmer's zeal, while others wondered if Palmer's zeal was a greater threat to the country than the radicals. In this document, Palmer defines what he sees as the Red threat.*

Like a prairie-fire, the blaze of revolution was sweeping over every American institution of law and order a year ago. It was eating its way into the homes of the American workman, its sharp tongues of revolutionary heat were licking into the altars of the churches, leaping into the belfry of the school bell, crawling into the sacred corners of American homes, seeking to replace marriage vows with libertine laws, burning up the foundations of society....

Upon these two basic certainties, first that the "Reds" were criminal aliens, and secondly that the American Government must prevent crime, it was decided that there could be no nice distinctions drawn between the theoretical ideals of the radicals and their actual violations of our national laws. An assassin may have brilliant intellectuality, he may be able to excuse his murder or robbery with fine oratory, but any theory which excuses crime is not wanted in America. This is no place for the criminal to flourish, nor will he do so, so long as the rights of common citizenship can be exerted to prevent him....

By stealing, murder and lies, Bolshevism has looted Russia not only of its material strength, but of its moral force. A small clique of outcasts from the East Side of New York has attempted this, with what success we all know. Because a disreputable alien— Leon Bronstein, the man who now calls himself Trotzky—can inaugurate a reign of terror from his throne room in the Kremlin: because this lowest of all types known to New

* From A. Mitchell Palmer, "The Case Against the Reds," *The Forum* 63 (February 1920): 63–75.

York can sleep in the Czar's bed, while hundreds of thousands in Russia are without food or shelter, should Americans be swayed by such doctrines?...

My information showed that communism in this country was an organization of thousands of aliens, who were direct allies of Trotzky. Aliens of the same misshapen cast of mind and indecencies of character, and it showed that they were making the same glittering promises of lawlessness, of criminal autocracy to Americans, that they had made to the Russian peasants. How the Department of Justice discovered upwards of 60,000 of these organized agitators of the Trotzky doctrine in the United States, is the confidential information upon which the Government is now sweeping the nation clean of such alien filth....

The whole purpose of communism appears to be a mass formation of the criminals of the world to overthrow the decencies of private life, to usurp property that they have not earned, to disrupt the present order of life regardless of health, sex, or religious rights....

These are the revolutionary tenets of Trotzky and the Communist Internationale. Their manifesto further embraces the various organizations in this country of men and women obsessed with discontent, having disorganized relations to American society. These include the I. W. W.'s, the most radical socialists, the misguided anarchists, the agitators who oppose the limitations of unionism, the moral perverts and the hysterical neurasthenic women who abound in communism. The phraseology of their manifesto is practically the same wording as was used by the Bolsheviks for their International Communist Congress.

...The Department of Justice will pursue the attack of these "Reds" upon the Government of the United States with vigilance, and no alien, advocating the overthrow of existing law and order in this country, shall escape arrest and prompt deportation.

It is my belief that while they have stirred discontent in our midst, while they have caused irritating strikes, and while they have infected our social ideas with the disease of their own minds and their unclean morals, we can get rid of them! And not until we have done so shall we have removed the menace of Bolshevism for good.

DOCUMENT ANALYSIS

1. How does Palmer characterize the Reds, and what harm does he suggest they pose to the United States? Does his characterization of their threat and power seem credible? Explain.

Twenty-five.2

Comprehensive Immigration Law
(1924)

This act limited immigration to two percent of those born in any given foreign country in the United States in 1890. In 1927 an even more restrictive law limited immigration to around 150,000 per year. (By contrast, between 1840 and 1920, on average, a half a million immigrants had entered the country per year.) Despite the act's stringency, immigration laws were not enforced strictly: in order to prevent labor shortages in the Southwest, Mexican workers were encouraged to cross the border to work in the United States. *

By the President of the United States of America

A Proclamation

Whereas it is provided in the act of Congress approved May 26, 1924, entitled "An act to limit the immigration of aliens into the United States, and for other purposes" that "The annual quota of any nationality shall be two per centum of the number of foreign-born individuals of such nationality resident in continental Untied States as determined by the United States Census of 1890, but the minimum quota of any nationality shall be 100 (Sec. 11 a)....

"The Secretary of State, the Secretary of Commerce, and the Secretary of Labor, jointly, shall, as soon as feasible after the enactment of this act, prepare a statement showing the number of individuals of the various nationalities resident in continental United States as determined by the United States Census of 1890, which statement shall be the population basis for the purposes of subdivision (a) of section 11 (Sec. 12 b).

"Such officials shall, jointly, report annually to the President the quota of each nation-

---

* From U.S. Bureau of Immigration, *Annual Report of the Commissioner-General of Immigration, 1924* (Washington, D.C.: Government Printing Office, 1924), 24 ff.

ality under subdivision (a) of section 11, together with the statements, estimates, and revisions provided for in this section. The President shall proclaim and make known the quotas so reported". (Sec. 12 e).

Now, therefore I, Calvin Coolidge, President of the United States of America acting under and by virtue of the power in me vested by the aforesaid act of Congress, do hereby proclaim and make known that on and after July 1, 1924, and throughout the fiscal year 1924–1925, the quota of each nationality provided in said act shall be as follows:

COUNTRY OR AREA OF BIRTH QUOTA 1924–1925

Afghanistan— 100
Albania— 100
Andorra— 100
Arabian peninsula (1, 2)— 100
Armenia— 124
Australia, including Papua, Tasmania, and all islands appertaining to Australia (3, 4)— 121
Austria— 785
Belgium (5)— 512
Bhutan— 100
Bulgaria— 100
Cameroon (proposed British mandate)— 100
Cameroon (French mandate)— 100
China— 100
Czechoslovakia— 3,073
Danzig, Free City of— 228
Denmark (5, 6)— 2,789
Egypt— 100
Estonia— 124
Ethiopia (Abyssinia)— 100
Finland— 170
France (1, 5, 6)— 3,954
Germany— 51,227
Great Britain and Northern Ireland (1, 3, 5, 6)— 34,007
Greece— 100
Hungary— 473
Iceland— 100
India (3)— 100
Iraq (Mesopotamia)— 100

Irish Free State (3)— 28,567
Italy, including Rhodes, Dodecanesia, and Castellorizzo (5)— 3,845
Japan— 100
Latvia—142
Liberia— 100
Liechtenstein— 100
Lithuania— 344
Luxemburg— 100
Monaco— 100
Morocco (French and Spanish Zones and Tangier)— 100
Muscat (Oman)— 100
Nauru (proposed British mandate) (4)— 100
Nepal— 100
Netherlands (1, 5, 6)— 1,648
New Zealand (including appertaining islands (3, 4)— 100
Norway (5)— 6,453
New Guinea, and other Pacific Islands under proposed Australian mandate (4)— 100
Palestine (with Trans-Jordan, proposed British mandate)— 100
Persia (1)— 100
Poland— 5,982
Portugal (1, 5)— 503
Ruanda and Urundi (Belgium mandate)— 100
Rumania— 603
Russia, European and Asiatic (1)— 2,248
Samoa, Western (4) (proposed mandate of New Zealand)— 100

San Marino— 100
Siam— 100
South Africa, Union of (3)— 100
South West Africa (proposed mandate
    of Union of South Africa)— 100
Spain (5)— 131
Sweden— 9,561
Switzerland— 2,081
Syria and The Lebanon (French
    mandate)— 100

Tanganyika (proposed British
    mandate)— 100
Togoland (proposed British mandate)—
    100
Togoland (French mandate)— 100
Turkey— 100
Yap and other Pacific islands (under
    Japanese mandate) (4)— 100
Yugoslavia— 671

GENERAL NOTE.—The immigration quotas assigned to the various countries and quota-areas should not be regarded as having any political significance whatever, or as involving recognition of new governments, or of new boundaries, or of transfers of territory except as the United States Government has already made such recognition in a formal and official manner....Calvin Coolidge.

DOCUMENT ANALYSIS

1. Based on the new immigration quota system contained in this law, what region of the world was to be allowed to send the most new immigrants to the United States annually? Where had most immigrants been coming from in the thirty years prior to the enactment of this legislation?

Twenty-five.3

Calvin Coolidge, Honoring Charles Lindbergh (1927)

Charles Lindbergh gained world fame in May 1927 when he flew his plane, the Spirit of St. Louis, *in the first solo flight across the Atlantic. He received a tremendous welcome in Paris, and American newspapers—in this age of sensational ballyhoo—heralded Lindbergh's flight with banner headlines and enthusiastic stories. When Lindbergh arrived back in the United States (by ship!), he was greeted by even more enthusiastic, adoring, cheering crowds. In Washington, President Calvin Coolidge delivered a speech welcoming Lindbergh back to his home country, and awarded Lindbergh the nation's Distinguished Flying Cross.**

M<small>Y</small> F<small>ELLOW</small> C<small>OUNTRYMEN</small>:

It was in America that the modern art of flying of heavier-than-air machines was first developed. As the experiments became successful, the airplane was devoted to practical purposes. It has been adapted to commerce in the transportation of passengers and mail and used for national defense by our land and sea forces. Beginning with a limited flying radius, its length has been gradually extended. We have made many flying records. Our Army flyers have circumnavigated the globe....Our own country has been traversed from shore to shore in a single flight.

It had been apparent for some time that the next great feat in the air would be a continuous flight from the mainland of America to the mainland of Europe. Two courageous Frenchmen made the reverse attempt and passed to a fate that is as yet unknown. Others were speeding their preparations to make the trial, but it remained for an unknown youth to tempt the elements and win. It is the same story of valor and victory by a son of the people that shines through every page of American history.

---

* From Address of President Coolidge Bestowing upon Charles A. Lindbergh the Distinguished Flying Cross, Washington, D.C., June 11, 1927 (Washington, D.C.: Government Printing Office, 1927).

Twenty five years ago there was born in Detroit, Michigan, a boy, representing the best traditions of this country, of a stock known for its deeds of adventure and exploration. His father, moved with a desire for public service, was a Member of Congress for several terms. His mother, who dowered her son with her own modesty and charm, is with us to-day. Engaged in the vital profession of school-teaching, she has permitted neither money nor fame to interfere with her fidelity to her duties. Too young to have enlisted in the World War, her son became a student at one of the big State universities. His interest in aviation led him to an Army aviation school; and in 1925 he was graduated as an airplane pilot. In November, 1926, he had reached the rank of captain in the Officers' Reserve Corps. Making his home in St. Louis, he had joined the One hundred and tenth Observation Squadron of the Missouri National Guard....

...Later he became connected with the United States Mail Service, where he exhibited marked ability, and from which he is now on leave of absence.

On a morning just three weeks ago yesterday, this wholesome, earnest, fearless, courageous product of America rose into the air from Long Island in a monoplane christened "The Spirit of St. Louis"...It was no haphazard adventure. After months of most careful preparation, supported by a valiant character, driven by an unconquerable will and inspired by the imagination and the spirit of his Viking ancestors, this reserve officer set wing across the dangerous stretches of the North Atlantic. He was alone. His destination was Paris.

Thirty-three hours and thirty minutes later, in the evening of the second day, he landed at his destination on the French flying field at Le Bourget. He had traveled over 3,600 miles and established a new and remarkable record. The execution of his project was a perfect exhibition of art.

This country will always remember the way in which he was received by the people of France, by their President, and by their Government. It was the more remarkable because they were mourning the disappearance of their intrepid countrymen, who had tried to span the Atlantic on a western flight.

Our messenger of peace and good will had broken down another barrier of time and space and brought two great peoples into closer communion. In less than a day and a half he had crossed the ocean over which Columbus had traveled for 69 days, and the Pilgrim Fathers for 66 days, on their way to the New World....

The absence of self-acclaim, the refusal to become commercialized, which has marked the conduct of this sincere and genuine exemplar of fine and noble virtues, has endeared him to everyone. He has returned unspoiled....

And now, my fellow citizens, this young man has returned. He is here. He has brought his unsullied fame home. It is our great privilege to welcome back to his native land, on behalf of his own people, who have a deep affection for him and have been thrilled by his splendid achievement, a colonel of the United States Officers' Reserve Corps, an illustrious citizen of our Republic, a conqueror of the air and strengthener of the ties which bind us to our sister nations across the sea, and, as President of the United States, I bestow the distinguished flying cross, as a symbol of appreciation for what he is and what he has done, upon Col. Charles A. Lindbergh.

DOCUMENT ANALYSIS

1. How does President Coolidge portray Charles Lindbergh's personal character?
2. In what ways does Coolidge link Lindbergh's accomplishments to a heroic tradition in American history? Is this connection convincing to you? Explain.

Twenty-five.4

Marcus Garvey, Aims and Objectives of the UNIA (1923)

Although born and raised in Jamaica, Marcus Garvey came to the United States in the mid-1910s and quickly established himself in Harlem as a major force in the African American community. He championed a movement for black cultural pride, set up a newspaper and several businesses to serve the black community, and organized the Universal Negro Improvement Association, with chapters throughout the country. In this document, Garvey describes the goals of the UNIA. Garvey would soon be arrested and convicted for mail fraud involving his shipping business, imprisoned, then exiled from the United States. Long after his exile, however, support for his message did not die.*

A ims and Objectives of UNIA
Carnegie Hall, 23 February 1923

Mr. Chairman and Fellow Citizens: I am here tonight as the President-General of the Universal Negro Improvement Association to explain the aims and objects of this organization and to defend its principles. Over five years ago the Universal Negro Improvement Association placed itself before the world as the movement through which the new and rising Negro would give expression of his feelings. This association adopts an attitude not of hostility to other races and peoples of the world, but an attitude of self-respect of manhood rights on behalf of 400,000,000 Negroes of the world.

MUCH MISUNDERSTANDING ABOUT THE U.N.I.A.

In advocating the principles of this association we find we have been very much misunderstood and very much misrepresented by men from within our own race, as well as

* From Marcus Garvey's speech, Aims and Objectives of the UNIA, February 23, 1923, given at Carnegie Hall, accessible online at http://www.marcusgarvey.com/wmview.php?ArtID=556&term=Carnegie Hall.

others from without. Any reform movement that seeks to bring about changes for the benefit of humanity is bound to be misrepresented by those who have always taken it upon themselves to administer to, and to lead the unfortunate—to lead and to direct those who may be placed under temporary disadvantages. It has been so in all other movements whether it is social or political; hence those of us in the Universal Negro Improvement Association who lead do not feel in any way embarrassed about this misrepresentation, about this misunderstanding as far as the Aims and Objects of the Universal Negro Improvement Association go. But those who probably would have taken kindly notice of this great movement have been led to believe that this movement seeks not to develop the good within the race, but to give expression to that which is most destructive and most harmful to society and to government.

A DENIAL OF THE MISREPRESENTATIONS

I am here tonight to deny that misrepresentation. I am here to remove the misunderstanding that has been created in the minds of the millions of people throughout the world in their relationship to the Universal Negro Improvement Association.

WHAT THE U.N.I.A. STANDS FOR

The Universal Negro Improvement Association stands for the bigger brotherhood; the Universal Negro Improvement Association stands for human rights, not only for Negroes, but for all races. The Universal Negro Improvement Association believes in the rights of not only the black race, but the white race, the yellow race and the brown race. The Universal Negro Improvement Association believes that the white man has as much right to be considered, the yellow man has as much right to be considered, the brown man has as much right to be considered as well as the black man of Africa. In view of the fact that the black man of Africa has contributed as much to the world as the white man of Europe, and the brown and yellow man of Asia, we of the Universal Negro Improvement Association demand that the white, yellow and brown races give to the black man his place in the civilization of the world. We ask for nothing more than the rights of 400,000,000 Negroes. We are not seeking, as I said before, to destroy or disrupt the society or the government of other races, but we are determined that 400,000,000 of us shall unite ourselves to free our motherland from the grasp of the invader. We of the Universal Negro Improvement Association are determined to unite 400,000,000 Negroes for their own industrial, political, social and religious emancipation. We of the Universal Negro Improvement Association are determined to unite the 400,000,000 Negroes of the world to give expression to their own feeling; we are determined to unite the 400,000,000 Negroes of the world for the purpose of building a civilization of their own....We are looking toward political freedom on the continent of Africa, the land of our fathers.

NOT SEEKING A GOVERNMENT WITHIN A GOVERNMENT

The Universal Negro Improvement Association is not seeking to build up another government within the bounds or borders of the United States of America. The Universal

Negro Improvement Association is not seeking to disrupt any organized system of government, but the association is determined to bring Negroes together for the building up of a nation of their own. And why? Because we have been forced to it....

THE DIFFERENCE BETWEEN THE U.N.I.A. AND OTHER ORGANIZATIONS

The difference between the Universal Negro Improvement Association and the other movements of this country and probably the world is that the Universal Negro Improvement Association seeks independence of government, while the other organizations seek to make the Negro a secondary part of existing governments. We differ from the organizations in America like the National Association for the Advancement of Colored People because they seek to subordinate the Negro as a secondary consideration in great civilization. The N.A.A.C.P. knows that in America the Negro will never reach his highest ambition; it knows that the Negro in America will never get all his constitutional rights....You and I can live in the United States of America for 100 more years and our generations may live for 200 years or for 5,000 years and so long as there is a black and white population, when the majority is on the side of the white race, you and I will never get political justice or get political equality in this country. Then why should a black man with rising ambition after preparing himself in every possible way to give expression to that highest ambition allow himself to be kept down by racial prejudice within a country? If I am as educated as the next man, if I am as prepared as the next man, if I have passed through the best schools and colleges and universities as the other fellow, why should I not have a fair chance to compete with the other fellow for the biggest position in the nation? That is where the Universal Negro Improvement Association differs from the National Association for the Advancement of Colored People. That association knows well that the Negro will never occupy anything else but a secondary position within the United States. The time will never come for the black man to be president of the United States. The time will never come for the black man to be secretary of state to the nation, nor to be attorney general of the United States. Why then should I limit my ambition to be street cleaner while the other fellow is president of the United States? I have feelings, I have blood, I have senses like the other fellow; I have ambition, I have hope. Why should he, because of some racial prejudice, keep me down and why should I concede to him the right to rise above me and to establish himself as my permanent master? God never created any master for the human race but Himself....

LIBERTY NOT WON BY BEGGING

Liberty is not won by begging; it is not won by praying for it; it is won by fighting and sometimes dying. That is how we differ again from the other organizations; they believe in petitions and mass meetings, we believe in solid organization when everybody is ready to make one big, long march. Instead of dissipating and wasting our energies here and there as fifteen millions in America, twelve millions in the West Indies, ten millions in Central and South America, that we come together as four hundred million Negroes and then demand the things that we want. That is the job that is too much for these fellows. It does not mean that the leaders of such a movement as this are going to get their reward in the present day and the present age, and these fellows want all that is coming to them now. That is just the difference. Marcus Garvey could be in an organization like the N.A.A.C.P. if he was satisfied to get a check from any philanthropist every six months or once a year, or get a salary of $5,000 a year, and live the best among Negroes and call himself a "dicty" aristocrat. That is what is called an easy job, but Marcus Garvey does not want an easy job. The job of Marcus Garvey means that sometimes he must be in jail and probably sometimes out of jail; that sometimes Marcus Garvey is not only in jail, but he must die prematurely for the cause that needs assistance. The jail is nothing to Marcus Garvey and those who lead the cause of Negro freedom.

The men of the N.A.A.C.P., who criticize the U.N.I.A., there is none of them from its president down to its secretary who has ever taken the chance of being ten miles near the jail. Some leaders, fighting for the liberty of the people, people oppressed, martyred and massacred all over the world, and the leaders feel that the nearest they must go is in a parlor of carpet and cushions. Yet Du Bois thinks himself an aristocrat because he has a wrong idea of leadership. Before a race is established or makes itself a nation, there is no aristocracy within that race or among that people, because aristocracy is not based upon assumption, it is built upon service. What service has Du Bois rendered to the race?...Those who lead the U.N.I.A. on the Executive Council today sometimes go for a year without any salary, but we have worked honestly and faithfully because of the conviction we have and the faith we have in this race of ours.

AN ASSOCIATION OF SACRIFICE

The difference between the N.A.A.C.P. and the U.N.I.A. is the one is an association of sacrifice, an association wherein its leaders are prepared not only to fight, but to die, for the accomplishments of its Aims and Objects. I am supposed to be different from Du Bois because I am prepared to go the limit. I have absolutely no cause to fear going to jail, or to fear arrest by the government. There is no government in the world that can say Marcus Garvey had anything in his private life to cause the police to come ten miles near his door; the only trouble that I am supposed to be in came from my services to the U.N.I.A. and my services to the race.

DOCUMENT ANALYSIS

1. How much hope did Marcus Garvey hold out for the eventual acceptance of blacks as full equals in American society?

2. How did Garvey contrast his organization, the Universal Negro Improvement Association, with the more established National Association for the Advancement of Colored People? Do you think Garvey's characterization of the NAACP is fair?

Chapter Study Questions

1. What factors contributed to making the Red Scare of 1919–1920 so intense? Why do you think it eventually died out?

2. To what extent might the quotas of the Comprehensive Immigration Law of 1924 tie back to attitudes evident during the Red Scare of 1919–1920?

3. Compare and contrast Palmer's description of a "Red" with President Coolidge's characterization of Charles A. Lindbergh.

4. What would explain why hundreds of thousands of African Americans joined Marcus Garvey's Universal Negro Improvement Association in the late 1910s and 1920s?

Twenty-six

Franklin D. Roosevelt and the New Deal

The 1929 stock-market crash was the catalyst for the worst depression in the nation's history. By the presidential election of 1932, 25 percent of the American workforce had lost their jobs, while per capita incomes had been halved. Franklin Delano Roosevelt won the presidency by appealing to the "forgotten man" and attacking rich businessmen. His New Deal programs did not end the depression, but perhaps more significantly, they did restore national confidence and faith in government.

During the first few years of the New Deal, the federal government established hundreds of new programs, many of them massive, and spent more money than had ever been spent before during peacetime. Although these programs assisted millions of suffering farmers, unemployed workers, and their families, they did not bring the Great Depression to an end. And these programs were sharply criticized by Republicans and conservative Democrats, who feared that Franklin Roosevelt was endangering free enterprise and personal liberty in the United States. A group of business and civic leaders, many of them Democrats unhappy with FDR, formed a group known as the Liberty League in 1934 to speak out against the New Deal. Among their spokesmen was Al Smith, the Democratic nominee for President in 1928.

While the Liberty League argued that the New Deal went too far in expanding the role of government, a far larger chorus of critics attacked the New Deal for not doing enough to solve the suffering of the Great Depression. Socialists and communists had some successes in gaining party members in the 1930s, but many other radical figures won far broader support. Huey Long, a Democratic U.S. Senator from Louisiana, led the largest populist protest. Long had supported FDR's candidacy in 1932, but became an early critic of the New Deal for, as he saw it, not doing enough for the common man.

Long gave stump speeches around the country, and won over millions of followers to his "Share Our Wealth" program, which promised a guaranteed income for all

Americans, and vowed to aggressively tax the rich. The broad outlines of Long's program are included as the third document. Long was a potential rival of Roosevelt's for the Democratic presidential nomination in 1936, but was assassinated in 1935. The depression did not affect everyone in the same way. Stories of middle-class people losing their homes, wealthy children being pulled from boarding schools, and the working class finding themselves on the streets did not represent the full range of experience during the Great Depression. Many people, for instance, noticed little change in their daily lives.

Franklin Roosevelt's wife, Eleanor, was a very unusual First Lady, who served as a close adviser to her husband, and traveled extensively to connect with the American people. Far more than her husband, she spoke out on behalf of liberal causes such as the rights of labor, women's rights, and civil rights. Three selections from her daily newspaper column, "My Day," are included as the final document in this chapter.

Twenty-six.1

Franklin D. Roosevelt, First Inaugural Address (1933)

Roosevelt's first inaugural address is very familiar and oft-quoted. It was gauged to reassure the American people, to remind them of their unique heritage, the primary task of government, and the spirit that had made the nation great.*

I am certain that my fellow Americans expect that on my induction into the Presidency I will address them with a candor and a decision which the present situation of our Nation impels. This is preeminently the time to speak the truth, the whole truth, frankly and boldly. Nor need we shrink from honestly facing conditions in our country today. This great Nation will endure as it has endured, will revive and will prosper. So, first of all, let me assert my firm belief that the only thing we have to fear is fear itself—nameless, unreasoning, unjustified terror which paralyzes needed efforts to convert retreat into advance. In every dark hour of our national life a leadership of frankness and vigor has met with that understanding and support of the people themselves which is essential to victory. I am convinced that you will again give that support to leadership in these critical days.

In such a spirit on my part and on yours we face our common difficulties. They concern, thank God, only material things. Values have shrunken to fantastic levels; taxes have risen; our ability to pay has fallen; government of all kinds is faced by serious curtailment of income; the means of exchange are frozen in the currents of trade; the withered leaves of industrial enterprise lie on every side; farmers find no markets for their produce; the savings of many years in thousands of families are gone.

More important, a host of unemployed citizens face the grim problem of existence, and an equally great number toil with little return. Only a foolish optimist can deny the dark reality of the movement.

* From Franklin D. Roosevelt, *Inaugural Address*, March 4, 1933.

Yet our distress comes from no failure or substance. We are stricken by no plague of locusts. Compared with the perils which our forefathers conquered because they believed and were not afraid, we have still much to be thankful for. Nature still offers her bounty and human efforts have multiplied it. Plenty is at our doorstep, but a generous use of it languishes in the very sight of the supply. Primarily this is because rulers of the exchange of mankind's goods have failed through their own stubbornness and their own incompetence, have admitted their failure, and have abdicated. Practices of the unscrupulous money changers stand indicted in the court of public opinion, rejected by the hearts and minds of men.

True they have tried, but their efforts have been cast in the pattern of an outworn tradition. Faced by failure of credit they have proposed only the lending of more money. Stripped of the lure of profit by which to induce our people to follow their leadership, they have resorted to exhortations, pleading tearfully for restored confidence. They have known only the rules of a generation of self-seekers. They have no vision, and when there is no vision the people perish.

The money changers have fled from their high seats in the temple of our civilization. We may now restore that temple to the ancient truths. The measure of the restoration lies in the extent to which we apply social values more noble than mere monetary profit.

Happiness lies not in the mere possession of money; it lies in the joy of achievement, in the thrill of creative effort. The joy and moral stimulation of work no longer must be forgotten in the mad chase of evanescent profits. These dark days will be worth all they cost us if they teach us that our true destiny is not to be ministered unto but to minister to ourselves and to our fellow men.

Recognition of the falsity of material wealth as the standard of success goes hand in hand with the abandonment of the false belief that public office and high political position are to be valued only by the standards of pride of place and personal profit; and there must be an end to a conduct in banking and in business which too often has given to a sacred trust the likeness of callous and selfish wrongdoing. Small wonder that confidence languishes, for it thrives only on honesty, on honor, on the sacredness of obligations, on faithful protection, on unselfish performance; without them it cannot live.

Restoration calls, however not for changes in ethics alone. This Nation asks for action, and action now.

Our greatest primary task is to put people to work. This is no unsolvable problem if we face it wisely and courageously. It can be accomplished in part by direct recruiting by the Government itself, treating the task as we would treat the emergency of a war, but at the same time, through this employment, accomplishing greatly needed projects to stimulate and reorganize the use of our natural resources.

Hand in hand with this we must frankly recognize the overbalance of population in our industrial centers and, by engaging on a national scale in a redistribution, endeavor to provide a better use of the land for those best fitted for the land. The task can be helped by definite efforts to raise the values of agricultural products and with this the power to purchase the output of our cities. It can be helped by preventing realistically the tragedy of the growing loss through foreclosure of our small homes and our farms. It can be helped by insistence that the Federal, State, and local governments act forthwith on the demand that their cost be drastically reduced. It can be helped by the uni-fying of relief activities which today are often scattered, uneconomical, and unequal. It can be helped by national planning for and supervision of all forms of transportation and of communications and other utilities which have a definitely public character. There are many ways in which it can be helped but it can never be helped merely by talking about it. We must act and act quickly.

Finally, in our progress toward a resumption of work we require two safeguards against a return of the evils of the old order: there must be a strict supervision of all banking an credits and investments, so that there will be an end to speculation with other people's money; and there must be provision for an adequate but sound currency.

These are the lines of attack. I shall presently urge upon a new Congress, in special session, detailed measures for their fulfillment, and I shall seek the immediate assistance of the several States.

Through this program of action we address ourselves to putting our own national house in order and making income balance outgo. Our international trade relations, though vastly important, are in point of time and necessity secondary to the establish-ment of a sound national economy. I favor as a practical policy the putting of first things first. I shall spare no effort to restore world trade by international economic readjust-ment, but the emergency at home cannot wait on that accomplishment.

The basic thought that guides these specific means of national recovery is not narrowly nationalistic. It is the insistence as a first consideration, upon the interdependence of the various elements in and parts of the United States—a recognition of the old and perma-nently important manifestation of the American spirit of the pioneer. It is the way to recov-ery. It is the immediate way. It is the strongest assurance that the recovery will endure.

In the field of world policy I would dedicate this Nation to the policy of the good neighbor—the neighbor who respects his obligations and respects the sanctity of his agreements in and with a world of neighbors.

If I read the temper of our people correctly, we now realize as we have never realized before our interdependence on each other; that we cannot merely take but we must give as well; that if we are to go forward, we must move as a trained and loyal army willing to sacrifice for the good of a common discipline, because without such discipline no progress is made, no leadership becomes effective. We are, I know, ready and willing to submit our lives and property to such discipline, because it makes possible a leadership which aims at a larger good. This I propose to offer, pledging that the larger purpose will bind upon us all as a sacred obligation with a unity of duty hitherto evoked only in time of armed strife.

With this pledge taken, I assume unhesitatingly the leadership of this great army of our people dedicated to a disciplined attack upon our common problems.

Action in this image and to this end is feasible under the form of government which we have inherited from our ancestors. Our Constitution is so simple and practical that it is possible always to meet extraordinary needs by changes in emphasis and arrange-ment without loss of essential form. That is why our constitutional system has proved itself the most superbly enduring political mechanism the modern world has produced. It has met every stress of vast expansion of territory, of foreign wars, of bitter internal strife, of world relations.

It is to be hoped that the normal balance of Executive and legislative authority may be wholly adequate to meet the unprecedented task before us. But it may be that an unprecedented demand and need for undelayed action may call for temporary departure from that normal balance of public procedure.

I am prepared under my constitutional duty to recommend the measures that a stricken Nation in the midst of a stricken world may require. These measures, or such other measures as the Congress may build out of its experience and wisdom, I shall seek, within my constitutional authority to bring to speedy adoption.

But in the event that the Congress shall fail to take one of these two courses and in the event that the national emergency is still critical, I shall not evade the clear course of duty that will then confront me. I shall ask the Congress for the one remaining instrument to meet the crisis—broad Executive power to wage a war against the emergency, as great as the power that would be given to me if we were in fact invaded by a foreign foe.

For the trust reposed in me I will return the courage and the devotion that befit the time. I can do no less.

We face the arduous days that lie before us in the warm courage of national unity; with the clear consciousness of seeking old and precious moral values; with the clear satisfaction that comes from the stern performance of duty by old and young alike. We aim at the assurance of a rounded and permanent national life.

We do not distrust the future of essential democracy. The people of the United States have not failed. In their need they have registered a mandate that they want direct, vigorous action. They have asked for discipline and direction under leadership. They have made me the present instrument of their wishes. In the spirit of the gift I take it.

In this dedication of a Nation we humbly ask the blessing of God. May He protect each and every one of us. May He guide me in the days to come.

Document Analysis

1. In his first inaugural address, who does Franklin Roosevelt blame for the severity of the nation's economic crisis?

2. Why would the public feel a renewed sense of confidence after hearing this speech? What specific plans does Roosevelt put forward to end the Great Depression?

Twenty-six.2

Huey Long, "Share Our Wealth"
(1935)

The charismatic Huey Long was elected governor of Louisiana in 1928, owing in large measure to his "Share Our Wealth" philosophy, which provided services to the poor, built hospitals and schools, and granted awesome powers to Long himself. In 1930 he became a U.S. Senator and, critical of Roosevelt, had ambitions to run for president before he was killed in 1935. His Share Our Wealth Society had more than 4.6 million members. This circular was addressed "To the Members and Well-Wishers of the Share Our Wealth Society" and was placed in the Congressional Record *in 1935.* *

Here is the whole sum and substance of the Share Our Wealth movement:

1. Every family to be furnished by the government a homestead allowance, free of debt, of not less than one-third the average family wealth of the country, which means, at the lowest, that every family shall have the reasonable comforts of life up to a value of from $5,000 to $6,000: No person to have a fortune of more than 100 to 300 times the average family fortune, which means that the limit to fortune is between $1,500,000 and $5,000,000, with annual capital levy taxes imposed on all above $1,000,000.

2. The yearly income of every family shall be not less than one-third of the average family income, which means that, according to the estimates of the statisticians of the U.S. Government and Wall Street, no family's annual income would be less than from $2,000 to $2,500: No yearly income shall be allowed to any person larger than from 100 to 300 times the size of the average family income, which means that no person would be allowed to earn in any year more than $600,000 to $1,800,000, all to be subject to present income tax laws.

* From Huey Long, "To the Members and Well-Wishers of the Share Our Wealth Society," *Congressional Record*, 1935 (Washington D.C.: U.S. Government Printing Office, 1935).

3. To limit or regulate the hours of work to such an extent as to prevent over-production; the most modern and efficient machinery would be encouraged so that as much would be produced as possible so as to satisfy all demands of the people, but also to allow the maximum time to the workers for recreation, convenience, education, and luxuries of life.

4. An old-age pension to the persons over 60.

5. To balance agricultural production with what can be consumed according to the laws of God, which includes the preserving and storing of surplus commodities to be paid for and held by the Government for emergencies when such are needed. Please bear in mind, however, that when the people of America have had money to buy things they needed, we have never had a surplus of any commodity. This plan of God does not call for destroying any of the things raised to eat or wear, nor does it countenance whole destruction of hogs, cattle or milk.

6. To pay the veterans of our wars what we owe them and to care for their disabled.

7. Education and training for all children to be equal in opportunity in all schools, colleges, universities, and other institutions for training in the professions and vocations of life; to be regulated on the capacity of children to learn, and not on the ability of parents to pay the costs. Training for life's work to be as much universal and thorough for all walks in life as has been the training in the arts of killing.

8. The raising of revenues and taxes for the support of this program to come from the reduction of swollen fortunes from the top, as well as for the support of public works to give employment whenever there may be any slackening necessary in private enterprise.

DOCUMENT ANALYSIS

1. What specific government guarantees did Huey Long propose to "Share Our Wealth"? How would the government afford Long's programs?

2. Does Long's "Share Our Wealth" program appeal to you? Why do you think it was so enormously popular among millions in the 1930s?

Twenty-six.3

Eleanor Roosevelt, from "My Day" Columns (1939)

*Eleanor Roosevelt challenged tradition, using her status as First Lady in unprecedented ways to fight for causes in which she believed. She also had her own newspaper column, "My Day," which dealt with a variety of topics, both personal and political. The selections below are three "My Day" columns from 1939. In the first selection, Eleanor is explaining her decision to give up her membership in the Daughters of the American Revolution. The DAR had recently denied the use of its concert hall in Washington to a famous African American singer, Marian Anderson, and Eleanor wanted to make it clear that she rejected this racial prejudice.** *

DAR Resignation

WASHINGTON, FEBRUARY 27, 1939—I am having a peaceful day. I drove my car a short distance out of the city this morning to pilot some friends of mine who are starting off for a vacation in Florida. I think this will be my only excursion out of the White House today, for I have plenty of work to do on an accumulation of mail, and I hope to get through in time to enjoy an evening of uninterrupted reading. I have been debating in my mind for some time, a question which I have had to debate with myself once or twice before in my life. Usually I have decided differently from the way in which I am deciding now. The question is, if you belong to an organization and disapprove of an action which is typical of a policy, should you resign or is it better to work for a changed point of view within the organization? In the past, when I was able to work actively in any organization to which I belonged, I have usually stayed until I had at least made a fight and had been defeated.

---

* From Eleanor Roosevelt, "My Day," February 27, 1939; July 14, 1939; September 2, 1939, © United Features Syndicate, in Franklin D. Roosevelt Library and Museum, Hyde Park, New York, accessible online at http://www.pbs.org/wgbh/amex/eleanor/sfeature/myday.html.

Even then, I have, as a rule, accepted my defeat and decided I was wrong or, perhaps, a little too far ahead of the thinking for the majority at that time. I have often found that the thing in which I was interested was done some years later. But in this case, I belong to an organization in which I can do no active work. They have taken an action which has been widely talked of in the press. To remain as a member implies approval of that action, and therefore I am resigning.

Prohibition

NEW YORK, July 14, 1939—A number of letters have come to me complaining bitterly about the fact that I said in an article recently that the repeal of prohibition had been a crusade carried on by women. I know quite well, of course that the Democratic Party took the stand in its platform that Prohibition should be repealed. I have always felt, however, that the women's organization for repeal, which was a nonpartisan organization, laid the groundwork which finally brought about the vote for repeal.

I was one of those who was very happy when the original prohibition amendment passed. I thought innocently that a law in this country would automatically be complied with, and my own observation led me to feel rather ardently that the less strong liquor anyone consumed the better it was. During prohibition I observed the law meticulously, but I came gradually to see that laws are only observed with the consent of the individuals concerned and a moral change still depends on the individual and not on the passage of any law.

Little by little it dawned upon me that this law was not making people drink any less, but it was making hypocrites and law breakers of a great number of people. It seemed to me best to go back to the old situation in which, if a man or woman drank to excess, they were injuring themselves and their immediate family and friends and the act was a violation against their own sense of morality and no violation against the law of the land.

I could never quite bring myself to work for repeal, but I could not oppose it, for intellectually I had to agree that it was the honest thing to do. My contacts are wide and I see a great many different groups of people, and I cannot say that I find that the change in the law has made any great change in conditions among young or old in the country today.

Invasion of Poland

HYDE PARK, SEPTEMBER 2, 1939—At 5 o'clock this morning, our telephone rang and it was the President in Washington to tell me the sad news that Germany had invaded Poland and that her planes were bombing Polish cities. He told me that Hitler was about to address the Reichstag, so we turned on the radio and listened until 6 o'clock.

Curiously enough, I had received a letter on my return last evening from a German friend who roomed with me in school in England. In this letter she said that when hate was rampant in the world, it was easy to believe harm of any nation, that she knew all the nations believed things that were not true about Germany, did not understand her position, and therefore hated her. She begged that we try to see Germany's point of view and not to judge her harshly.

As I listened to Hitler's speech, this letter kept returning to my mind. How can you feel kindly toward a man who tells you that German minorities have been brutally treated, first in Czechoslovakia and then in Danzig, but that never can Germany be accused of being unfair to a minority? I have seen evidence with my own eyes of what this same man has done to people belonging to a minority group—not only Jews, but Christians, who have long been German citizens.

Can one help but question his integrity? His knowledge of history seems somewhat sketchy too, for, after all, Poland possessed Danzig many years prior to the time that it ever belonged to Germany. And how can you say that you do not intend to make war on women and children and then send planes to bomb cities?

No, I feel no bitterness against the German people. I am deeply sorry for them, as I am for the people of all other European nations facing this horrible crisis. But for the man who has taken this responsibility upon his shoulders I can feel little pity. It is hard to see how he can sleep at night and think of the people in many nations whom he may send to their deaths.

DOCUMENT ANALYSIS

1. What sense do you get of Eleanor Roosevelt from these three columns?

2. How does Eleanor distinguish between the actions of the German government and her attitude toward the German people?

Chapter Study Questions

1. In his first inaugural address, Roosevelt said that Americans had "nothing to fear but fear itself." Why did millions of people in the 1930s have real, legitimate fears far beyond "fear itself"?

2. How did Franklin Roosevelt and Huey Long view the role of the government during the crisis of the Great Depression? Which approach appeals to you the most, and why?

3. Eleanor Roosevelt stepped well beyond the bounds of the usual role of First Lady, making her a controversial figure. Why do you think so many loved her, while others disliked her intensely? What role do you think the spouse of the President should play in public affairs?

Twenty-seven

America and the World, 1921–1945

W orld War II catapulted the United States into the international arena after several decades of relative isolation. When the war began in 1939, America was forced to rethink its global responsibilities and relationships and narrow its comfortable distance from world events. Rumors that the Germans were building an atomic bomb added to the pressure to act. Franklin Roosevelt, restrained by the neutrality acts and popular isolationism and pacifism, was not able to do very much to aid the British or the French.

However, by January 1941, when Roosevelt delivered his State of the Union address after winning reelection for an unprecedented third term, war seemed imminent. In his address (reprinted here) Roosevelt warned the nation of the threat posed by fascism in Germany, Italy, and Japan. He also proposed his Lend-Lease program, designed to circumvent the neutrality acts, through which the United States would "lend" munitions to England without expecting payment in return. Lend-Lease passed Congress, in March, and American involvement in the war escalated.

The best-known organization opposing U.S. entry into World War II was the America First Committee. Many business, civic, and academic leaders joined this isolationist group, which held rallies and pressured Congress to maintain neutrality even as the Axis Powers conquered more of Europe and Asia. A key spokesman for America First was the aviator Charles A. Lindbergh. As the United States moved closer to war in the late summer of 1941, Lindbergh delivered a speech in Des Moines, Iowa, in which he sharply criticized what he saw as the three key forces promoting American intervention. Lindbergh's speech is included as the third document in this chapter.

On the heels of the depression's upheavals, World War II brought further dramatic changes to American society. Foremost among these was that a critical shortage in the labor supply for war production allowed American women to enter the workforce in unprecedented numbers; by the end of the war, nineteen million women had gone to work outside the home, many at jobs that had been traditionally closed to them. Two interviews included in this chapter describe the experiences of some of these women, who were collectively nicknamed "Rosie the Riveters" after a popular song.

While over one million African Americans would serve in uniform for the United States in World War II, and millions more would contribute on the home front, racial tensions persisted throughout the war. The U.S. armed forces remained racially segregated, with blacks most often assigned the most labor-intensive and least desirable tasks. A race riot in Detroit over government housing in 1943 was a national embarrassment, and other incidents occurred throughout the country. Some African Americans called for a "Double-V Campaign," arguing that there should be a simultaneous fight against the Axis Powers abroad and racial injustice here at home. A similar call for blacks to force the federal government to make changes during the war was pressed by A. Philip Randolph, a civil rights leader and president of the Brotherhood of Sleeping Car Porters union. The fourth document in this chapter is from Randolph's 1942 speech calling for a wartime march on Washington, much like he had threatened before the war.

While American women, and to a lesser extent blacks, made significant gains in the 1940s, no group in American society suffered more from World War II than Japanese Americans. The American government, acting on racial hatred and irrational rumors, interned over 110,000 Japanese Americans—most of whom were American citizens—in "relocation centers" in the American West. Japanese Americans lost their homes, property, and businesses and were humiliated and ill-treated in the camps.

The final document in this chapter is from the Supreme Court's decision in the case of *Korematsu v. U.S.* (1944), in which the court ruled that the federal government's relocation and internment of Japanese Americans during World War II was justified.

Twenty-seven.1

Albert Einstein, Letter to President Roosevelt (1939)

This letter from Albert Einstein warned Franklin Roosevelt that German researchers were close to making an atomic bomb. Inspired by Einstein (and his fellow scientists), Roosevelt organized a secret project (known later as the Manhattan project), to ensure that the United States had a bomb before Germany. In later life, Albert Einstein, committed to peace, regretted sending this letter. *

Albert Einstein
Old Grove Rd.
Nassau Point
Peconic, Long Island
August 2nd, 1939

F. D. Roosevelt,
President of the United States,
White House
Washington, D.C.

Sir:

Some recent work by E. Fermi and L. Szilard, which has been communicated to me in manuscript, leads me to expect that the element uranium may be turned into a new and important source of energy in the immediate future. Certain aspects of the situation which has arisen seem to call for watchfulness and, if necessary, quick action on the part

* Reprinted from Otton Nathan and Heinz Noren, eds. *Einstein on Peace* (New York: Simon and Schuster, 1960), 290.

of the Administration. I believe therefore that it is my duty to bring to your attention the following facts and recommendations:

In the course of the last four months it has been made probable—through the work of Joliot in France as well as Fermi and Szilard in America—that it may become possible to set up a nuclear chain reaction in a large mass of uranium, by which vast amount of power and large quantities of new radium-like elements would be generated. Now it appears almost certain that this could be achieved in the immediate future.

This new phenomenon would also lead to the construction of bombs, and it is conceivable—though much less certain—that extremely powerful bombs of a new type may thus be constructed. A single bomb of this type, carried by boat and exploded in a port, might very well destroy the whole port together with some of the surrounding territory. However, such bombs might very well prove to be too heavy for transportation by air.

The United States has only very poor ores of uranium in moderate quantities. There is some good ore in Canada and the former Czechoslovakia, while the most important source of uranium is the Belgian Congo.

In view of this situation you may think it desirable to have some permanent contact maintained between the Administration and the group of physicists working on chain reactions in America. One possible way of achieving this might be for you to entrust with this task a person who has your confidence and who could perhaps serve in an inofficial capacity. His task might comprise the following:

a) to approach Government Departments, keep them informed of the further development, and put forward recommendations for Government action, giving particular attention to the problem of securing a supply of uranium ore for the United States:

b) to speed up the experimental work, which is at present being carried on within the limits of the budgets of University laboratories, by providing funds, if such funds be required, through his contacts with private persons who are willing to make contributions for this cause, and perhaps also by obtaining the co-operation of industrial laboratories which have the necessary equipment.

I understand that Germany has actually stopped the sale of uranium from the Czechoslovakian mines which she has taken over. That she should have taken such early action might perhaps be understood on the ground that the son of the German Under-Secretary of State, von Weizsacker, is attached to the Kaiser-Wilhelm Institut in Berlin where some of the American work on uranium is now being repeated.

Yours very truly,

[signed] Albert Einstein

DOCUMENT ANALYSIS

1. Why did Albert Einstein feel that it was imperative to alert President Roosevelt to the potential of a new bomb?

2. When Einstein wrote this letter, why does he refer to "the former Czechoslovakia"?

Twenty-seven.2

Franklin D. Roosevelt, The Four Freedoms
(1941)

*This selection from Roosevelt's annual address to Congress is his argument for American involvement in the war, tied to his Lend-Lease act which provided military supplies for England.**

Armed defense of democratic existence is now being gallantly waged in four continents. If that defense fails, all the population and all the resources of Europe, Asia, Africa and Australia will be dominated by the conquerors. The total of those populations and their resources...greatly exceeds the sum total of the population and the resources of the whole of the Western Hemisphere—many times over.

In times like these it is immature—and incidentally untrue—for anybody to brag that an unprepared America, single-handed, and with one hand tied behind its back, can hold off the whole world.

No realistic American can expect from a dictator's peace international generosity, or return of true independence, or world disarmament, or freedom of expression, or freedom of religion—or even good business....

The need of the moment is that our actions and our policy should be devoted primarily—almost exclusively—to meeting this foreign peril. For all our domestic problems are now a part of the great emergency.

Just as our national policy in internal affairs has been based upon a decent respect for the rights and the dignity of all our fellow men within our gates, so our national policy in foreign affairs has been based on a decent respect for the rights and dignity of all nations, large and small. And the justice of morality must and will win in the end.

Our national policy is this:

First, by an impressive expression of the public will and without regard to partisanship, we are committed to all-inclusive national defense.

* From Franklin D. Roosevelt, "Annual Message to Congress," January 6, 1941, *Congressional Record*, 77th Cong. 1st sess., LXXXVII, pt. I, 45–47.

Second, by an impressive expression of the public will and without regard to partisanship, we are committed to full support of all those resolute peoples, everywhere, who are resisting aggression and are thereby keeping war away from our hemisphere. By this support, we express our determination that the democratic cause shall prevail, and we strengthen the defense and security of our own nation.

Third, by an impressive expression of the public will and without regard to partisanship, we are committed to the proposition that principles of morality and considerations for our own security will never permit us to acquiesce in a peace dictated by aggressors and sponsored by appeasers. We know that enduring peace cannot be bought at the cost of other people's freedom....

I also ask this Congress for authority and for funds sufficient to manufacture additional munitions and war supplies of many kinds, to be turned over to those nations which are now in actual war with aggressor nations.

Our most useful and immediate role is to act as an arsenal for them as well as for ourselves. They do not need man power. They do need billions of dollars' worth of the weapons of defense....

Let us say to the democracies, "We Americans are vitally concerned in your defense of freedom. We are putting forth our energies, our resources, and our organizing powers to give you the strength to regain and maintain a free world. We shall send you, in ever-increasing numbers, ships, planes, tanks, guns. This is our purpose and our pledge."...

There is nothing mysterious about the foundations of a healthy and strong democracy. The basic things expected by our people of their political and economic systems are simple. They are:

Equality of opportunity for youth and for others.

Jobs for those who can work.

Security for those who need it.

The ending of special privilege for the few.

The preservation of civil liberties for all.

The enjoyment of the fruits of scientific progress in a wider and constantly rising standard of living.

These are the simple and basic things that must never be lost sight of in the turmoil and unbelievable complexity of our modern world. The inner and abiding strength of our economic and political systems is dependent upon the degree to which they fulfill these expectations....

In the future days, which we seek to make secure, we look forward to a world founded upon four essential human freedoms.

The first is freedom of speech and expression everywhere in the world.

The second is freedom of every person to worship God in his own way everywhere in the world.

The third is freedom from want, which, translated into world terms, means economic understandings which will secure to every nation a healthy peacetime life for its inhabitants everywhere in the world.

The fourth is freedom from fear—which, translated into world terms, means a world-wide reduction of armaments to such a point and in such a thorough fashion that no nation will be in a position to commit an act of physical aggression against any neighbor—anywhere in the world.

That is no vision of a distant millennium. It is a definite basis for a kind of world attainable in our own time and generation. That kind of world is the very antithesis of the so-called new order of tyranny which the dictators seek to create with the crash of a bomb.

To that new order we oppose the greater conception—the moral order. A good society is able to face schemes of world domination and foreign revolutions alike without fear.

Since the beginning of our American history we have been engaged in change—in a perpetual peaceful revolution—a revolution which goes on steadily, quietly adjusting itself to changing conditions—without the concentration camp or the quicklime in the ditch. The world order which we seek is the cooperation of free countries, working together in a friendly, civilized society.

DOCUMENT ANALYSIS

1. What are the "four freedoms" that FDR claims the United States will fight to protect?

2. What is Roosevelt asking of Congress as he makes this speech?

Twenty-seven.3

Charles A. Lindbergh,
from Des Moines Speech
(1941)

Charles Lindbergh's solo flight across the Atlantic in 1927 had made him a great hero, but his life became less ideal in the following years. In the early 1930s, his infant son was kidnapped and murdered. Later in that decade, Lindbergh made well-publicized trips to Nazi Germany, and spoke approvingly of how Hitler had reinvigorated the German economy. After the outbreak of World War II in Europe in 1939, Lindbergh joined the America First Committee, dedicated to keeping the United States out of the war. In this speech he gave in Des Moines, Iowa, in September 1941, Lindbergh made controversial claims as to why the United States was on the verge of war. His reputation was tarnished permanently as a result of these comments.*

It is now two years since this latest European war began. From that day in September, 1939, until the present moment, there has been an over-increasing effort to force the United States into the conflict.

That effort has been carried on by foreign interests, and by a small minority of our own people; but it has been so successful that, today, our country stands on the verge of war.

At this time, as the war is about to enter its third winter, it seems appropriate to review the circumstances that have led us to our present position. Why are we on the verge of war? Was it necessary for us to become so deeply involved? Who is responsible for changing our national policy from one of neutrality and independence to one of entanglement in European affairs?…

Here, I would like to point out to you a fundamental difference between the groups who advocate foreign war, and those who believe in an independent destiny for America.

If you will look back over the record, you will find that those of us who oppose intervention have constantly tried to clarify facts and issues; while the interventionists have

---

* From Charles A. Lindbergh, Des Moines Speech, September 11, 1941, accessible at http://www.pbs.org/wgbh/amex/lindbergh/filmmore/reference/primary/desmoinesspeech.html or at http://www.charleslindbergh.com/americanfirst/speech.asp.

tried to hide facts and confuse issues....

When this war started in Europe, it was clear that the American people were solidly opposed to entering it. Why shouldn't we be? We had the best defensive position in the world; we had a tradition of independence from Europe; and the one time we did take part in a European war left European problems unsolved, and debts to America unpaid....

The three most important groups who have been pressing this country toward war are the British, the Jewish and the Roosevelt administration.

Behind these groups, but of lesser importance, are a number of capitalists, Anglophiles, and intellectuals who believe that the future of mankind depends upon the domination of the British empire. Add to these the Communistic groups who were opposed to intervention until a few weeks ago, and I believe I have named the major war agitators in this country.

I am speaking here only of war agitators, not of those sincere but misguided men and women who, confused by misinformation and frightened by propaganda, follow the lead of the war agitators.

As I have said, these war agitators comprise only a small minority of our people; but they control a tremendous influence. Against the determination of the American people to stay out of war, they have marshaled the power of their propaganda, their money, their patronage.

Let us consider these groups, one at a time.

First, the British: It is obvious and perfectly understandable that Great Britain wants the United States in the war on her side. England is now in a desperate position. Her population is not large enough and her armies are not strong enough to invade the continent of Europe and win the war she declared against Germany.

Her geographical position is such that she cannot win the war by the use of aviation alone, regardless of how many planes we send her. Even if America entered the war, it is improbable that the Allied armies could invade Europe and overwhelm the Axis powers. But one thing is certain. If England can draw this country into the war, she can shift to our shoulders a large portion of the responsibility for waging it and for paying its cost.

As you all know, we were left with the debts of the last European war; and unless we are more cautious in the future than we have been in the past, we will be left with the debts of the present case. If it were not for her hope that she can make us responsible for the war financially, as well as militarily, I believe England would have negotiated a peace in Europe many months ago, and be better off for doing so....

The second major group I mentioned is the Jewish.

It is not difficult to understand why Jewish people desire the overthrow of Nazi Germany. The persecution they suffered in Germany would be sufficient to make bitter enemies of any race.

No person with a sense of the dignity of mankind can condone the persecution of the Jewish race in Germany. But no person of honesty and vision can look on their pro-war policy here today without seeing the dangers involved in such a policy both for us and for them. Instead of agitating for war, the Jewish groups in this country should be opposing it in every possible way for they will be among the first to feel its consequences.

Tolerance is a virtue that depends upon peace and strength. History shows that it cannot survive war and devastations. A few far-sighted Jewish people realize this and stand opposed to intervention. But the majority still do not.

Their greatest danger to this country lies in their large ownership and influence in our motion pictures, our press, our radio and our government.

I am not attacking either the Jewish or the British people. Both races, I admire. But I am saying that the leaders of both the British and the Jewish races, for reasons which are as understandable from their viewpoint as they are inadvisable from ours, for reasons which are not American, wish to involve us in the war....

The Roosevelt administration is the third powerful group which has been carrying this country toward war. Its members have used the war emergency to obtain a third presidential term for the first time in American history. They have used the war to add unlimited billions to a debt which was already the highest we have ever known. And they have just used the war to justify the restriction of congressional power, and the assumption of dictatorial procedures on the part of the president and his appointees.

The power of the Roosevelt administration depends upon the maintenance of a wartime emergency....

In selecting these three groups as the major agitators for war, I have included only those whose support is essential to the war party. If any one of these groups—the British, the Jewish, or the administration—stops agitating for war, I believe there will be little danger of our involvement.

When hostilities commenced in Europe, in 1939, it was realized by these groups that the American people had no intention of entering the war. They knew it would be worse than useless to ask us for a declaration of war at that time. But they believed that this country could be entered into the war in very much the same way we were entered into the last one.

They planned: first, to prepare the United States for foreign war under the guise of American defense; second, to involve us in the war, step by step, without our realization; third, to create a series of incidents which would force us into the actual conflict. These plans were of course, to be covered and assisted by the full power of their propaganda.

Our theaters soon became filled with plays portraying the glory of war. Newsreels lost all semblance of objectivity. Newspapers and magazines began to lose advertising if they carried anti-war articles. A smear campaign was instituted against individuals who opposed intervention. The terms "fifth columnist," "traitor," "Nazi," "anti-Semitic" were thrown ceaselessly at any one who dared to suggest that it was not to the best interests of the United States to enter the war. Men lost their jobs if they were frankly anti-war. Many others dared no longer speak.

Before long, lecture halls that were open to the advocates of war were closed to speakers who opposed it. A fear campaign was inaugurated....Propaganda was in full swing.

There was no difficulty in obtaining billions of dollars for arms under the guise of defending America. Our people stood united on a program of defense. Congress passed appropriation after appropriation for guns and planes and battleships, with the approval of the overwhelming majority of our citizens. That a large portion of these appropriations was to be used to build arms for Europe, we did not learn until later. That was another step.

We have become involved in the war from practically every standpoint except actual shooting. Only the creation of sufficient "incidents" yet remains...

Men and women of Iowa; only one thing holds this country from war today. That is the rising opposition of the American people. Our system of democracy and representative government is on test today as it has never been before. We are on the verge of a war in which the only victor would be chaos and prostration.

We are on the verge of a war for which we are still unprepared, and for which no one has offered a feasible plan for victory—a war which cannot be won without sending our soldiers across the ocean to force a landing on a hostile coast against armies stronger than our own.

We are on the verge of war, but it is not yet too late to stay out. It is not too late to show that no amount of money, or propaganda, or patronage can force a free and independent people into war against its will. It is not yet too late to retrieve and to maintain the independent American destiny that our forefathers established in this new world.

The entire future rests upon our shoulders. It depends upon our action, our courage, and our intelligence. If you oppose our intervention in the war, now is the time to make your voice heard.

Document Analysis

1. What three groups did Lindbergh single out as being most responsible for pushing the United States toward war in the autumn of 1941?

2. What evidence of pro-war propaganda does Lindbergh claim is being used by these groups?

Twenty-seven.4

A. Philip Randolph, "Why Should We March?" (1942)

*In 1941, the civil rights leader A. Philip Randolph, threatened to lead a massive march of African Americans on Washington to protest discrimination against blacks by U.S. defense industries. Randolph met with President Roosevelt, and made it clear he would not back down. Roosevelt, wanting to avoid such a divisive march, issued Executive Order 8802, establishing a Fair Employment Practices Committee, and requiring that defense industries hire black workers. During the war, Randolph continued his campaign to end discrimination by the government and defense industries, and kept up the idea of a march for justice.**

Though I have found no Negroes who want to see the United Nations lose this war, I have found many who, before the war ends, want to see the stuffing knocked out of white supremacy and of empire over subject peoples. American Negroes, involved as we are in the general issues of the conflict, are confronted not with a choice but with the challenge both to win democracy for ourselves at home and to help win the war for democracy the world over.

There is no escape from the horns of this dilemma. There ought not to be escape. For if the war for democracy is not won abroad, the fight for democracy cannot be won at home. If this war cannot be won for the white peoples, it will not be won for the darker races.

Conversely, if freedom and equality are not vouchsafed the peoples of color, the war for democracy will not be won. Unless this double-barreled thesis is accepted and applied, the darker races will never wholeheartedly fight for the victory of the United Nations. That is why those familiar with the thinking of the American Negro have sensed his lack of enthusiasm, whether among the educated or uneducated, rich or poor, professional or nonprofessional, religious or secular, rural or urban, north, south, east or west.

* From A. Philip Randolph, "Why Should We March?" (1942), accessible online at http://occawlonline.pearsoned.com/bookbind/pubbooks/divine5e/chapter27/medialib/primarysources1_27_2.html.

That is why questions are being raised by Negroes in church, labor union and fraternal society; in poolroom, barbershop, schoolroom, hospital, hair-dressing parlor; on college campus, railroad, and bus. One can hear such questions asked as these: What have Negroes to fight for? What's the difference between Hitler and that "cracker" Talmadge of Georgia? Why has a man got to be Jim Crowed to die for democracy? If you haven't got democracy yourself, how can you carry it to somebody else?

What are the reasons for this state of mind? The answer is: discrimination, segregation, Jim Crow. Witness the navy, the army, the air corps; and also government services at Washington. In many parts of the South, Negroes in Uncle Sam's uniform are being put upon, mobbed, sometimes even shot down by civilian and military police, and on occasion lynched. Vested political interests in race prejudice are so deeply entrenched that to them winning the war against Hitler is secondary to preventing Negroes from winning democracy for themselves. This is worth many divisions to Hitler and Hirohito. While labor, business, and farm are subjected to ceilings and doors and not allowed to carry on as usual, these interests trade in the dangerous business of race hate as usual.

When the defense program began and billions of the taxpayers' money were appropriated for guns, ships, tanks and bombs, Negroes presented themselves for work only to be given the cold shoulder. North as well as South, and despite their qualifications, Negroes were denied skilled employment. Not until their wrath and indignation took the form of a proposed protest march on Washington, scheduled for July 1, 1941, did things begin to move in the form of defense jobs for Negroes. The march was postponed by the timely issuance (June 25, 1941) of the famous Executive Order No. 8802 by President Roosevelt. But this order and the President's Committee on Fair Employment Practice, established thereunder, have as yet only scratched the surface by way of eliminating discriminations on account of race or color in war industry. Both management and labor unions in too many places and in too many ways are still drawing the color line.

It is to meet this situation squarely with direct action that the March on Washington Movement launched its present program of protest mass meetings. Twenty thousand were in attendance at Madison Square Garden, June 16; sixteen thousand in the Coliseum in Chicago, June 26; nine thousand in the City Auditorium of St. Louis, August 14. Meetings of such magnitude were unprecedented among Negroes. The vast throngs were drawn from all walks and levels of Negro life—businessmen, teachers, laundry workers, Pullman porters, waiters, and red caps; preachers, crapshooters, and social workers; jitterbugs and Ph.D.'s. They came and sat in silence, thinking, applauding only when they considered the truth was told, when they felt strongly that something was going to be done about it.

The March on Washington Movement is essentially a movement of the people. It is all Negro and pro-Negro, but not for that reason anti-white or anti-Semitic, or anti-Catholic, or anti-foreign, or anti-labor. Its major weapon is the non-violent demonstration of Negro mass power. Negro leadership has united back of its drive for jobs and justice. "Whether Negroes should march on Washington, and if so, when?" will be the focus of a forthcoming national conference. For the plan of a protest march has not been abandoned. Its purpose would be to demonstrate that American Negroes are in deadly earnest, and all out for their full rights. No power on earth can cause them today to abandon their fight to wipe out every vestige of second class citizenship and the dual standards that plague them.

A community is democratic only when the humblest and weakest person can enjoy the highest civil, economic, and social rights that the biggest and most powerful possess. To trample on these rights of both Negroes and poor whites is such a commonplace in the South that it takes readily to anti-social, anti-labor, anti-Semitic and anti-Catholic propaganda. It was because of laxness in enforcing the Weimar constitution in republican Germany that Nazism made headway. Oppression of the Negroes in the United States, like suppression of the Jews in Germany, may open the way for a fascist dictatorship.

By fighting for their rights now, American Negroes are helping to make America a moral and spiritual arsenal of democracy. Their fight against the poll tax, against lynch law, segregation, and Jim Crow, their fight for economic, political, and social equality, thus becomes part of the global war for freedom.

DOCUMENT ANALYSIS

1. What does Randolph argue is the reason behind African Americans marching during World War II? How does he adopt Roosevelt's phrase of making America an "arsenal of democracy"? Is Randolph's argument persuasive?

Twenty-seven.5

Korematsu v. United States
(1944)

The removal of all Japanese Americans from the West Coast of the United States by Executive Order 9066 in 1942 was, according to the federal government, justified by wartime necessity. Fred Korematsu, an American citizen and a second-generation Japanese American, challenged this policy, and his case made it to the Supreme Court. Although hardly united, the Court issued a 6–3 decision in 1944, acquiescing in the government's decision against an entire group.

Exclusion of those of Japanese origin was deemed necessary because of the presence of an unascertained number of disloyal members of the group, most of whom we have no doubt were loyal to this country. It was because we could not reject the finding of the military authorities that it was impossible to bring about an immediate segregation of the disloyal from the loyal that we sustained the validity of the curfew order as applying to the whole group. In the instant case, temporary exclusion of the entire group was rested by the military on the same ground. The judgement that exclusion of the whole group was for the same reason a military imperative answers the contention that the exclusion was in the nature of group punishment based on antagonism to those of Japanese origin. That there were members of the group who retained loyalties in Japan has been confirmed by investigations made subsequent to the exclusion. Approximately five thousand American citizens of Japanese ancestry refused to swear unqualified allegiance to the United States and to renounce allegiance to the Japanese Emperor, and several thousand evacuees requested repatriation to Japan.

We uphold the exclusion order as of the time it was made and when the petitioner violated it....In doing so, we are not unmindful of the hardships imposed by it upon a large group of American citizens....But hardships are part of war, and war is an aggregation of hardships. All citizens alike, both in and out of uniform, feel the impact of war in greater or lesser measure. Citizenship has its responsibilities as well as its privileges,

* From 323 U.S. 214 (1944).

and in time of war the burden is always heavier. Compulsory exclusion of large groups of citizens from their homes, except under circumstances of direct emergency and peril, is inconsistent with our basic governmental institutions. But when under conditions of modern warfare our shores are threatened by hostile forces, the power to protect must be commensurate with the threatened danger....

It is said that we are dealing here with the case of imprisonment of a citizen in a concentration camp solely because his ancestry, without evidence or inquiry concerning his loyalty and good disposition towards the United States. Our task would be simple, our duty clear, were this a case involving the imprisonment of a loyal citizen in a concentration camp because of racial prejudice. Regardless of the true nature of the assembly and relocation centers—and we deem it unjustifiable to call them concentration camps with all the ugly connotations that term implies—we are dealing specifically with nothing but an exclusion order. To cast this case into outlines of racial prejudice, without reference to the real military dangers which were presented, merely confuses the issue. Korematsu was not excluded from the Military Area because of hostility to him or his race. He *was* excluded because we are at war with the Japanese Empire, because the properly constituted military authorities feared an invasion of our West Coast and felt constrained to take proper security measures, because they decided that the military urgency of the situation demanded that all citizens of Japanese ancestry be segregated from the West Coast temporarily, and finally, because Congress, reposing its confidence in this time of war in our military leaders—as inevitably it must—determined that they should have the power to do just this. There was evidence of disloyalty on the part of some, the military authorities considered that the need for action was great, and time was short. We cannot—by availing ourselves of the calm perspective of hindsight—now say that at that time these actions were unjustified.

Justice Murphy, dissenting.

This exclusion of "all persons of Japanese ancestry, both alien and non-alien," from the Pacific Coast area on a plea of military necessity in the absence of martial law ought not to be approved. Such exclusion goes over "the very brink of constitutional power" and falls into the ugly abyss of racism.

In dealing with matters relating to the prosecution and progress of a war, we must accord great respect and consideration to the judgments of the military authorities who are on the scene and who have full knowledge of the military facts. The scope of their discretion must, as a matter of necessity and common sense, be wide. And their judgments ought not to be overruled lightly by those whose training and duties ill-equip them to deal intelligently with matters so vital to the physical security of the nation....

No one denies, of course, that there were some disloyal persons of Japanese descent on the Pacific Coast who did all in their power to aid their ancestral land. Similar disloyal activities have been engaged in by many persons of German, Italian and even more pioneer stock in our country. But to infer that examples of individual disloyalty prove group disloyalty and justify discriminatory action against the entire group is to deny that under our system of law individual guilt is the sole basis for deprivation of rights....To give constitutional sanction to that inference in this case, however well-intentioned may have been the military command on the Pacific Coast, is to adopt one of the cruelest of the rationales used by our enemies to destroy the dignity of the individual and to encourage and open the door to discriminatory actions against other minority groups...

I dissent, therefore, from this legalization of racism. Racial discrimination in any form and in any degree has no justifiable part whatever in our democratic way of life. It is unattractive in any setting but it is utterly revolting among a free people who have embraced the principles set forth in the Constitution of the United States. All residents of this nation are kin in some way by blood or culture to a foreign land. Yet they are primarily and necessarily a part of the new and distinct civilization of the United States. They must accordingly be treated at all times as the heirs of the American experiment and as entitled to all the rights and freedoms guaranteed by the Constitution.

DOCUMENT ANALYSIS

1. According to the majority opinion, why was it justifiable for Korematsu and other Japanese Americans to be removed from the West Coast after Pearl Harbor? Is his argument persuasive?

2. What is the essential point of Justice Murphy's dissenting opinion?

Chapter Study Questions

1. Why do you think Einstein and other scientists who fled Europe were especially concerned about the prospect of Germany obtaining an atomic weapon?

2. Compare Franklin Roosevelt's Four Freedoms speech to Woodrow Wilson's Fourteen Points in Chapter 24. Do you find Roosevelt equally idealistic in the ultimate goals for the world he presents, or more realistic? Explain.

3. What do you think caused such an outcry against Charles Lindbergh following his Des Moines speech in 1941?

4. How does A. Philip Randolph's push for racial equality and the debate over the *Korematsu v. United States* case relate to Franklin Roosevelt's Four Freedoms? Do you see any irony here? Explain.

Twenty-eight

The Onset of the Cold War

At the end of World War II, only two nations possessed the military and economic power to assume positions of leadership. For both the United States and the Soviet Union, the war colored their actions in the period immediately following. Neither nation wanted to suffer the horrors of war again. The Soviets began to surround themselves with a barrier of buffer states—Czechoslovakia, North Korea, and East Germany were among the first—in order to protect themselves, while the United States, responding aggressively to the Soviets' expansion, adopted a policy of "containment" (as articulated in George Kennan's famous telegram from the U.S. embassy in Moscow).

Each nation perceived the other as a threat to world peace and its own national security. By 1947, with most of Eastern Europe under the control of the communists, President Harry Truman had come to believe that an "Iron Curtain," as Winston Churchill described it, had descended on Eastern Europe and would soon also move southward. In Turkey and Greece, British-supported governments appeared to be falling under Soviet pressure as their British military and economic support dried up. Communists fought against monarchists in Greece and the Soviets vied for control of the passage from the Black Sea to the Mediterranean in Turkey. In response Truman argued that America should step in where Britain had left off, and furthermore act to stem the spread of communism and Soviet power anywhere else in the world. This so-called Truman Doctrine would exert enormous influence on American foreign policy for many years to come.

The Truman Doctrine was not the only policy through which the United States sought to counter Soviet global influence. Perhaps the most successful American program of the postwar period was formulated by Secretary of State George Marshall. The economic problems of Western Europe worried Marshall; like Truman, he feared that economic instability would lead to political turmoil and provide new political opportunities for the communists. Thus the rapid economic recovery of Europe was crucial, and the Marshall Plan was constructed to provide massive economic assistance to Western Europe. Part of its ingenuity was that the plan was designed not only to fuel European recovery but also to create markets for American goods. Approved by Congress, the Marshall Plan sent $15 billion in economic assistance to American allies in Europe.

The Cold War pervaded all aspects of American life but was particularly trenchant in domestic politics. Aggressive anticommunist rhetoric fostered paranoias and in political debates, Republicans were quick to accuse the Democrats of being "soft on communism." Some even believed that Roosevelt had given Eastern Europe to the Soviet Union at the Yalta conference. And in 1947, Truman established the Federal Employee Loyalty probe—an investigation into the patriotism of all federal employees.

In this climate of suspicion and fear the House Un-American Activities Committee began a series of hearings focusing on the loyalty of the entertainment community. Over a four-year period, scores of Hollywood writers, directors, actors and actresses were asked to testify about the infiltration of communists into the industry. Some, most notably the Hollywood Ten, refused to testify and were sent to prison. For years afterward, suspected communists were virtually unable to work in the film community.

The HUAC hearings encouraged Americans to see communist influence and conspiracy in myriad institutions. This paranoia was intensified in the Red scare led by Senator Joseph R. McCarthy. In his speeches and in hearings he led from 1950 to 1954, McCarthy fanned the flames of national fear, by inspecting libraries, subpoenaing witnesses, and in the end, attacking army leaders in a fervent effort to root out communists. The selection included here is from the very beginning of McCarthy's short-lived fame; it is the first instance in which he hints at the presence of communists in the State Department.

McCarthy's charges led some Democrats to hide in fear, while some fellow Republicans, knowing McCarthy was something of a reckless demagogue, refused to speak out against him as they appreciated his effectiveness in smearing Democrats. Senator Margaret Chase Smith, a Republican from Maine, was one of a group of Republicans who did speak out early against the character assassinations being made by McCarthy. Smith issued a Declaration of Conscience in June 1950, which, without naming McCarthy by name, rejected the types of unsubstantiated charges and character assassinations for which McCarthy was becoming famous. Portions of this Declaration of Conscience are included as the fourth document in this chapter. McCarthy would not back down, however, and continued a reign of terror until 1954, when the Senate finally voted to censure him for conduct unbecoming a Senator.

The final document in the chapter is from the autobiography of Whittaker Chambers, an admitted ex-communist, who became famous in the late 1940s when he appeared before HUAC and alleged that Alger Hiss, a well-known Democrat who had worked for the U.S. State Department in the Roosevelt administration, had also been a communist. Hiss vehemently denied the charge, but was eventually convicted of perjury for lying under oath about his communist past. To Chambers, communism was the embodiment of evil, and he felt a religious duty to write the story of how he came to see it for what it was.

Twenty-eight.1

Harry S Truman, The Truman Doctrine (1947)

World War II left Europe economically devastated and politically unstable. Early in 1947, it appeared that Turkey and Greece would fall under Soviet influence. In this famous speech, Truman outlines his support for a policy of aggressive containment of the Soviet Union not only in Turkey and Greece, but all over the world. In the words of his secretary of state, Dean Acheson, the Truman administration worried that "like apples in a barrel infected by one rotten one, the corruption of Greece would infect Iran and all of the east."*

At the present moment in world history nearly every nation must choose between alternative ways of life. The choice is too often not a free one.

One way of life is based upon the will of the majority, and is distinguished by free institutions, representative government, free elections, guaranties of individual liberty, freedom of speech and religion, and freedom from political oppression.

The second way of life is based upon the will of a minority forcibly imposed upon the majority. It relies upon terror and oppression, a controlled press and radio, fixed elections, and the suppression of personal freedoms.

I believe that it must be the policy of the United States to support free peoples who are resisting attempted subjugation by armed minorities or by outside pressures.

I believe that we must assist free peoples to work out their own destinies in their own way.

I believe that our help should be primarily through economic and financial aid, which is essential to economic stability and orderly political processes.

The world is not static, and the status quo is not sacred. But we cannot allow changes in the status quo in violation of the Charter of the United Nations by such methods as coercion, or by such subterfuges as political infiltration. In helping free and independ-

* From Harry S Truman, "Speech, March 12, 1947," in *Public Papers of the Presidents, Harry S Truman, 1947* (Washington, D.C.: U.S. Government Printing Office, 1963), 176–180.

ent nations to maintain their freedom, the United States will be giving effect to the principles of the Charter of the United Nations....

The seeds of totalitarian regimes are nurtured by misery and want. They spread and grow in the evil soil of poverty and strife. They reach their full growth when the hope of a people for a better life has died.

We must keep that hope alive.

The free peoples of the world look to us for support in maintaining their freedoms.

If we falter in our leadership, we may endanger the peace of the world—and we shall surely endanger the welfare of our own Nation.

DOCUMENT ANALYSIS

1. What does Truman define as the choice that all countries must make in this early Cold War era?

2. How did the Truman Doctrine define American foreign policy and America's role in foreign affairs?

Twenty-eight.2

George Marshall, The Marshall Plan (1947)

In this speech, delivered at the Harvard University commencement in 1947, Secretary of State Marshall articulated a plan for American aid to Europe. The plan was designed to fill the power vacuum in Europe and to help Europe reconstruct itself after the devastation of war. Marshall even extended the promise of aid to the Soviet-dominated countries of Eastern Europe. The program was remarkably successful and by the early 1950s the Western European economy was much recovered. *

The truth of the matter is that Europe's requirements for the next three or four years of foreign food and other essential products—principally from America—are so much greater than her present ability to pay that she must have substantial additional help or face economic, social, and political deterioration of a very grave character....

Aside from the demoralizing effect on the world at large and the possibilities of disturbances arising as a result of the desperation of the people concerned, the consequences of the economy of the United States should be apparent to all. It is logical that the United States should do whatever it is able to do to assist in the return of normal economic health in the world, without which there can be no political stability and no assured peace. Our policy is directed not against any country or doctrine but against hunger, poverty, desperation, and chaos. Its purpose should be the revival of a working economy in the world so as to permit the emergence of political and social conditions in which free institutions can exist.

Such assistance, I am convinced, must not be on a piecemeal basis as various crises develop. Any assistance that this Government may render in the future should provide a cure rather than a mere palliative. Any government that is willing to assist in the task of recovery will find full cooperation, I am sure, on the part of the United States

* From George Marshall, Speech of June 5, 1947, *Department of State Bulletin* 16 (June 15, 1947), 1159–1160.

Government. Any government which maneuvers to block the recovery of other countries cannot expect help from us. Furthermore, governments, political parties, or groups which seek to perpetuate human misery in order to profit there from politically or otherwise will encounter the opposition of the United States.

It is already evident that, before the United States Government can proceed much further in its efforts to alleviate the situation and help start the European world on its way to recovery, there must be some agreement among the countries of Europe as to the requirements of the situation and the part those countries themselves will take in order to give proper effect to whatever action might be undertaken by this Government.

It would be neither fitting nor efficacious for this Government to undertake to draw up unilaterally a program designed to place Europe on its feet economically. This is the business of the Europeans. The initiative, I think, must come from Europe. The role of this country should consist of friendly aid in the drafting of a European program and of later support of such a program so far as it may be practical for us to do so. The program should be a joint one, agreed to by a number, if not all, European nations.

DOCUMENT ANALYSIS

1. What does Marshall suggest might happen in Europe if American financial aid is not provided? Does his argument seem convincing to you? Explain.

Twenty-eight.3

Joseph R. McCarthy, from Speech Delivered to the Women's Club of Wheeling, West Virginia (1950)

This speech, delivered in February 1950 and addressed to the Women's Club of Wheeling, West Virginia, gained Senator McCarthy national attention. Initially, McCarthy claimed he could identify 205 known Communists in the State Department; in this version of the speech, submitted into the Congressional Record, *he has reduced the number to 57. McCarthy's speech attacks in particular the State Department, then headed by Dean Acheson. Acheson was one of McCarthy's favorite victims, in part because of his relationship with Alger Hiss (a former State Department official later accused of spying for the Soviet Union and convicted of perjury). McCarthy later called Acheson and his predecessor, George Marshall (then secretary of defense), leaders or "executioners" in a "great conspiracy" directed by Moscow intended to "diminish the United States."**

F ive years after a world war has been one, men's hearts should anticipate a long peace, and men's minds should be free from the heavy weight that comes from war. But this is not such a period—for this is not a period of peace. This is a time of the "cold war." This is a time when all the world is split into two vast, increasingly hostile armed camps....

The reason why we find ourselves in a position of impotency is not because our only powerful potential enemy has sent men to invade our shores, but rather because of the traitorous actions of those who have been treated so well by this Nation. It has not been the less fortunate or members of minority groups who have been selling this Nation out, but rather those who have had all the benefits that the wealthiest nation on earth has to offer—the finest homes, the finest college education, and the finest jobs in Government.

This is glaringly true in the State Department. There the bright young men who are born with silver spoons in their mouths are the ones who have been the worst....In my

* From Joseph McCarthy, Remarks, *Congressional Record*, 81st Congress, 1st sess, 1951, 6556–6603.

opinion, the State Department, which is one of the most important government departments, is thoroughly infested with Communists.

I have in my hand 57 cases of individuals who would appear to be either card carrying members or certainly loyal to the Communist Party, but who nevertheless are still helping to shape our foreign policy....

As you know, very recently the Secretary of State proclaimed his loyalty to a man guilty of what has always been considered as the most abominable of all crimes—of being a traitor to the people who gave him a position of great trust. The Secretary of State in attempting to justify his continued devotion to the man who sold out the Christian world to the atheistic world, referred to Christ's Sermon on the Mount as a justification and reason therefor, and the reaction of the American people to this would have made the heart of Abraham Lincoln happy.

When this pompous diplomat in striped pants, with a phony British accent, proclaimed to the American people that Christ on the Mount endorsed communism, high treason, and a betrayal of a sacred trust, the blasphemy was so great that it awakened the dormant indignation of the American people.

He has lighted the spark which is resulting in a moral uprising and will end only when the whole sorry mess of twisted, warped thinkers are swept from the national scene so that we may have a new birth of national honesty and decency in government.

DOCUMENT ANALYSIS

1. Why were the charges made by McCarthy in this 1950 speech so explosive? What is he accusing the Truman administration of allowing to happen?

2. How is McCarthy using populist rhetoric to attack those he considers communists?

Twenty-eight.4

Margaret Chase Smith,
from "Declaration of Conscience"
(1950)

Following McCarthy's Wheeling speech in early 1950, the Senate held a special session to investigate his serious charges of communist infiltration of the State Department, only to discover that McCarthy could not produce the evidence. A short time later, several Republican senators signed on to a Declaration of Conscience offered by Maine Senator Margaret Chase Smith, a moderate Republican. *

Mr. President:

I would like to speak briefly and simply about a serious national condition. It is a national feeling of fear and frustration that could result in national suicide and the end of everything that we Americans hold dear....

I speak as a Republican. I speak as a woman. I speak as a United States Senator. I speak as an American.

The United States Senate has long enjoyed worldwide respect as the greatest deliberative body in the world. But recently that deliberative character has too often been debased to the level of a forum of hate and character assassination sheltered by the shield of congressional immunity.

It is ironical that we Senators can in debate in the Senate directly or indirectly, by any form of words, impute to any American who is not a Senator any conduct or motive unworthy or unbecoming an American—and without that non-Senator American having any legal redress against us—yet if we say the same thing in the Senate about our colleagues we can be stopped on the grounds of being out of order.

It is strange that we can verbally attack anyone else without restraint and with full protection and yet we hold ourselves above the same type of criticism here on the Senate

* From U.S. Congress, Senate, *Congressional Record*, 81st Congress, 2nd sess., pp. 7894–7895, accessible online at http://www.americanrhetoric.com/speeches/margaretchasesmithconscience.html.

Floor. Surely the United States Senate is big enough to take self-criticism and self-appraisal. Surely we should be able to take the same kind of character attacks that we "dish out" to outsiders.

I think that it is high time for the United States Senate and its members to do some soul-searching—for us to weigh our consciences—on the manner in which we are performing our duty to the people of America—on the manner in which we are using or abusing our individual powers and privileges.

I think that it is high time that we remembered that we have sworn to uphold and defend the Constitution. I think that it is high time that we remembered that the Constitution, as amended, speaks not only of the freedom of speech but also of trial by jury instead of trial by accusation.

Whether it be a criminal prosecution in court or a character prosecution in the Senate, there is little practical distinction when the life of a person has been ruined.

Those of us who shout the loudest about Americanism in making character assassinations are all too frequently those who, by our own words and acts, ignore some of the basic principles of Americanism:

> The right to criticize;

> The right to hold unpopular beliefs;

> The right to protest;

> The right of independent thought.

The exercise of these rights should not cost one single American citizen his reputation or his right to a livelihood nor should he be in danger of losing his reputation or livelihood merely because he happens to know someone who holds unpopular beliefs. Who of us doesn't? Otherwise none of us could call our souls our own. Otherwise thought control would have set in.

The American people are sick and tired of being afraid to speak their minds lest they be politically smeared as "Communists" or "Fascists" by their opponents. Freedom of speech is not what it used to be in America. It has been so abused by some that it is not exercised by others.

The American people are sick and tired of seeing innocent people smeared and guilty people whitewashed. But there have been enough proved cases, such as the Amerasia case, the Hiss case, the Coplon case, the Gold case, to cause the nationwide distrust and strong suspicion that there may be something to the unproved, sensational accusations.

As a Republican, I say to my colleagues on this side of the aisle that the Republican Party faces a challenge today that is not unlike the challenge that it faced back in Lincoln's day. The Republican Party so successfully met that challenge that it emerged from the Civil War as the champion of a united nation—in addition to being a Party that unrelentingly fought loose spending and loose programs.

Today our country is being psychologically divided by the confusion and the suspicions that are bred in the United States Senate to spread like cancerous tentacles of "know nothing, suspect everything" attitudes. Today we have a Democratic Administration that has developed a mania for loose spending and loose programs.

History is repeating itself—and the Republican Party again has the opportunity to emerge as the champion of unity and prudence.

The record of the present Democratic Administration has provided us with sufficient campaign issues without the necessity of resorting to political smears. America is rapidly losing its position as leader of the world simply because the Democratic Administration has pitifully failed to provide effective leadership.

The Democratic Administration has completely confused the American people by its daily contradictory grave warnings and optimistic assurances—that show the people that our Democratic Administration has no idea of where it is going.

The Democratic Administration has greatly lost the confidence of the American people by its complacency to the threat of communism here at home and the leak of vital secrets to Russia though key officials of the Democratic Administration. There are enough proved cases to make this point without diluting our criticism with unproved charges.

Surely these are sufficient reasons to make it clear to the American people that it is time for a change and that a Republican victory is necessary to the security of this country. Surely it is clear that this nation will continue to suffer as long as it is governed by the present ineffective Democratic Administration.

Yet to displace it with a Republican regime embracing a philosophy that lacks political integrity or intellectual honesty would prove equally disastrous to this nation. The nation sorely needs a Republican victory. But I don't want to see the Republican Party ride to political victory on the Four Horsemen of Calumny—Fear, Ignorance, Bigotry, and Smear.

DOCUMENT ANALYSIS

1. What are the concerns Smith raises about some of her Republican colleagues? What criticisms does she offer of the Democrats?

2. Why do you think Smith chooses not to name Joe McCarthy in this criticism?

Twenty-eight.5

Whittaker Chambers, from Foreword to *Witness* (1952)

In 1948, a frumpy senior editor for Time *magazine appeared before HUAC and described his involvement with the communist party in the 1930s. He had admitted this involvement long ago, but he stunned the committee by naming Alger Hiss, a well-respected former State Department employee and diplomat, as a fellow communist from years earlier. The Hiss-Chambers case made headlines as a gripping spy drama, and Hiss was eventually found guilty of perjury. Chambers wrote a gripping autobiography in 1952 in which he described his reasons for leaving the communist party, and what he believed to be at the heart of the fight between democracy versus communism.* *

B eloved Children,

I am sitting in the kitchen of the little house at Medfield, our second farm which is cut off by the ridge and a quarter-mile across the fields from our home place, where you are. I am writing a book. In it I am speaking to you. But I am also speaking to the world. To both I owe an accounting.

It is a terrible book. It is terrible in what it tells about men. If anything, it is more terrible in what it tells about the world in which you live. It is about what the world calls the Hiss-Chambers Case, or even more simply, the Hiss Case. It is about a spy case. All the props of an espionage case are there—foreign agents, household traitors, stolen documents, microfilm, furtive meetings, secret hideaways, phony names, an informer, investigations, trials, official justice.

But if the Hiss Case were only this, it would not be worth my writing about or your reading about....

---

* From Whittaker Chambers, *Witness* (Chicago: Regnery Gateway, 1952), pp. 3–9.

For it was more than human tragedy. Much more than Alger Hiss or Whittaker Chambers was on trial in the trials of Alger Hiss. Two faiths were on trial. Human societies, like human beings, live by faith and die when faith dies....

At heart, the Great Case was this critical conflict of faiths; that is why it was a great case. On a scale personal enough to be felt by all, but big enough to be symbolic, the two irreconcilable faiths of our time—Communism and Freedom—came to grips in the persons of two conscious and resolute men. Indeed, it would have been hard, in a world still only dimly aware of what the conflict is about, to find two other men who knew so clearly. Both had been schooled in the same view of history (the Marxist view). Both were trained by the same party in the same selfless, semisoldierly discipline. Neither would nor could yield without betraying, not himself, but his faith; and the different character of these faiths was shown by the different conduct of the two men toward each other throughout the struggle. For, with dark certitude, both knew, almost from the beginning, that the Great Case could end only in the destruction of one or both of the contending figures, just as the history of our times (both men had been taught) can end only in the destruction of one or both of the contending forces.

...My children, as long as you live, the shadow of the Hiss Case will brush you....In time, therefore, when the sum of your experience of life gives you authority, you will ask yourselves the question: What was my father?

I will give you an answer: I was a witness. I do not mean a witness for the Government or against Alger Hiss and the others. Nor do I mean the short, squat, solitary figure, trudging through the impersonal halls of public buildings to testify before Congressional committees, grand juries, loyalty boards, courts of law. A man is not primarily a witness *against* something. That is only incidental to the fact that he is a witness *for* something. A witness, in the sense that I am using the word, is a man whose life and faith are so completely one that when the challenge comes to step out and testify for his faith, he does so, disregarding all risks, accepting all consequences....

But a man may also be an involuntary witness. I do not know any way to explain why God's grace touches a man who seems unworthy of it. But neither do I know any other way to explain how a man like myself—tarnished by life, unprepossessing, not brave— could prevail so far against the powers of the world arrayed almost solidly against him, to destroy him and defeat his truth. In this sense, I am an involuntary witness to God's grace and to the fortifying power of faith.

It was my fate to be in turn a witness to each of the two great faiths of our time. And so we come to the terrible word, Communism. My very dear children, nothing in all these pages will be written so much for you, though it is so unlike anything you would want to read. In nothing shall I be so much a witness, in no way am I so much called upon to fulfill my task, as in trying to make clear to you (and to the world) the true nature of Communism and the source of its power, which was the cause of my ordeal as a man, and remains the historic ordeal of the world in the 20th century. For in this century, within the next decades, will be decided for generations whether all mankind is to become Communist, whether the whole world is to become free, or whether, in the struggle, civilization as we know it is to be completely destroyed or completely changed. It is our fate to live upon that turning point in history....

I see in Communism the focus of the concentrated evil of our time. You will ask: Why, then, do men become Communists? How did it happen that you, our gentle and loved father, were once a Communist? Were you simply stupid? No, I was not stupid. Were you morally depraved? No, I was not morally depraved. Indeed, educated men become Communists chiefly for moral reasons. Did you not know that the crimes and horrors of Communism are inherent in Communism? Yes, I knew that fact. Then why did you become a Communist? It would help more to ask: How did it happen that this movement, once a mere muttering of political outcasts, became this immense force that now contests the mastery of mankind? Even when all the chances and mistakes of history are allowed for, the answer must be: Communism makes some profound appeal to the human mind.

In the Hiss trials, where Communism was a haunting specter, but which did little or nothing to explain Communism. Communists were assumed to be criminals, pariahs, clandestine men who lead double lives under false names, travel on false passports, deny traditional religion, morality, the sanctity of oaths, preach violence and practice treason. These things are true about Communists, but they are not what Communism is about.

The revolutionary heart of Communism is not the theatrical appeal: "Workers of the world, unite. You have nothing to lose but your chains. You have a world to gain." It is a simple statement of Karl Marx, further simplified for handy use: "Philosophers have explained the world; it is necessary to change the world." Communists are bound together by no secret oath. The tie that binds them across the frontiers of nations, across barriers of language and differences of class and education, in defiance of religion, morality, truth, law, honor, the weaknesses of the body and the irresolutions of the mind, even unto death, is a simple conviction: It is necessary to change the world. Their power, whose nature baffles the rest of the world, because in a large measure the rest of the world has lost that power, is the power to hold convictions and to act on them. It is the same power that moves mountains; it is also an unfailing power to move men. Communists are that part of mankind which has recovered the power to live or die—to bear witness—for its faith. And it is a simple, rational faith that inspires men to live or die for it....

The Communist vision is the vision of Man without God.

It is the vision of man's mind displacing God as the creative intelligence of the world. It is the vision of man's liberated mind, by the sole force of its rational intelligence, redirecting man's destiny and reorganizing man's life and the world. It is the vision of man, once more the central figure of the Creation, not because God made man in His image, but because man's mind makes him the most intelligent of the animals.

DOCUMENT ANALYSIS

1. According to Chambers, why does he refer to himself as a "witness"?

2. What does Chambers claim is at the heart of the communist ideology? Why does Chambers, who had been a committed communist himself in the 1930s, now reject it entirely?

Chapter Study Questions

1. How did the Truman Doctrine and Marshall Plan both use foreign economic aid to promote U.S. foreign policy? Is this a good use of taxpayers' dollars? Explain.

2. Why were so many Americans willing to believe McCarthy's charges, even when he couldn't substantiate his claims? Why do you think Margaret Chase Smith and other Republicans worried that McCarthy was actually helping communists?

3. How did the Korean War, which began in June 1950, make people even more willing to believe McCarthy?

4. Analyze how and why McCarthy and Chambers see the fight against communism in religious terms.

Twenty-nine

Affluence and Anxiety

African Americans entered the postwar era with expectations of an end to segregation and racial equality. The New Deal and the war had increased employment opportunities for African Americans; during the war millions of blacks moved north and west to cities like New York, Los Angeles, Detroit, and Chicago to work in wartime industries. They established roots, and friends and family often followed to take advantage of the jobs created by the expanding American economy. Your text shows how racism still prevailed throughout the nation—Jim Crow still held fast in the South and *de facto* segregation and discrimination marked life in the North—but that social currents made increased opportunity and equality for African Americans inevitable.

In 1947, Jackie Robinson became the first African American to play major-league baseball and in 1948, President Harry Truman put an end to segregation in the armed services. The most significant event, however, was the Supreme Court's landmark 1954 *Brown v. Board of Education* decision. Culminating a three-year legal struggle led by the NAACP, the Court's decision rejected segregated schools as "inherently unequal."

The white South's reaction to Brown was, of course, almost universally negative. In 1956, a group of 100 white southern congressmen and senators signed what came to be known as the Southern Manifesto, which detailed their opposition to Brown based upon legal precedent. It is not an emotional document, but a point-by-point list of what they believed to be the inherent flaws in the decision. Echoes of the cries of "states' rights" resound throughout the document.

Until the 1950s, blacks' struggle for civil rights concentrated on challenging segregation's legal bases through the courts. In the 1950s, though, it became a more populist cause. The Civil Rights movement of the 1950s, characterized by boycotts, peaceful protests, and attempts to secure voting rights and put an end to segregation, began a new, more activist phase of the struggle for opportunity and equality. The Montgomery, Alabama, bus boycott precipitated by Rosa Parks traditionally marks the beginning of this phase of the Civil Rights era. It also marks the emergence of Martin Luther King, Jr., as the spokesperson and primary figurehead for the movement.

After the successful Montgomery boycott, King organized the Southern Christian Leadership Conference (SCLC) in 1957. The SCLC and King advocated nonviolent direct action as a means of winning equality for black Americans.

Twenty-nine.1

Brown v. Board of Education
(1954)

This landmark Supreme Court decision was the outcome of three years of litigation by the father of Linda Brown, an elementary school student from Topeka, Kansas. In this decision, the Court declared segregated schools unconstitutional. In subsequent decisions, it ruled that schools be desegregated with "all deliberate speed." Somewhat reluctantly, President Dwight Eisenhower oversaw the process in the South in the 1950s, which culminated in the dramatic desegregation of the Little Rock, Arkansas, high school in 1957 under the protection of the National Guard. *

Mr. Chief Justice Warren delivered the opinion of the Court

These cases come to us from the States of Kansas, South Carolina, Virginia, and Delaware. They are premised on different facts and different local conditions, but a common legal question justifies their consideration together in this consolidated opinion.

In each of the cases, minors of the Negro race, through their legal representatives, seek the aid of the courts in obtaining admission to the public schools of their community on a nonsegregated basis. In each instance, they had been denied admission to schools attended by white children under laws requiring or permitting segregation according to race. This segregation was alleged to deprive the plaintiffs of the equal protection of the laws under the Fourteenth Amendment. In each of the cases other than the Delaware case, a three-judge federal district court denied relief to the plaintiffs on the so-called "separate but equal" doctrine announced by this Court in *Plessy v. Ferguson*, 163 U.S. 537. Under that doctrine, equality of treatment is accorded when the races are provided substantially equal facilities, even though these facilities be separate. In the Delaware case, the Supreme Court of Delaware adhered to that doctrine, but ordered that the plaintiffs be admitted to the white schools because of their superiority to the Negro schools.

* From NAACP Legal Defense and Education Fund, Inc., "Summary of Argument," in the Supreme Court of the United States *Brown v. Board of Education of Topeka*, 347 U.S. 483 (1954).

The plaintiffs contended that segregated public schools are not "equal" and cannot be made "equal," and that hence they are deprived of the equal protection of the laws....

In the first cases in this Court construing the Fourteenth Amendment, decided shortly after its adoption, the Court interpreted it as proscribing all state-imposed discriminations against the Negro race. The doctrine of "separate but equal" did not make its appearance in this Court until 1896 in the case of *Plessy v. Ferguson, supra,* involving not education but transportation. American courts have since labored with the doctrine for over half a century. In this Court, there have been six cases involving the "separate but equal" doctrine in the field of public education....In none of these cases was it necessary to examine the doctrine to grant relief to the Negro plaintiff. And in *Sweatt v. Painter*...the Court expressly reserved decision on the question of whether *Plessy v. Ferguson* should be held inapplicable to public education.

In the instant cases, that question is directly presented. Here, unlike *Sweatt v. Painter,* there are findings below that the Negro and white schools involved have been equalized, or are being equalized, with respect to buildings, curricula, qualifications and salaries of teachers, and other "tangible" factors. Our decision, therefore, cannot turn on merely a comparison of these tangible factors in the Negro and white schools involved in each of the cases. We must look instead to the effect of segregation itself on public education.

In approaching this problem, we cannot turn the clock back to 1868 when the Amendment was adopted, or even to 1896 when *Plessy v. Ferguson* was written. We must consider public education in the light of its full development and its present place in American life throughout the Nation. Only in this way can it be determined if segregation in public schools deprives these plaintiffs of the equal protection of the laws.

Today, education is perhaps the most important function of state and local governments. Compulsory school attendance laws and the great expenditures for education both demonstrate our recognition of the importance of education to our democratic society. It is required in the performance of our most basic public responsibilities, even service in the armed forces. It is the very foundation of good citizenship. Today it is a principal instrument in awakening the child to cultural values, in preparing him for later professional training, and in helping him to adjust normally to his environment. In these days, it is doubtful that any child may reasonably be expected to succeed in life if he is denied the opportunity of an education. Such an opportunity, where the state has undertaken to provide it, is a right which must be made available to all on equal terms.

We come then to the question presented: Does segregation of children in public schools solely on the basis of race, even though the physical facilities and other "tangible" factors may be equal, deprive the children of the minority group of equal education opportunities? We believe that it does.

In *Sweatt v. Painter*...in finding that a segregated law school for Negroes could not provide them equal education opportunities, the Court relied in large part on "those qualities which are incapable of objective measurement but which make for greatness in a law school." In *McLaurin v. Oklahoma State Regents*...the Court, in requiring that a Negro admitted to a white graduate school be treated like all other students, again resorted to intangible considerations: "...his ability to study, to engage in discussions and exchange views with other students, and in general, to learn his profession." Such considerations apply with added force to children in grade and high schools. To separate them from others of similar age and qualifications solely because of their race generates a feeling of inferiority as to their status in the community that may affect their hearts and minds in a way unlikely ever to be undone. The effect of this separation on their educational opportunities was well stated by a finding in the Kansas case by a court which nevertheless felt compelled to rule against the Negro plaintiffs:

Segregation of white and colored children in public schools has a detrimental effect upon the colored children. The impact is greater when it has the sanction of the law; for the policy of separating the races is usually interpreted as denoting the inferiority of the Negro group. A sense of inferiority affects the motivation of a child to learn. Segregation with the sanction of law, therefore, has a tendency to retard the education and mental development of negro children and to deprive them of some of the benefits they would receive in a racial[ly] integrated school system.

Whatever may have been the extent of psychological knowledge at the time of *Plessy v. Ferguson*, this finding is amply supported by modern authority. Any language in *Plessy v. Ferguson* contrary to this finding is rejected.

We conclude that in the field of public education the doctrine of "separate but equal" has no place. Separate educational facilities are inherently unequal. Therefore, we hold that the plaintiffs and others similarly situated for whom the actions have been brought are, by reason of the segregation complained of, deprived of the equal protection of the laws guaranteed by the Fourteenth Amendment. This disposition makes unnecessary any discussion whether such segregation also violates the Due Process Clause of the Fourteenth Amendment.

DOCUMENT ANALYSIS

1. According to the Supreme Court ruling in this case, why is "separate but equal" not equal?

Twenty-nine.2

The Southern Manifesto
(1956)

The landmark 1954 U.S. Supreme Court decision in Brown v. Board of Education *mandated an end to public school segregation in the United States. Popular reaction throughout the South, especially, was predictable. One very public response to the decision was the Southern Manifesto, read before Congress, preserved in the* Congressional Record, *and published in newspapers throughout the country. One hundred southern senators and representatives signed the Manifesto, which detailed their objection to the* Brown *decision.*

Declaration of Constitutional Principles

The unwarranted decision of the Supreme Court in the public school cases is now bearing the fruit always produced when men substitute naked power for established law.

The Founding Fathers gave us a Constitution of checks and balances because they realized the inescapable lesson of history that no man or group of men can be safely entrusted with unlimited power. They framed this Constitution with its provisions for change by amendment in order to secure the fundamentals of government against the dangers of temporary popular passion or the personal predilections of public officeholders.

We regard the decision of the Supreme Court in the school cases as a clear abuse of judicial power. It climaxes a trend in the Federal judiciary undertaking to legislate, in derogation of the authority of Congress, and to encroach upon the reserved rights of the States and the people.

The original Constitution does not mention education. Neither does the 14th Amendment nor any other amendment. The debates preceding the submission of the 14th Amendment clearly show that there was no intent that it should affect the systems of education maintained by the States.

The very Congress which proposed the amendment subsequently provided for segregated schools in the District of Columbia.

When the amendment was adopted, in 1868, there were 37 States of the Union. Every one of the 26 States that had any substantial racial differences among its people either approved the operation of segregated schools already in existence or subsequently established such schools by action of the same lawmaking body which considered the 14th Amendment.

As admitted by the Supreme Court in the public school case (*Brown v. Board of Education*), the doctrine of separate but equal schools "apparently originated in *Roberts v. City of Boston*...(1849), upholding school segregation against attack as being violative of a State constitutional guarantee of equality." This constitutional doctrine began in the North—not in the South, and it was followed not only in Massachusetts, but in Connecticut, New York, Illinois, Indiana, Michigan, Minnesota, New Jersey, Ohio, Pennsylvania, and other northern States until they, exercising their rights as States through the constitutional processes of local self-government, changed their school systems.

In the case of *Plessy v. Ferguson*, in 1896, the Supreme Court expressly declared that under the 14th Amendment no person was denied any of his rights if the States provided separate but equal public facilities. This decision has been followed in many other cases. It is notable that the Supreme Court, speaking through Chief Justice Taft, a former President of the United States, unanimously declared, in 1927, in *Lum v. Rice*, that the "separate but equal" principle is "within the discretion of the State in regulating its public schools and does not conflict with the 14th amendment."

This interpretation, restated time and again, became a part of the life of the people of many of the States and confirmed their habits, customs, traditions, and way of life. It is founded on elemental humanity and common sense, for parents should not be deprived by Government of the right to direct the lives and education of their own children.

Though there has been no constitutional amendment or act of Congress changing this established legal principle almost a century old, the Supreme Court of the United States, with no legal basis for such action, undertook to exercise their naked judicial power and substituted their personal political and social ideas for the established law of the land.

This unwarranted exercise of power by the Court, contrary to the Constitution, is creating chaos and confusion in the States principally affected. It is destroying the amicable relations between the white and Negro races that have been created through 90 years of patient effort by the good people of both races. It has planted hatred and suspicion where there has been heretofore friendship and understanding.

Without regard to the consent of the governed, outside agitators are threatening immediate and revolutionary changes in our public-school systems. If done, this is certain to destroy the system of public education in some of the States.

With the gravest concern for the explosive and dangerous condition created by this decision and inflamed by outside meddlers:

We reaffirm our reliance on the Constitution as the fundamental law of the land.

We decry the Supreme Court's encroachments on rights reserved to the States and to the people, contrary to established law and to the Constitution.

We commend the motives of those States which have declared the intention to resist forced integration by any lawful means.

We appeal to the States and people who are not directly affected by these decisions to consider the constitutional principles involved against the time when they, too, on issues vital to them, may be the victims of judicial encroachment.

Even though we constitute a minority in the present Congress, we have full faith that a majority of the American people believe in the dual system of Government which has enabled us to achieve our greatness and will in time demand that the reserved rights of the State and of the people be made secure against judicial usurpation.

We pledge ourselves to use all lawful means to bring about a reversal of this decision which is contrary to the Constitution and to prevent the use of force in its implementation.

In this trying period, as we all seek to right this wrong, we appeal to our people not to be provoked by the agitators and troublemakers invading our States and to scrupulously refrain from disorders and lawless acts.

Signed by:

[Nineteen] Members of the United States Senate

[Eighty-one] Members of the United States House of Representatives

DOCUMENT ANALYSIS

1. What is the basis of the opposition to the *Brown* decision as expressed in this document?

2. What kinds of precedent does the Manifesto rely upon for its argument?

Twenty-nine.3

Jo Ann Gibson Robinson,
The Montgomery Bus Boycott
(1955)

In this memoir, Jo Ann Gibson Robinson recalls her role in the Montgomery, Alabama, bus boycott begun by Rosa Parks, a seamstress and member of the NAACP. Women, like Parks and Robinson, were actively involved in the Southern Civil Rights Movement. *

In the afternoon of Thursday, December 1, [1955] a prominent black woman named Mrs. Rosa Parks was arrested for refusing to vacate her seat for a white man. Mrs. Parks was a medium-sized, cultured mulatto woman; a civic and religious worker; quiet unassuming, and pleasant in manner and appearance; dignified and reserved; of high morals and a strong character. She was—and still is, for she lives to tell the story—respected in all black circles. By trade she was a seamstress, adept and competent in her work.

Tired from work, Mrs. Parks boarded a bus. The "reserved seats" were partially filled, but the seats just behind the reserved section were vacant, and Mrs. Parks sat down in one. It was during the busy evening rush hour. More black and white passengers boarded the bus, and soon all the reserved seats were occupied. The driver demanded that Mrs. Parks get up and surrender her seat to a white man, but she was tired from her work. She remained seated. In a few minutes, police summoned by the driver appeared, placed Mrs. Parks under arrest and took her to jail.

It was the first time the soft-spoken, middle-aged woman had been arrested. She maintained her decorum and poise, and the word of her arrest spread. Mr. E. D. Nixon, a longtime stalwart of our NAACP branch, along with liberal white attorney Clifford Durr and his wife Virginia, went to the jail and obtained Mrs. Parks's release on bond. Her trial was scheduled for Monday, December 5, 1955.

The news traveled like wildfire into every black home. Telephones jangled; people congregated on street corners and in homes and talked. But nothing was done. A numb-

* From Jo Ann Gibson Robinson, *The Montgomery Bus Boycott and the Women Who Started It: The Memoir of Jo Ann Gibson Robinson*, ed. David J. Garrow (Knoxville: University of Tennessee Press, 1987), 43–45.

ing helplessness seemed to paralyze everyone. Very few stayed off the buses the rest of that day or the next. There was fear, discontent, and uncertainty. Everyone seemed to wait for someone to *do* something, but nobody made a move. For that day and a half, black Americans rode the buses as before, as if nothing had happened. They were sullen and uncommunicative, but they rode the buses. There was a silent, tension-filled waiting. For blacks were not talking loudly in public places—they were quiet, sullen, waiting. Just waiting!

Thursday evening came and went. Thursday night was far spent, when, at about 11:30 P.M., I sat in my peaceful, single-family dwelling on a side street. I was thinking about the situation. Lost in thought, I was startled by the telephone's ring. Black attorney Fred Gray, who had been out of town all day, had just gotten back and was returning the phone message I had left him about Mrs. Parks's arrest. Attorney Gray, though a very young man, had been one of my most active colleagues in our previous meetings with bus company officials and Commissioner Birmingham. A Montgomery native who had attended Alabama State and been one of my students, Fred Gray had gone on to law school in Ohio before returning to his hometown to open a practice with the only other black lawyer in Montgomery, Charles Langford.

Fred Gray and his wife Bernice were good friends of mine, and we talked often. In addition to being a lawyer, Gray was a trained, ordained minister of the gospel, actively serving as assistant pastor of Holt Street Church of Christ.

Tonight his voice on the phone was very short and to the point. Fred was shocked by the news of Mrs. Parks's arrest. I informed him that I already was thinking that the WPC [Women's Political Council] should distribute thousands of notices calling for all bus riders to stay off the buses on Monday, the day of Mrs. Parks's trial. "Are you ready?" he asked. Without hesitation, I assured him that we were. With that he hung up, and I went to work.

I made some notes on the back of an envelope: "The Women's Political Council will not wait for Mrs. Parks's consent to call for a boycott of city buses. On Friday, December 2, 1955, the women of Montgomery will call for a boycott to take place on Monday, December 5."

DOCUMENT ANALYSIS

1. What event triggered the Montgomery bus boycott? Why did the driver summon police for such a minor situation?

2. According to Robinson, was the Montgomery bus boycott a spontaneous uprising or a well-planned protest?

Chapter Study Questions

1. How did the Supreme Court's decision in *Brown v. Board of Education* in 1954 and the Civil Rights Act of 1964 reflect a tremendous change in the willingness of the federal government to enforce the Fourteenth Amendment, enacted after the Civil War? Why do you think this new willingness to enforce racial equality occurred in the 1950s and 1960s?

2. Compare the *Brown* decision to the Southern Manifesto. What issues do they approach from opposite points? What is the real point of disagreement in the Manifesto?

3. What made the Montgomery bus boycott, the sit-ins, marches, and the desegregation of Birmingham so successful?

Thirty

The Turbulent Sixties

Your text shows how foreign policy—centered on and dictated by the Cold War and the Vietnam War—dominated the presidency from 1960 to 1976. While significant changes occurred in domestic life, global issues occupied center stage in the administrations of Kennedy, Johnson, Nixon, and Ford and proved to be the downfall of Johnson. This was a generation of presidents who remembered the lessons of World War II.

American policy in Southeast Asia was based on the domino theory, the foundation of which lay in American fears of unchecked aggression and its consequences. American involvement in Southeast Asia and in Vietnam in particular dated back to the Eisenhower administration. Under the leadership of communist Ho Chi Minh, nationalist rebels had been fighting from the puppet regime dominated by France, the country's former colonial ruler. But despite fears that a victory for the communists would signify an expansion of the Soviets' influence, Eisenhower refused to commit American ground troops to the aid of the French at the battle of Dien Bien Phu in 1954, predicting that it would involve the United States in a war impossible to win. A few years later, however, after the French withdrawal and the division of Vietnam into North and South, the Eisenhower administration began plying the South Vietnam's anticommunist government with aid, military advisors, and equipment in an attempt to stave off a communist takeover by the North.

While President Kennedy continued Eisenhower's low-level involvement in Vietnam, his defining Cold War moment came in a standoff with the Soviets over Cuba. JFK's handling of Cuba has alternately been described as his greatest triumph and his greatest blunder. Whatever the case, it was often seen to be the closest that the United States and Soviet Union came to making the Cold War a hot one. The Bay of Pigs invasion, in April of 1961, was certainly a failure. In this invasion, 2,000 Cuban exiles were sent to invade Cuba, where they were quickly forced to give up their arms. The Cuban Missile

Crisis, in October of the following year, occurred after the Soviet Union planned to move missiles onto Cuban soil. Kennedy, acting aggressively, announced that the navy would turn back the Soviet ships bringing weapons to Cuba and that all work on the missile bases must be stopped. After a few days of tension, the Soviets capitulated, leading to a softening of the tense relationship between the two countries.

Meanwhile, in Vietnam, American involvement gradually escalated between the Eisenhower years and Kennedy's assassination in 1963. The number of military advisors, for example, grew from some 675 to 16,000. But it was not until shortly after the Kennedy assassination that the United States became a major player in Vietnam. President Johnson declared that he wouldn't be the president who lost in Vietnam and dramatically increased American military presence. If there was an "official" beginning to the Vietnam War, it would have to be the Gulf of Tonkin incident—a supposed attack on an American destroyer in the Gulf of Tonkin in northern Vietnam. The Gulf of Tonkin incident provided Johnson with an ideal entrée into Vietnam. In response to it, the number of American troops in country rose to 530,000.

The 1960s opened on a hopeful note of change and expectation. John F. Kennedy's election brought a promise of a new society—a New Frontier, as he put it, where the country could resolve its problems at home and provide leadership abroad. It was an era of activists—an activist presidency, growth of activist government, and a generation of young people increasingly (sometimes radically) involved with the political process.

John Kennedy and his successor, Lyndon Johnson, shared a vision of government working to jump-start the economy, alleviate poverty, and end racial discrimination. During his administration Kennedy was unable to get much of his social legislation— including the first major Civil Rights bill since Reconstruction—through Congress. But following Kennedy's assassination in Dallas in 1963, Lyndon Johnson pushed through Congress an aggressive series of legislative initiatives called the Great Society plan, which included anti-poverty programs, the Job Corps, Medicare (medical care for senior citizens), the Voting Rights Act, Head Start, minimum-wage laws, the National Foundations for the Arts and Humanities, a new immigration act, and Medicaid (medical care for the poor).

Voices against America's status quo were heard throughout the 1960s and 1970s, as students, African Americans, Latinos, and women demanded to be politically, economically and socially enfranchised. Students became active in the free-speech movements and, through organizations such as the Students for a Democratic Society, protested against the war in Vietnam, among others issues, and staged marches, strikes, and university takeovers. African Americans radicalized, especially after riots in Watts in 1965, New York and Chicago in 1966, and Newark in 1967, and the murder of Martin Luther King, Jr., in 1968. Mexican Americans began to organize in the West, and in 1965, under the leadership of César Chávez, staged an important strike against grape farmers, demanding higher wages, union recognition, and improved working conditions.

Women, who were slighted and marginalized in both the student and Civil Rights movements, began to organize groups such as the National Organization for Women (NOW) to promote equality between the sexes, including fighting for an Equal Rights

Amendment, changes in divorce laws and laws concerning rape and domestic violence, the legalization of abortion, and easier access to child care.

The Student Nonviolent Coordinating Committee (SNCC), formed in 1960 as a younger offshoot of the SCLC, grew out of the SCLC's marches and sit-ins. It directed its energies into voter registration drives in the Deep South, where it met with entrenched and violent resistance. Such confrontations convinced some that nonviolence would not work. For while many had adopted nonviolence as an effective tool, they did not share the deep moral and religious commitment to it held by King, and others. As the fifties became the sixties, many SNCC field workers began to question not just the tactic of nonviolence but also the goal of integration.

By the time of the March on Washington in August 1963, SNCC was thoroughly disillusioned with the Kennedy administration, which had demonstrated only lukewarm support for Civil Rights and had failed to protect Civil Rights workers in the South. King's famous "I have a dream" speech delivered at the march, emphasized nonviolence. He was out of step with a growing number of people within SNCC.

Even after the March on Washington and the passage of the Civil Rights and Voting Rights Acts, racism and inequity remained causing some within the Civil Rights movement to become impatient with the pace and the method of change. After a group of SNCC-organized African

American activists offering themselves as an alternative to the all-white Mississippi delegation—the Freedom Democratic Party—were not seated at the 1964 Democratic National Convention in Atlantic City, increasing numbers of activists became disillusioned with traditional political action.

Thirty.1

John F. Kennedy, Cuban Missile Address (1962)

This is an excerpt from the television address President Kennedy gave on October 22, 1962, to the American people, letting them know about the security threat posed by the Soviets in Cuba and his willingness to take strong aggressive action against it. It is interesting to note that while all this transpired the Soviet Union already had missiles stationed in Siberia which were within range of the West Coast and that the United States had missiles in Europe that were certainly within range of the Soviet Union's major population centers.*

Good evening, my fellow citizens. This Government, as promised, has maintained the closest surveillance of the Soviet military build-up on the island of Cuba. Within the past week unmistakable evidence has established the fact that a series of offensive missile sites is now in preparation on that imprisoned island. The purposes of these bases can be none other than to provide a nuclear strike capability against the Western Hemisphere.

Upon receiving the first preliminary hard information of this nature last Tuesday morning [October 16] at 9:00 A.M., I directed that our surveillance be stepped up. And now having confirmed and completed our evaluation of the evidence and our decision on a course of action, this Government feels obliged to report this new crisis to you in fullest detail.

The characteristics of these new missile sites indicate two distinct types of installations. Several of them include medium-range ballistic missiles capable of carrying a nuclear warhead for a distance of more than 1,000 nautical miles. Each of these missiles, in short, is capable of striking Washington, D.C., the Panama Canal, Cape Canaveral, Mexico City, or any other city in the southeastern part of the United States, in Central America, or in the Caribbean area.

---

* From *The Public Papers of the Presidents, John F. Kennedy*, 1962 (Washington, D.C.: Government Printing Office, 1963).

Additional sites not yet completed appear to be designed for intermediate-range ballistic missiles capable of traveling more than twice as far—and thus capable of striking most of the major cities in the Western Hemisphere, ranging as far north as Hudson Bay, Canada, and as far south as Lima, Peru. In addition, jet bombers, capable of carrying nuclear weapons, are now being uncrated and assembled in Cuba, while the necessary air bases are being prepared.

This urgent transformation of Cuba into an important strategic base—by the presence of these large, long-range, and clearly offensive weapons of sudden mass destruction—constitutes an explicit threat to the peace and security of all the Americas, in flagrant and deliberate defiance of the Rio Pact of 1947, the traditions of this nation and Hemisphere, the Joint Resolution of the Eighty-seventh Congress, the Charter of the United Nations, and my own public warnings to the Soviets on September 4 and 13.

This action also contradicts the repeated assurances of Soviet spokesmen, both publicly and privately delivered, that the arms build-up in Cuba would retain its original defensive character and that the Soviet Union had no need or desire to station strategic missiles on the territory of any other nation....

In that sense missiles in Cuba add to an already clear and present danger—although it should be noted the nations of Latin America have never previously been subjected to a potential nuclear threat.

But this secret, swift, and extraordinary build-up of Communist missiles—in an area well known to have a special and historical relationship to the United States and the nations of the Western Hemisphere, in violation of Soviet assurances, and in defiance of American and hemispheric policy—this sudden, clandestine decision to station strategic weapons for the first time outside of Soviet soil—is a deliberately provocative and unjustifiable change in the status quo which cannot be accepted by this country if our courage and our commitments are ever to be trusted again by either friend or foe.

DOCUMENT ANALYSIS

1. According to President Kennedy, why are the Soviet missiles in Cuba of grave danger?

Thirty.2

The Tonkin Gulf Incident
(1964)

In August 1964, President Lyndon Johnson declared that an American destroyer had been fired upon while sailing in international waters in the Gulf of Tonkin off northern Vietnam. Not until later was it revealed that the destroyer had really been in North Vietnamese territorial waters—just thirty miles from shore—assisting South Vietnamese soldiers. Included here are the text of Johnson's message to Congress requesting support for increased involvement and the Congress's resolution granting it, which passed in the House 416–0 and the Senate 88–2. *

President Johnson's Message to Congress

Last night I announced to the American people that North Vietnamese regime had conducted further deliberate attacks against U.S. naval vessels operating in international waters, and that I had therefore directed air action against gunboats and supporting facilities used in these hostile operations. This air action has now been carried out with substantial damage to the boats and facilities. Two U.S. aircraft were lost in the action.

After consultation with the leaders of both parties in the Congress, I further announced a decision to ask the Congress for a resolution expressing the unity and determination of the United States in supporting freedom and in protecting peace in southeast Asia.

These latest actions of the North Vietnamese regime have given a new and grave turn to the already serious situation in southeast Asia. Our commitments in that area are well known to the Congress. They were first made in 1954 by President Eisenhower. They were further defined in the Southeast Asia Collective Defense Treaty approved by the Senate in February 1955.

* From President Johnson's Message to Congress, and Joint Resolution of Congress, H. J. Res. 1145 *Department of State Bulletin*, August 24, 1964.

This treaty with its accompanying protocol obligates the United States and other members to act in accordance with their constitutional processes to meet Communist aggression against any of the parties or protocol states.

Our policy in southeast Asia has been consistent and unchanged since 1954. I summarized it on June 2 in our simple propositions:

1. America keeps her word. Here as elsewhere, we must and shall honor our commitments.

2. The issue is the future of southeast Asia as a whole. A threat to any nation in that region is a threat to all, and a threat to us.

3. Our purpose is peace. We have no military, political, or territorial ambitions in the area.

4. This is not just a jungle war, but a struggle for freedom on every front of human activity. Our military and economic assistance to South Vietnam and Laos in particular has the purpose of helping these countries to repel aggression and strengthen their independence.

The threat to the free nations of southeast Asia has long been clear. The North Vietnamese regime has constantly sought to take over South Vietnam and Laos. This Communist regime has violated the Geneva accords for Vietnam. It has systematically conducted a campaign of subversion, which included the direction, training, and supply of personnel and arms for the conduct of guerrilla warfare in South Vietnamese territory. In Laos, the North Vietnamese regime has maintained military forces, used Laotian territory for infiltration into South Vietnam, and most recently carried out combat operations—all in direct violation of the Geneva agreements of 1962.

In recent months, the actions of the North Vietnamese regime have become steadily more threatening....

As President of the United States I have concluded that I should now ask the Congress, on its part, to join in affirming the national determination that all such attacks will be met, and that the United States will continue in its basic policy of assisting the free nations of the area to defend their freedom.

As I have repeatedly made clear, the United States intends no rashness, and seeks no wider war. We must make it clear to all that the United States is united in its determination to bring about the end of Communist subversion and aggression in the area. We seek the full and effective restoration of the international agreements signed in Geneva in 1954, with respect to South Vietnam, and again in Geneva in 1962, with respect to Laos....

Joint Resolution of Congress

To promote the maintenance of international peace and security in southeast Asia.

Whereas naval units of the Communist regime in Vietnam, in violation of the principles of the Charter of the United Nations and of international law, have deliberately and repeatedly attacked United States naval vessels lawfully present in international waters, and have thereby created a serious threat to international peace; and

Whereas these attacks are part of a deliberate and systematic campaign of aggression that the Communist regime in North Vietnam has been waging against its neighbors and the nations joined with them in the collective defense of their freedom; and

Whereas the United States is assisting the peoples of southeast Asia to protect their freedom and has no territorial, military or political ambitions in that area, but desires only that these peoples should be left in peace to work out their own destinies in their own way; Now, therefore, be it

Resolved by the Senate and House of Representatives of the United States of America in Congress assembled, that the Congress approves and supports the determination of the President, as Commander in Chief, to take all necessary measures to repel any armed attack against the forces of the United States and to prevent further aggression.

SEC. 2. The United States regards as vital to its national interest and to world peace the maintenance of international peace and security in southeast Asia. Consonant with the Constitution of the United States and the Charter of the United Nations and in accordance with its obligations under the Southeast Asia Collective Defense Treaty, the United States is, therefore, prepared, as the President determines, to take all necessary steps, including the use of armed force, to assist any member or protocol state of the Southeast Asia Collective Defense Treaty requesting assistance in defense of its freedom.

SEC. 3. This resolution shall expire when the President shall determine that the peace and security of the area is reasonably assured by international conditions created by action of the United Nations or otherwise, except that it may be terminated earlier by concurrent resolution of the Congress.

DOCUMENT ANALYSIS

1. According to President Johnson, why is it necessary for the United States to play a major role in Vietnam and southeast Asia? Do you find his argument persuasive?

2. How does the Tonkin Gulf Resolution extend the powers of the executive branch? Why do you think Congress was willing to give the President such power, yet never declare war in Vietnam?

Thirty.3

Lyndon Johnson, The War on Poverty (1964)

Lyndon Johnson had served in Roosevelt's New Deal administrations and believed in the power of government to provide for the poor and to solve social problems. His Great Society package became the most massive reform movement in America's history, and its effects would touch more groups than any other reform movement. It is not an understatement to say that the Great Society changed the very face and to a certain extent structure of American society. The Economic Opportunity Act, proposed in this speech to Congress, was a $947.5 million appropriation to wage war on poverty. It included establishing the Job Corps, VISTA (Volunteers in Service to America), and new education programs including work-study for college students and grants for elementary education in poor districts.*

I have called for a national war on poverty. Our objective: total victory.

There are millions of Americans—one fifth of our people—who have not shared in the abundance which has been granted to most of us, and on whom the gates of opportunity have been closed.

What does this poverty mean to those who endure it?

It means a daily struggle to secure the necessities for even a meager existence. It means that the abundance, the comforts, the opportunities they see all around them are beyond their grasp.

Worst of all, it means hopelessness for the young.

The young man or woman who grows up without a decent education, in a broken home, in a hostile and squalid environment, in ill health or in the face of racial injustice—that young man or woman is often trapped in a life of poverty.

He does not have the skills demanded by a complex society. He does not know how

* From *Public Papers of the Presidents of the United States, Lyndon B. Johnson, 1965* (Washington, D.C.: Government Printing Office, 1966).

to acquire those skills. He faces a mounting sense of despair which drains initiative and ambition and energy....

The war on poverty is not a struggle simply to support people, to make them dependent on the generosity of others.

It is a struggle to give people a chance.

It is an effort to allow them to develop and use their capacities, as we have been allowed to develop and use ours, so that they can share, as others share, in the promise of this nation.

We do this, first of all, because it is right that we should.

For the establishment of public education and land grant colleges through agricultural extension and encouragement to industry, we have pursued the goal of a nation with full and increasing opportunities for all its citizens.

The war on poverty is a further step in that pursuit.

We do it also because helping some will increase the prosperity of all.

Our fight against poverty will be an investment in the most valuable of our resources—the skills and strength of our people.

And in the future, as in the past, this investment will return its cost many fold to our entire economy.

If we can raise the annual earnings of 10 million among the poor by only $1,000 we will have added $14 billion a year to our national output. In addition we can make important reductions in public assistance payments which now cost us $4 billion a year, and in the large costs of fighting crime and delinquency, disease and hunger.

This is only part of the story.

Our history has proved that each time we broaden the base of abundance, giving more people the chance to produce and consume, we create new industry, higher production, increased earnings and better income for all.

Giving new opportunity to those who have little will enrich the lives of all the rest.

Because it is right, because it is wise, and because, for the first time in our history, it is possible to conquer poverty, I submit, for the consideration of the Congress and the country, the Economic Opportunity Act of 1964.

The Act does not merely expand old programs or improve what is already being done.

It charts a new course.

It strikes at the causes, not just the consequences of poverty.

It can be a milestone in our one-hundred-eighty-year search for a better life for our people.

DOCUMENT ANALYSIS

1. President Johnson explains his expensive War on Poverty as a national investment. Is this characterization persuasive? What specifics does he provide here?

Thirty.4

Students for a Democratic Society, Port Huron Statement (1962)

Students for a Democratic Society (SDS) was organized in 1960 and became one of the largest and best-organized groups in the student movement of the 1960s, involved in the Berkeley Free Speech movement in 1965, the Columbia strike in 1968, and other protests designed to liberalize university policies and demonstrate opposition to the Vietnam War. The Port Huron Statement is a statement of political ideology, drafted by leaders of the SDS, written primarily by Tom Hayden (a student at the University of Michigan who is now a state legislator in California), and adopted by SDS at its national convention in Port Huron, Michigan, in 1962.*

We are the people of this generation, bred in at least modest comfort, housed now in the universities, looking uncomfortably to the world we inherit.

When we were kids the United States was the wealthiest and strongest country in the world; the only one with the atom bomb, the least scarred by modern war, an initiator of the United Nations that we thought would distribute Western influence throughout the world. Freedom and equality for each individual, government of, by, and for the people—these American values we found good, principles by which we could live as men. Many of us began maturing in complacency.

As we grew, however, our comfort was penetrated by events too troubling to dismiss. First, the permeating and victimizing fact of human degradation, symbolized by the Southern struggle against racial bigotry, compelled most of us from silence to activism. Second, the enclosing fact of the Cold War, symbolized by the presence of the Bomb, brought awareness that we ourselves, and our friends, and millions of abstract "others" we knew more directly because of our common peril, might die at any time. We might deliberately ignore, or avoid or fail to feel all other human problems, but not these two, for these were too immediate and crushing in their impact, too challenging in the demand that we as individuals take the responsibility for encounter and resolution.

* From the Port Huron Statement. Reprinted by permission of Tom Hayden.

DOCUMENT ANALYSIS

1. What issues dominated the Port Huron Statement? Do they appeal to you? Why, or why not?

2. What American ideals are celebrated by the SDS in the Port Huron Statement? To what extent is it those ideals that have led it to criticize the country?

Thirty.5

Curtis Sitcomer, "Harvest of Discontent"
(1967)

Among the new voices in American politics emerging in the 1960s were those of Mexican Americans. Concentrated primarily in the Southwest, Mexican Americans had suffered centuries of economic, social and political discrimination. In the sixties, however, they began to fight back. Raza Unida, one of several grassroots Latino organizations in the Southwest, became a strong political force while other smaller groups formed to pressure for close-to-home bilingual education in the public schools. But perhaps no one better symbolized this new militancy than César Chávez, who took on what appeared to be an impossible task; the unionization of migrant workers. Despite the odds, Chávez was successful in leading these marginalized workers in strikes and boycotts to improve their working and living conditions. "Harvest of Discontent," a selection from an article that appeared in 1967 in The Christian Science Monitor, *described the conditions of the workers and Chávez's fight.* *

The broiling summer sun bakes this central California valley with one-hundred-ten-degree temperatures.

It's preharvest time. And out in the hot, muggy fields a lush grape crop and a labor movement are ripening together.

At stake is a half-million dollars in grapes and the fortunes of eighty thousand migrants who pick them.

What happens may force a redirection of California's $3.8-billion-a-year agricultural economy, which peaks right here in this fiery furnace in late August and September.

César Chávez's farm labor union has been picking up momentum for two years—since its dramatic grape strike here in the fall of 1965. At the same time, [the] migrant workers' civil rights movement also crystallized.

CONTRACT PUSH PLANNED

Now with tens of thousands of acres of fruit ready for harvesting, the union plans its greatest push ever for collective-bargaining contracts.

Some three hundred growers in the San Joaquin Valley will be under pressure. Many may be forced to sign with the union or lose their crop for lack of labor.

Other factors make this perhaps the most meaningful harvest ever for the growers. In recent years, their profits have steadily dwindled as overhead soared. Higher labor costs, forced by unionization, could drive some growers out of business.

A successful union thrust in the next few weeks could mean [for the migrants] higher wages,…a better standard of living, improved housing, and a boost from society's cellar.

But if the union drive fails, the entire farm labor movement and its attendant civil rights cause may be set back for a decade.…

LA CAUSA HITS

Then came La Causa.

…The Mexican farm worker, virtually silent and anonymous for more than half a century, sprang from beneath the arbors and demanded a share of "the good life." He called his uprising La Causa.

He was prodded by the simple but pungent dialogue of one of his own kind, soft-spoken César Chávez, a man whom an admirer called "a quiet explosion."…

INROADS MADE

Through his new union, the migrants asked for reform. From the grower, he demanded guaranteed wages, better working conditions, and collective-bargaining agreements with a union contract and closed shop. From the government, he demanded coverage under the National Labor Relations Act, unemployment and disability insurance, and Social Security.…

GOAL DESCRIBED

For the migrant, César embodies the *Huelga*—the union's two-year-long strike for recognition by three hundred growers in California's lush San Joaquin Valley.

And he embodies La Causa—the dramatic civil rights-type movement aimed at pulling the poverty-stricken, uneducated, and up to now almost ignored, Spanish-speaking migrant into labor's mainstream.

César is short and sturdy. He has wavy, black hair and a dark, youthful complexion.

His eyes are searching and penetrating. And they seem to add to the credibility of the simple but sometimes explosively eloquent phrases which verbalize La Causa.

"We are more than a union," he says. "But we are also less than a union."

In the first instance, he is talking about an extra dimension which most other unions don't possess. Some of the Chávez associates here call this "social conscience." He himself refers to it as "personalized service."

ACTIVITIES LISTED

...In some ways, César Chávez, as a union leader, is reminiscent of the past. He is the union—much in the tradition of Samuel Gompers and, later, John L. Lewis.

BATTLE ALREADY WON

...The migratory worker is not covered under the National Labor Relations Act. He is usually ineligible for unemployment insurance. He is without specific health and welfare protection. And he has no guaranteed minimum wage.

RECOGNITION SOUGHT

Against this backdrop, La Causa fights the migrant's battle on three fronts. It presses the grower for union recognition and collective-bargaining contracts. It lobbies the state and federal governments for legislation to protect the agricultural worker. And it makes a broad appeal to the public to end social discrimination against the migrant.

"Our aims are still very elementary," explains Mr. Chávez. "The big goal is union recognition by the growers. And even when we get this, we have to teach the growers the very meaning of negotiations. Hopeful, they will then get together themselves and set up management-labor relations departments. Now they have no such thing."

Legislation giving benefits to migrants as a group [is] almost nonexistent.

"What we need in a state like California," says Mr. Chávez, "is a Little Wagner Act which would spell out our right to organize and engage in collective bargaining."

"On the national level—for the past thirty years—federal policy has said that workers in general have a right to join a union. We want this extended specifically to farm workers."

The soft-spoken migrant leader is optimistic that such coverage will come. "We have history on our side," he says.

CHANGE ANSWERED

...César Chávez is a patient man. He realizes that it may take ten years or longer for his union to make real headway. In its first two years of operation, UFWOC has signed with only three of the three hundred growers in central California.

And although he doesn't particularly like to think of La Causa as a civil rights movement, Mr. Chávez knows that constant public exposure of the abject poverty and deprivation of the farm worker is essential to the momentum of his movement.

"Our situation," he says, "is really no different from that which exists in the Negro ghettos in other parts of the country."...

DOCUMENT ANALYSIS

1. What was "La Causa"? Why do you think it suddenly grew to strength in the 1960s?
2. What were the goals of César Chávez and the UFW?

National Organization for Women, Statement of Purpose (1966)

There was no one organization that spoke for women in the 1960s and 1970s. Many were formed, but one of the first and certainly most influential was the National Organization for Women. NOW was a mainstream organization, founded by professional women including Betty Friedan (author of the ground-breaking The Feminine Mystique*), focused on raising consciousness and correcting the legal, economic, and political inequities facing women. Organized in 1966, NOW used the Equal Employment Act and the Civil Rights Act of 1964 to initiate social changes to benefit women. This is the statement of purpose adopted at the NOW organizing conference in Washington D.C., in October 1966.* *

We, men and women who hereby constitute ourselves as the National Organization for Women, believe that the time has come for a new movement toward true equality for all women in America, and toward a fully equal partnership of the sexes, as part of the worldwide revolution of human rights now taking place within and beyond our national borders.

The purpose of **NOW** is to take action to bring women into full participation in the mainstream of American society now, exercising all the privileges an responsibilities thereof in truly equal partnership with men.

WE BELIEVE the time has come to move beyond the abstract argument, discussion, and symposia over the status and special nature of women which have raged in America in recent years; the time has come to confront, with concrete action, the conditions that now prevent women from enjoying the equality of opportunity and freedom of choice which is their right, as individual Americans, and as human beings.

NOW is dedicated to the proposition that women, first and foremost, are human beings, who, like all other people in our society, must have the chance to develop their

---

* Reprinted from the National Organization for Women, "Statement of Purpose." It should be noted that this is a historical document and does not reflect all current NOW policies and priorities.

fullest human potential. We believe that women can achieve such equality only by accepting to the full the challenges and responsibilities they share with all other people in our society, as part of the decision-making mainstream of American political, economic, and social life.

WE ORGANIZE to initiate or support action, nationally, or in any part of this nation, by individuals or organizations, to break through the silken curtain of prejudice and discrimination against women in government, industry, the professions, the churches, the political parties, the judiciary, the labor unions, in education, science, medicine, law, religion, and every other field of importance in American society....

Despite all the talk about the status of American women in recent years, the actual position of women in the United States has declined, and is declining, to an alarming degree throughout the 1950's and 1960's....Working women are becoming increasingly—not less—concentrated on the bottom of the job ladder. As a consequence full-time women workers today earn on the average only 60% of what men earn, and that wage gap has been increasing over the past twenty-five years in every major industry group....

Further, with higher education increasingly essential in today's society, too few women are entering and finishing college or going on to graduate or professional school....

In all the professions considered of importance to society, and in the executive ranks of industry and government, women are losing ground. Where they are present it is only a token handful....

Official pronouncement of the advance in the status of women hide not only the reality of this dangerous decline, but the fact that nothing is being done to stop it. The excellent reports of the President's Commission on the Status of Women and of the State Commissions have not been fully implemented. Such Commissions have power only to advise. They have no power to enforce their recommendations; nor have they the freedom to organize American women and men to press for action on them. The reports of these commissions have, however, created a basis upon which it is now possible to build.

Discrimination in employment on the basis of sex is now prohibited by federal law, in Title VII of the Civil Rights Act of 1964....Until now, too few women's organizations and official spokesmen have been willing to speak out against these dangers facing women. Too many women have been restrained by the fear of being called "feminist."

There is no civil rights movement to speak for women, as there has been for Negroes and other victims of discrimination. The National Organization for Women must therefore begin to speak.

WE BELIEVE that the power of American law, and the protection guaranteed by the U.S. Constitution to the civil rights of all individuals, must be effectively applied and enforced to isolate and remove patterns of sex discrimination, to ensure equality of opportunity in employment and education, and equality of civil and political rights and responsibilities on behalf of women, as well as for Negroes and other deprived groups.

WE REALIZE that women's problems are linked to many broader questions of social justice; their solution will require concerted action by many groups....

WE DO NOT ACCEPT the token appointment of a few women to high-level positions in government and industry as a substitute for a serious continuing effort to recruit and advance women according to their individual abilities. To this end, we urge American government and industry to mobilize the same resources of ingenuity and command with which they have solved problems of far greater difficulty than those now impeding the progress of women.

WE BELIEVE that this nation has a capacity at least as great as other nations, to innovate new social institutions which will enable women to enjoy true equality of opportunity and responsibility in society, without conflict with their responsibilities as mothers and homemakers....

...WE REJECT the assumption that these problems are the unique responsibility of each individual woman, rather than a basic social dilemma which society must solve....

WE BELIEVE that it is an essential for every girl to be educated to her full potential of human ability as it is for every boy—with the knowledge that such education is the key to effective participation in today's economy and that, for a girl as for a boy, education can only be serious where there is expectation that it will be used in society....

WE REJECT the current assumptions that a man must carry the sole burden of supporting himself, his wife, and family, and that a woman is automatically entitled to lifelong support by a man upon her marriage, or that marriage, home, and family are primarily woman's world and responsibility—hers to dominate—his to support. We believe that a true partnership between the sexes demands a different concept of marriage, and equitable sharing of the responsibilities of home and children and of the economic burdens of their support. We believe that proper recognition should be given to the economic and social value of homemaking and child care....

WE BELIEVE that women must now exercise their political rights and responsibilities as American citizens. They must refuse to be segregated on the basis of sex into separate-and-not-equal ladies' auxiliaries in the political parties, and they must demand representation according to their numbers in the regularly constituted party committees—at local, state, and national levels—and in the informal power structure, participating fully in the selection of candidates and political decision making, and running for office themselves....

NOW WILL HOLD ITSELF INDEPENDENT OF ANY POLITICAL PARTY in order to mobilize the political power of all women and men intent on our goals....

WE BELIEVE that women will do most to create a new image of women by acting now, and by speaking out in behalf of their own equality, freedom, and human dignity—not in pleas for special privilege, nor in enmity toward men, who are also victims of the current, half-equality between the sexes—but in an active, self-respecting partnership with men. By so doing, women will develop confidence in their own ability to determine actively, in partnership with men, the conditions of their life, their choices, their future, and their society.

DOCUMENT ANALYSIS

1. In its statement of purpose, what changes does NOW want to see in the role women play in society?

2. How radical were the list of goals put forward by NOW in this statement? Are they still radical today? Explain.

Chapter Study Questions

1. Why didn't President Kennedy order an invasion of Cuba, given the fact that it is so close to the Florida coast, and we already were sending thousands of military advisers to Vietnam during his administration?

2. Why were the programs of the War on Poverty so controversial? To what extent did the War on Poverty build on FDR's New Deal?

3. How are the Port Huron Statement, NOW's Statement of Purpose, and the United Farm Workers' struggle all indicative of a new emphasis on broadening rights in the sixties? How do you think these groups learned and borrowed from one another? How effective were they in achieving their goals?

4. Why was the Tonkin Gulf incident so controversial? Why is it the "official" beginning of the war?

Thirty-one

To a New Conservatism, 1969–1988

D omestic opposition to America's role in Vietnam became increasingly vocal and strident in the late 1960s. Hundreds of thousands marched on New York and Washington to protest the war. Such opposition was not without merit, for after the Tet offensive in 1968, it became apparent to many that the United States could not win the war. The experiences of one Marine, Kevin MacCauley, who endured the siege of Khe Sahn in early 1968, are included here. Bowing to domestic pressures, Richard Nixon in 1968 pledged to "Vietnamize" the war and pull U.S. troops out gradually. A few days before his reelection in 1972, his secretary of state, Henry Kissinger, announced that "peace was at hand." Peace was declared, but anti-government opposition and a withering of trust in public officials was still in the air. American involvement in Vietnam continued until 1975.

Richard Nixon was forced to resign in 1974, following disclosure of his role in the Watergate cover-up. His resignation haunted the administration of Gerald Ford; most certainly, Ford's decision to pardon Nixon factored heavily in Ford's defeat in 1976 by Jimmy Carter. Carter, the governor of Georgia, rode strong antigovernment sentiments to the presidency. Unfortunately, his "outsider" status hurt his ability to lead the nation through difficult economic and diplomatic times.

The 1970s also saw changes in Americans' private lives and perhaps no issue was more controversial than abortion. In the late 1960s and early 1970s, a few states— including New York and California— passed laws de-criminalizing abortion. The overwhelming majority of states, however, had laws making abortion a crime, both in performing the procedure and in undergoing it. A woman given the pseudonym Jane Roe sued the state of Texas for denying her the right to terminate her pregnancy. The case, known as *Roe v. Wade*, made it all the way to the U.S. Supreme Court. In a surprise ruling in January 1973, the nation's highest court ruled that during the first trimester of pregnancy, states could not interfere with a woman's right to choose to abort. Most women's rights supporters hailed the move, while many other Americans criticized the Supreme Court for inventing this right, which was not spelled out anywhere in the Constitution. An excerpt from the majority opinion in *Roe v. Wade* is included in this chapter.

Your text notes how Ronald Reagan's presidency ushered in a new era when he was elected with the support of an unlikely coalition of fiscal and social conservatives. The 1980 election showed for the first time the new power of so-called Christian conservatives, who overwhelmingly voted for Reagan (although Jimmy Carter was himself a Christian fundamentalist). Though he had promised voters fiscal responsibility, by the end of his administration Ronald Reagan had produced the largest deficit in America's history. Reagan spent increasing amounts of money on defense, while promising to shrink the federal government (in fact government grew in the 1980s) and implemented supply-side economics. Such an economic policy basically dictated that taxes would be lowered for the wealthy on the theory that they would invest and spend, thus stimulating the economy. The result was an era in which conspicuous consumption was in vogue and American society became polarized into the rich and the poor.

Thirty-one.1

Kevin MacCauley,
Oral History on the 1968 Siege of Khe Sanh

In January 1968, just days before the outbreak of the Tet offensive, the North Vietnamese began a massive assault on the U.S. Marines air base in Khe Sanh. For more than two months, the Marines withstood a constant onslaught of shelling, suffering heavy losses. One of the thousands who endured the siege of Khe Sanh was Corporal Kevin MacCauley of New York. *

In addition to what was called a PRC 25 radio, which weighed about twenty-five, thirty pounds, I carried a spare battery. Then I carried food for the duration of the patrol, six to eight days. I would carry water in quart canteens. All our pack and our cartridge belt and all the armaments and ammo that we carried with us was about seventy to eighty pounds for the regular grunt soldiers and with the radio, mine was close to one hundred pounds. The area that we were in Khe Sanh was a very hilly, mountainous area. You went from triple canopy jungle to what they called elephant grass. The insects, the flora and fauna, was something that was totally alien to anything that I had experienced. The elephant grass has such sharp edges that you would be cut to shreds just walking through it. The animals out there were just absolutely amazing. One patrol, we were waiting for the helicopters to pick us up and an eight-and-half-foot-long Bengal tiger came out in front of us, not more than six feet away. I had a rifle ready to shoot it in case it jumped at us and I was aiming all over the sky, I was so nervous. Another occasion we had elephants in the area. We had apes.

When monsoon season hit us, I don't think I've been colder in my entire life. Khe Sanh was socked in by clouds, and you'd have a mist, twenty-three out of twenty-four hours a day. I'm wrapped in a sleeping bag, wearing a field jacket because it was so cold. And the temperature dropped from daytime to nighttime, a good thirty to forty degrees. It really was cold up there at night. Out in the bush you were just totally

* From "Kevin MacCauley," in Ron Steinman, *The Soldier's Story: Vietnam in Their Own Words* (New York: T.V. Books, 1999), pp.105–109.

exposed to the elements. We didn't carry ponchos because when the rain hit the ponchos, it made too much noise. So we just laid out there. If it rained, we got wet. It was hot, we baked. It was cold, we shivered....

We took a lot of casualties in January and February. It seemed as though the guys who would kill were killed. We took nineteen guys killed during that period of time, and we just took wounded day after day after day. I sent people out on working parties, and they wouldn't come back. Some guy would go out and get something, and he wouldn't come back. And you never saw the wounded, so that added to a certain degree of demoralization.

The bunker that got hit was a bad experience. It's not nice ripping a bunker apart and finding only pieces left of people you had been talking to fifteen minutes earlier. As we got the top off, I found one guy who was just picked up by the blast and pushed up against the ceiling of the bunker, which was basically runway matting. And I never saw a person bleed as much as what this poor guy did. He survived but he was terribly wounded. And the four guys who were killed were horribly mangled. You're never really prepared for your first view of a dead person. And you got close with guys such that you would make plans for one another. And unfortunately, a lot of the plans were totally destroyed by what happened to us. So there are a number of experiences that I went through that still cause nightmares and still cause a lot of heartache.

Morale, at times, was very, very high, and morale, at times, was very, very low. We thought we were invincible. We didn't like the idea of being held on the base because everybody said that, you know, the marines are hard chargers. We should be out there in the bush, going after the North Vietnamese. But on the other side of the coin, we would sit there and say, all right. Come on. Come on at us. Come at us. We'll take as many of you with us before we go than what they could afford. So our morale was high as far as that's concerned. But it never came about. There never was the actual big ground battle at Khe Sanh.

Basically it was hell. There was no place that was safe. One day we took over seventeen hundred rounds of mixed artillery and rocket fire. Another day we took in the neighborhood of six hundred rounds over the space of a four-hour period. And you're sitting in a bunker supposedly safe, ten feet below the ground. The safety just wasn't there. The 24th of January we had one of our bunkers hit. Had twenty-two guys in it. Eighteen were wounded and four were killed. And we thought we were safe inside and we weren't. Day after day we would constantly fill sandbags. You got so tired that you did sleep some. But the rats running around inside the bunker and on top in and around the sandbags, it really didn't make for much sleeping. You figure a room, not even a room, a space of about maybe ten feet wide by about six foot high by maybe thirty feet long and you'd have eighteen, nineteen, twenty guys inside that space. You'd be lying next to, on top of, underneath the guys in your platoon or squad, however many people could fit in the bunker. That's where we existed. It wasn't a pleasant situation, but it was the only situation that we had. It was the only way we could keep ourselves safe from the small pieces of shrapnel that were flying around, it seemed like all the time.

I went from November until probably the end of March without taking a shower. ...Really never had the opportunity the better part of five months to wash your clothes. It would rot off on you, and you'd get a resupply. The water we did have was specifically for drinking. You really didn't use it for washing clothes or taking showers. There was a whole bunch of us who looked really strange with little tufts of hair growing out of our adolescent faces that we thought looked like the most macho beards and mustaches but we looked ridiculous, to say the least....

Semper Fi meant "Always Faithful," but it was always faithful to the guy next to you. You would do anything for the guy next to you. You would lay down your life for the guy next to you. There were never any grandiose thoughts of, you know, we're over here fighting for the American way of life, for apple pie and mother. We were fighting basically for the guy next to us. You would fight because you were afraid of what the guy next to you might think if you didn't fight. I don't ever remember meeting a coward in Vietnam. A lot of guys dealt with things a different way, but you wanted to be part of a team. You wanted to part of a platoon, and the only way that you could do that was being faithful, *Semper Fi*, to the guy next to you. And that was the most important thing for us.

DOCUMENT ANALYSIS

1. What was life like in Vietnam for Kevin MacCauley and his fellow Marines in Khe Sanh?

2. What does MacCauley say that, above all, he and his fellow troops were fighting for?

Richard M. Nixon,
Speech on Vietnamization Policy
(1969)

When Richard Nixon ran for President in 1968, he promised the American people that he had a "secret plan" to end the war in Vietnam. Once Nixon took office, however, the U.S. death toll continued to climb, and he sought to find a way out of the quagmire through various means. In what proved to be a popular strategy—although too slow for opponents of the war— he began a process called "Vietnamization" of the war in 1969. This involved a gradual with- drawal of U.S. forces, and better training of the South Vietnamese force so they could fight for themselves. Nixon described Vietnamization and his resolve to stay committed to Vietnam in a televised speech in the autumn of 1969. **

G ood evening, my fellow Americans:
   Tonight I want to talk to you on a subject of deep concern to all Americans and to many people in all parts of the world—the war in Vietnam.
   I believe that one of the reasons for the deep division about Vietnam is that many Americans have lost confidence in what their Government has told them about our policy. The American people cannot and should not be asked to support a policy which involves the overriding issues of war and peace unless they know the truth about that policy....
   Now, let me begin by describing the situation I found when I was inaugurated on January 20.
   —The war had been going on for 4 years.
   —31,000 Americans had been killed in action.
   —The training program for the South Vietnamese was behind schedule.
   —540,000 Americans were in Vietnam with no plans to reduce the number.
   —No progress had been made at the negotiations in Paris and the United States had not put forth a comprehensive peace proposal.

* From Richard Nixon, Address to the Nation on the War in Vietnam, November 3, 1969, Nixon Library and Historical Birthplace, accessible online at http://www.nixonfoundation.org.

—The war was causing deep division at home and criticism from many of our friends as well as our enemies abroad.

In view of these circumstances there were some who urged that I end the war at once by ordering the immediate withdrawal of all American forces.

From a political standpoint this would have been a popular and easy course to follow. After all, we became involved in the war while my predecessor was in office. I could blame the defeat which would be the result of my action on him and come out as the Peacemaker. Some put it to me quite bluntly: This was the only way to avoid allowing Johnson's war to become Nixon's war.

But I had a greater obligation than to think only of the years of my administration and of the next election. I had to think of the effect of my decision on the next generation and on the future of peace and freedom in America and in the world....

We Americans are a do-it-yourself people. We are an impatient people. Instead of teaching someone else to do a job, we like to do it ourselves. And this trait has been carried over into our foreign policy.

In Korea and again in Vietnam, the United States furnished most of the money, most of the arms, and most of the men to help the people of those countries defend their freedom against Communist aggression.

Before any American troops were committed to Vietnam, a leader of another Asian country expressed this opinion to me when I was traveling in Asia as a private citizen. He said: "When you are trying to assist another nation defend its freedom, U.S. policy should be to help them fight the war but not to fight the war for them."

Well, in accordance with this wise counsel, I laid down in Guam three principles as guidelines for future American policy toward Asia:

—First, the United States will keep all of its treaty commitments.

—Second, we shall provide a shield if a nuclear power threatens the freedom of a nation allied with us or of a nation whose survival we consider vital to our security.

—Third, in cases involving other types of aggression, we shall furnish military and economic assistance when requested in accordance with our treaty commitments. But we shall look to the nation directly threatened to assume the primary responsibility of providing the manpower for its defense.

After I announced this policy, I found that the leaders of the Philippines, Thailand, Vietnam, South Korea, and other nations which might be threatened by Communist aggression, welcomed this new direction in American foreign policy.

The defense of freedom is everybody's business—not just America's business. And it is particularly the responsibility of the people whose freedom is threatened. In the previous administration, we Americanized the war in Vietnam. In this administration, we are Vietnamizing the search for peace.

The policy of the previous administration not only resulted in our assuming the primary responsibility for fighting the war, but even more significantly did not adequately stress the goal of strengthening the South Vietnamese so that they could defend themselves when we left....

Let me now turn to our program for the future.

We have adopted a plan which we have worked out in cooperation with the South

Vietnamese for the complete withdrawal of all U.S. combat ground forces, and their replacement by South Vietnamese forces on an orderly scheduled timetable. This withdrawal will be made from strength and not from weakness. As South Vietnamese forces become stronger, the rate of American withdrawal can become greater.

I have not and do not intend to announce the timetable for our program. And there are obvious reasons for this decision which I am sure you will understand. As I have indicated on several occasions, the rate of withdrawal will depend on developments on three fronts.

One of these is the progress which can be or might be made in the Paris talks. An announcement of a fixed timetable for our withdrawal would completely remove any incentive for the enemy to negotiate an agreement. They would simply wait until our forces had withdrawn and then move in.

The other two factors on which we will base our withdrawal decisions are the level of enemy activity and the progress of the training programs of the South Vietnamese forces. And I am glad to be able to report tonight progress on both of these fronts has been greater than we anticipated when we started the program in June for withdrawal. As a result, our timetable for withdrawal is more optimistic now than when we made our first estimates in June. Now, this clearly demonstrates why it is not wise to be frozen in on a fixed timetable....

And now I would like to address a word, if I may, to the young people of this Nation who are particularly concerned, and I understand why they are concerned, about this war.

I respect your idealism.

I share your concern for peace.

I want peace as much as you do.

There are powerful personal reasons I want to end this war. This week I will have to sign 83 letters to mothers, fathers, wives, and loved ones of men who have given their lives for America in Vietnam. It is very little satisfaction to me that this is only one-third as many letters as I signed the first week in office. There is nothing I want more than to see the day come when I do not have to write any of those letters.

—I want to end the war to save the lives of those brave young men in Vietnam.

—But I want to end it in a way which will increase the chance that their younger brothers and their sons will not have to fight in some future Vietnam someplace in the world.

—And I want to end the war for another reason. I want to end it so that the energy and dedication of you, our young people, now too often directed into bitter hatred against those responsible for the war, can be turned to the great challenges of peace, a better life for all Americans, a better life for all people on this earth.

I have chosen a plan for peace. I believe it will succeed.

If it does succeed, what the critics say now won't matter. If it does not succeed, anything I say then won't matter.

I know it may not be fashionable to speak of patriotism or national destiny these days. But I feel it is appropriate to do so on this occasion.

Two hundred years ago this Nation was weak and poor. But even then, America was the hope of millions in the world. Today we have become the strongest and richest nation in the world. And the wheel of destiny has turned so that any hope the world has for the survival of peace and freedom will be determined by whether the American people have the moral stamina and the courage to meet the challenge of free world leadership.

Let historians not record that when America was the most powerful nation in the world we passed on the other side of the road and allowed the last hopes for peace and freedom of millions of people to be suffocated by the forces of totalitarianism.

And so tonight—to you, the great silent majority of my fellow Americans—I ask for your support.

I pledged in my campaign for the Presidency to end the war in a way that we could win the peace. I have initiated a plan of action which will enable me to keep that pledge.

The more support I can have from the American people, the sooner that pledge can be redeemed; for the more divided we are at home, the less likely the enemy is to negotiate at Paris.

Let us be united for peace. Let us also be united against defeat. Because let us understand: North Vietnam cannot defeat or humiliate the United States. Only Americans can do that.

Fifty years ago, in this room and at this very desk, President Woodrow Wilson spoke words which caught the imagination of a war-weary world. He said: "This is the war to end war." His dream for peace after World War I was shattered on the hard realities of great power politics and Woodrow Wilson died a broken man.

Tonight I do not tell you that the war in Vietnam is the war to end wars. But I do say this: I have initiated a plan which will end this war in a way that will bring us closer to that great goal to which Woodrow Wilson and every American President in our history has been dedicated—the goal of a just and lasting peace.

DOCUMENT ANALYSIS

1. Why does President Nixon oppose an immediate U.S. withdrawal from Vietnam?
2. How does Nixon distinguish his new Vietnamization policy from President Johnson's policies?

Thirty-one.3

House Judiciary Committee, Conclusion on Impeachment Resolution (1974)

During the 1972 presidential race, several employees of the Committee to Re-Elect the President (CREEP), Richard Nixon's reelection campaign, broke into the Democratic Party headquarters, searched through files, and installed listening devices. They were caught. Nixon initially denied that anyone in the White House was involved. But after one of the burglars admitted during his trial that Republican officials had known about their activities, several White House officials admitted their involvement and resigned. As more disclosures followed, it became clear that Nixon administration officials had committed many illegal acts against political opponents and journalists, and paid off the Watergate burglars to ensure their silence. Newspapers, a Senate committee, and a Special Counsel investigated Nixon's involvement in the break-in, and John Dean, the former White House counsel, testified that the president had known about the cover-up. When it was revealed that he had tape-recorded all his meetings in the White House, the investigators sought those tapes in order to find out what Nixon knew. In the end, it took a Supreme Court ruling to force Nixon to hand over the tapes. The following is the conclusion of the House Judiciary Committee on the first of three articles of Impeachment, prepared before Nixon was ordered by the Court to release the tapes. Nixon resigned less than a month after this report was issued.*

After the Committee on the Judiciary had debated whether or not it should rec-ommend Article I to the House of Representatives, 27 of the 38 Members of the Committee found that the evidence before it could only lead to one conclusion: that Richard M. Nixon, using the powers of his high office, engaged, personally and through his subordinates and agents, in a course of conduct or plan designed to delay,

---

* House Judiciary Committee, *Conclusion on the Impeachment Resolution for President Nixon*, 1974, H. Rept. 93-1305, art. I, 133, 135–136.

impede, and obstruct the investigation of the unlawful entry on June 17, 1972, into the headquarters of the Democratic National Committee; to cover up, conceal and protect those responsible; and to conceal the existence and scope of other unlawful activities.

This finding is the only one that can explain the President's involvement in a pattern on undisputed acts that occurred after the break-in and that cannot otherwise be rationally explained.

1. The President's decision on June 20, 1972, not to meet with his Attorney General, his chief of staff, his counsel, his campaign director, and his assistant, John Ehrlichman, whom he had put in charge of the investigation—when the subject of their meeting was the Watergate matter.

2. The erasure of that portion of the recording of the President's conversation with White House chief of staff H. R. Haldeman on June 20, 1972, which dealt with Watergate—when the President stated that the tapes had been under his "sole and personal control."

3. The President's public denial on June 22, 1972, of the involvement of members of the Committee for the Re-election of the President [CREEP] or of the White House staff in the Watergate burglary, in spite of having discussed Watergate, on or before June 22, 1972, with Haldeman, special counsel Charles Colson, and former attorney general John Mitchell [head of CREEP]—all persons aware of that involvement.

4. The President's directive to Haldeman on June 23, 1972, to have the CIA request the FBI to curtail its Watergate investigation.

5. The President's refusal, on July 6, 1972, to inquire and inform himself what Patrick Gray, Acting Director of the FBI, meant by his warning that some of the President's aides were "trying to mortally wound him."

6. The President's discussion with Ehrlichman on July 8, 1972, of clemency for the Watergate burglars, more than two months before the return of any indictments.

7. The President's public statement on August 29, 1972, a statement later shown to be untrue, that an investigation by [White House counsel] John Dean "indicates no one in the White House staff, no one in the Administration, presently employed, was involved in this very bizarre incident."

8. The President's statement to Dean on September 14, 1972, the day that the Watergate indictments were returned without naming high CRP [CREEP] and White House officials, that Dean had handled his work skillfully, "putting your fingers in the dike every time that leaks have sprung here and sprung there," and that "you just try to button it up as well as you can and hope for the best."…

In addition to this evidence, there was before the Committee the following evidence:

1. Beginning immediately after June 17, 1972, the involvement of each of the President's top aides and political associates, Haldeman, Mitchell, Ehrlichman, Colson, Dena, LaRue, Mardinan, Magruder, in the Watergate coverup.…

Finally, there was before the Committee a record of public statement by the President between June 22, 1972 and June 9, 1974, deliberately contrived to deceive the courts, the Department of Justice, the Congress and the American people.

President Nixon's course of conduct following the Watergate break-in, as described in Article I, caused action not only by his subordinates but by the agencies of the United States, including the Department of Justice, the FBI, and the CIA. It required perjury, destruction of evidence, obstruction of justice, all crimes. But, most important, it required deliberate, contrived, and continuing deception of the American people.

President Nixon's actions resulted in manifest injury to the confidence of the nation and great prejudice to the cause of law and justice, and was subversive of constitutional government. His actions were contrary to his trust as President and unmindful of the solemn duties of his high office. It was this serious violation of Richard M. Nixon's constitutional obligations as President, and not the fact that violations of Federal criminal statutes occurred, that lies at the heart of Article I.

The Committee find, based upon clear and convincing evidence, that this conduct, detailed in the foregoing pages of this report, constitutes "high crimes and misdemeanors" as that term is used in Article II, Section 4 of the Constitution. Therefore, the Committee recommends that the House of Representatives exercise its constitutional power to impeach Richard M. Nixon.

DOCUMENT ANALYSIS

1. What are the most serious charges alleged against President Richard Nixon in this summary by the House Judiciary Committee? Do they strike you as sufficiently serious to warrant impeachment? Why, or why not?

Thirty-one.4

Roe v. Wade
(1973)

One of the most controversial decisions by the United States Supreme Court in the twentieth century was issued in 1973. Most states, including Texas, had laws making abortions illegal. After hearing arguments on a Texas case, Roe v. Wade, on appeal, the court ruled 7–2 that all state laws that denied women the right to terminate a pregnancy in the first trimester were unconstitutional. Ironically, the woman, given the pseudonym Jane Roe in this case, gave birth to a child before the appeal was granted, and later became an outspoken opponent of abortion. *

. . . We forthwith acknowledge our awareness of the sensitive and emotional nature of the abortion controversy, of the vigorous opposing views, even among physicians, and of the deep and seemingly absolute convictions that the subject inspires. One's philosophy, one's experiences, one's exposure to the raw edges of human existence, one's religious training, one's attitudes toward life and family and their values, and the moral standards one establishes and seeks to observe, are all likely to influence and to color one's thinking and conclusions about abortion.

In addition, population growth, pollution, poverty, and racial overtones tend to complicate and not to simplify the problem.

Our task, of course, is to resolve the issue by constitutional measurement, free of emotion and of predilection. We seek earnestly to do this, and, because we do, we [410 U.S. 113, 117] have inquired into, and in this opinion place some emphasis upon, medical and medical-legal history and what that history reveals about man's attitudes toward the abortion procedure over the centuries. We bear in mind, too, Mr. Justice Holmes' admonition in his now-vindicated dissent in *Lochner v. New York*, 198 U.S. 45, 76 (1905):

"[The Constitution] is made for people of fundamentally differing views, and the

* From 410 U.S. 113 (1973), accessible online at wps.ablongman.com/wps/media/objects/1676/1716309/documents/doc_t143.html.

accident of our finding certain opinions natural and familiar or novel and even shock-
ing ought not to conclude our judgment upon the question whether statutes embody-
ing them conflict with the Constitution of the United States."

The Constitution does not explicitly mention any right of privacy. However, the
Court has recognized that a right of personal privacy, or a guarantee of certain areas
or zones of privacy, does exist under the Constitution. In varying contexts, the Court
or individual Justices have, indeed, found at least the roots of that right in the First
Amendment; in the Fourth and Fifth Amendments; in the penumbras of the Bill of
Rights; in the Ninth Amendment; or in the concept of liberty guaranteed by the first
section of the Fourteenth Amendment. These decisions make it clear that only personal rights that can be deemed "fundamental" or "implicit in the concept of ordered
liberty" are included in this guarantee of personal privacy. They also make it clear that
the right has some extension to activities relating to marriage, procreation, contracep-
tion, family relationships, and child rearing and education.

This right of privacy, whether it be founded in the 14th Amendment's concept of
personal liberty and restrictions upon state action, as we feel it is, or, as the District
Court determined, in the Ninth Amendment's reservation of rights to the people, is
broad enough to encompass a woman's decision whether or not to terminate her pregnancy. The detriment that the State would impose upon the pregnant woman by denying this choice altogether is apparent. Specific and direct harm medically diagnosable
even in early pregnancy may be involved. Maternity, or additional offspring, may force
upon the woman a distressful life and future. Psychological harm may be imminent.
Mental and physical health may be taxed by child care. There is also the distress, for all
concerned, associated with the unwanted child, and there is the problem of bringing a
child into a family already unable, psychologically and otherwise, to care for it. In other
cases, as in this one, the additional difficulties and continuing stigma of unwed mother-
hood may be involved. All these are factors the woman and her responsible physician
necessarily will consider in consultation....

...In view of all this, we do not agree that, by adopting one theory of life, Texas
may override the rights of the pregnant woman that are at stake. We repeat, however,
that the State does have an important and legitimate interest in preserving and protecting the health of the pregnant woman, whether she be a resident of the State or a
nonresident who seeks medical consultation and treatment there, and that it has still
another important and legitimate interest in protecting the potentiality of human life.
These interests are separate and distinct. Each grows in substantiality as the woman
approaches [410 U.S. 113, 163] term and, at a point during pregnancy, each becomes
"compelling."

With respect to the State's important and legitimate interest in the health of the
mother, the "compelling" point, in the light of present medical knowledge, is at
approximately the end of the first trimester. This is so because of the now-established
medical fact...that until the end of the first trimester mortality in abortion may be less
than mortality in normal childbirth. It follows that, from and after this point, a State
may regulate the abortion procedure to the extent that the regulation reasonably relates
to the preservation and protection of maternal health. Examples of permissible state

regulation in this area are requirements as to the qualifications of the person who is to perform the abortion; as to the licensure of that person; as to the facility in which the procedure is to be performed, that is, whether it must be a hospital or may be a clinic or some other place of less-than-hospital status; as to the licensing of the facility; and the like.

This means, on the other hand, that, for the period of pregnancy prior to this "compelling" point, the attending physician, in consultation with his patient, is free to determine, without regulation by the State, that, in his medical judgment, the patient's pregnancy should be terminated. If that decision is reached, the judgment may be effectuated by an abortion free of interference by the State....

...To summarize and to repeat:

1. A state criminal abortion statute of the current Texas type, that excepts from criminality only a life-saving procedure on behalf of the mother, without regard to pregnancy stage and without recognition of the other interests involved, is violative of the Due Process Clause of the Fourteenth Amendment.

(a) For the stage prior to approximately the end of the first trimester, the abortion decision and its effectuation must be left to the medical judgment of the pregnant woman's attending physician.

(b) For the stage subsequent to approximately the end of the first trimester, the State, in promoting its interest in the health of the mother, may, if it chooses, regulate the abortion procedure in ways that are reasonably related to maternal health.

(c) For the stage subsequent to viability, the State in promoting its interest in the potentiality of human life [410 U.S. 113, 165] may, if it chooses, regulate, and even proscribe, abortion except where it is necessary, in appropriate medical judgment, for the preservation of the life or health of the mother.

DOCUMENT ANALYSIS

1. On what constitutional grounds does the Supreme Court find that women have the right to terminate their pregnancy during the first trimester?

2. In its written opinion in the *Roe* case, to what extent does the Supreme Court acknowledge the strongly divided public opinion on the sensitive issue of abortion?

Thirty-one.5

Ronald Reagan, Speech to the House of Commons (1982)

Ronald Reagan gave this speech, dubbed the "evil empire" speech for its description of the Soviet Union, to the British House of Commons while there in 1982. As president, Reagan portrayed himself as tough on communism and increased military spending dramatically while in office. This speech showcases his fabulous speechmaking abilities—his use of humor, humanizing anecdotes, and aggressive anticommunism.*

We're approaching the end of a bloody century plagued by a terrible political invention—totalitarianism. Optimism comes less easily today, not because democracy is less vigorous, but because democracy's enemies have refined their instruments of repression. Yet optimism is in order because day by day democracy is proving itself to be a not at all fragile flower. From Stettin on the Baltic to Varna on the Black Sea, the regimes planted by totalitarianism have had more than thirty years to establish their legitimacy. But none—not one regime—has yet been able to risk free elections. Regimes planted by bayonets do not take root.

The strength of the Solidarity movement in Poland demonstrates the truth told in an underground joke in the Soviet Union. It is that the Soviet Union would remain a one-party nation even if an opposition party were permitted because everyone would join the opposition party....

If history teaches us anything, it teaches self-delusion in the face of unpleasant facts is folly. We see around us the marks of our terrible dilemma—predictions of doomsday, antinuclear demonstrations, an arms race in which the West must, for its own protection, be an unwilling participant. At the same time we see totalitarian forces in the world who seek subversion and conflict around the globe to further their barbarous assault on the human spirit. What, then, is our course? Must civilization perish in a hail of fiery

---

* From the *Public Papers of the Presidents, Ronald Reagan*, 1982 (Washington, D.C.: National Archives, 1982).

248

atoms? Must freedom wither in a quiet, deadening accommodation with totalitarian evil?...

It may not be easy to see; but I believe we live now at a turning point.

In an ironic sense Karl Marx was right. We are witnessing today a great revolutionary crisis, a crisis where the demands of the economic order are conflicting directly with those of the political order. But the crisis is happening not in the free, non-Marxist West, but in the home of Marxism-Leninism, the Soviet Union. It is the Soviet Union that runs against the tide of history by denying human freedom and human dignity to its citizens. It is also deep in economic difficulty. The rate of growth in the national product has been steadily declining since the fifties and is less than half of what it was then.

The dimensions of this failure are astounding: a country which employs one-fifth of its population in agriculture is unable to feed its own people....The decay of the Soviet experiment should come as no surprise to us. Wherever the comparisons have been made between free and closed societies—West Germany and East Germany, Austria and Czechoslovakia, Malaysia and Vietnam—it is the democratic countries that are prosperous and responsive to the needs of their people....

Our military strength is a prerequisite to peace, but let it be clear we maintain this strength in the hope it will never be used, for the ultimate determinant in the struggle that's now going on in the world will not be bombs and rockets but a test of wills and ideas, a trial of spiritual resolve, the values we hold, the beliefs we cherish, the ideals to which we are dedicated....

I've often wondered about the shyness of some of us in the West about standing for these ideals that have done so much to ease the plight of man and the hardships of our imperfect world. This reluctance to use those vast resources at our command reminds me of the elderly lady whose home was bombed in the Blitz. As the rescuers moved about, they found a bottle of brandy she'd stored behind the staircase, which was all that was left standing. And since she was barely conscious, one of the workers pulled the cork to give her a taste of it. She came around immediately and said, "Here now—there now, put it back. That's for emergencies."

Well, the emergency is upon us. Let us be shy no longer. Let us go to our strength. Let us offer hope. Let us tell the world that a new age is not only possible but probable.

DOCUMENT ANALYSIS

1. How does President Reagan describe communist governments? Why does he see the 1980s as a historical turning point for communism?

2. How does Reagan use humor to help him make his points? Do you think this helps to explain his political success?

Thirty-one.6

Donald E. Wildmon,
The Conscience of a Conservative Christian
(1985)

Beginning in the 1970s, conservative Christians became actively involved in politics. One of the movement's early and most influential leaders, the Rev. Jerry Falwell, founded the Moral Majority in 1979 to oppose "abortion, pornography, the drug epidemic, the breakdown of the traditional family, the establishment of homosexuality as an accepted alternate lifestyle, and other moral cancers that are causing our society to rot from within." Conservative Christians were important supporters of Ronald Reagan in the 1980 election. Televangelists, including Pat Robertson, who would later be the founder of the Christian Coalition, Oral Roberts, and Jim Bakker, were popular political as well as religious figures in the mid-1980s, until they were struck by scandals. Right-wing evangelicals became increasingly important in the 1990s after their successes in grassroots organizing and the election of a number of their supporters in the congressional elections of 1994. This selection is from Donald Wildmon's book, The Home Invaders, *describing his decision to become involved in grassroots activism.**

One night during the Christmas holidays of 1976, I decided to watch television with my family. Gathered around the set in our den, shortly after 7 P.M., we prepared ourselves for a relaxing time of entertainment. We turned on the set and sat back to be entertained.

Not far into the program was a scene of adultery. I reacted to the situation in the manner I had been taught. I asked one of the children to change channels. Getting involved in the second program, we were shocked with some crude profanity. Once again reacting in the prescribed manner, I asked one of the children to change the channel. We got involved in a mystery when, without warning, on came a totally unexpected scene in which one man had another tied down and was working him over with a hammer. I again reacted as I had been instructed. I asked one of the children to turn off the set.

* From Donald E. Wildmon, *The Home Invaders* (Wheaton, Ill: Victor Books, 1983), 7–8, 44–7. Copyright © 1985 by Scripture Press Publications, Wheaton, IL 60187. Reprinted by permission.

As I sat in my den that night, I became angry. I had been disturbed by the deterioration of morals I had witnessed in the media and society during the previous twenty-five years. This was accompanied by a dramatic rise in crime, a proliferation of pornography, increasingly explicit sexual lyrics in music, increasing numbers of broken homes, a rise in drug and alcohol use among the youth, and various other negative factors. I had managed to avoid those unpleasant changes to a large degree by staying away, turning my head, justifying my actions with the reasons most commonly expressed—freedom of speech, pluralism, tolerance.

Realizing that these changes were being brought into the sanctity of my home, I decided I could and would no longer remain silent. I decided to do something even though at that time I had no idea what that something would be. Little did I realize the magnitude of my decision....

Out of that decision came the National Federation for Decency (and out of the NFD came the Coalition for Better Television). For nearly three years I dealt with what I perceived to be the problems with television—sex, violence, and profanity. But the more I dealt with the problems, the more I realized that I was dealing only with symptoms—not the disease....

We Americans are caught up in a great struggle unlike any with which we have faced before. Our struggle is not with an enemy from beyond our shores as it has been in the past; it is being waged inside our very borders. The outcome will determine the direction our country will take for the next several centuries.

This great struggle is one of values—particularly which ones will be the standard for our society and a base for our system of justice in the years to come. For 200 years our country has based its morals, its sense of right and wrong, on the Christian view of man. The Ten Commandments and the Sermon on the Mount have been our solid foundation. To be sure, we have never managed to get the system perfect in practice. Nor will we ever be able to do so no regardless of what base we use. But it has been the most perfect system ever devised in the history of mankind.

Today there are those who would have us change; go in new directions; directions, they are convinced, that will free man from his chains of oppression. They are tired of this old system. They want a new one. And the new one will be based on what they perceive to be right and wrong. The standards for society will come from within themselves. They will decide for themselves and, consequently, for society, what kinds of conduct are acceptable and unacceptable. The old Christian morals will be cast aside in pursuit of a new society....

If within the next five years we fail to turn the tide of this humanist value system which seeks to replace our Christian heritage, then we have—in my opinion—lost the struggle and it will be generations, if at all, before the Christian view of man will be the norm again. I don't like making such a statement. But I must write what I perceive to be the truth.

As a young minister I remember how cold chills ran over my body when I discovered what happened to unwanted bodies in Rome at the time of Christ. They were thrown into the sewer! And even in enlightened Athens unwanted children were discarded in the woods for the animals to eat. I thought about how much we have changed since then, how civilized we have become, how much more compassionate we are today than 2,000 years ago. Then I am told that every year there are more than one million abortions in this country. We haven't changed that much. We wouldn't dare throw a baby in the sewer. Today, we kill babies in the sterile atmosphere of a modern hospital or an abortion clinic and put the bodies in trash bags for disposal in garbage bins. It is so respectable that we even allocate tax money to help cover the expense. We aren't more civilized, only more efficient in our cruelty. Jesus' words, "Suffer the little children to come unto Me," seem out of place in this new society.

DOCUMENT ANALYSIS

1. What does Wildmon see as the great struggle going on in society? What does he see as the key adversary to the Christian values he embraces?

Chapter Study Questions

1. How does Kevin MacCauley's version of the war in Vietnam differ from what you've seen in movies or read in books?

2. How does President Nixon's Vietnamization speech of 1969 echo some of the same points made by President Johnson in his address to Congress about the Gulf of Tonkin incident five years earlier?

3. By invoking Woodrow Wilson, how was President Nixon attempting to link his policies to a long tradition? Is this linkage effective? Why, or why not?

4. In what ways was President Nixon's downfall due to the Watergate scandal tied to other broader events of the 1960s and early 1970s? In other words, was he forced to resign for crimes beyond those he and his aides committed?

5. What was the basis of the *Roe* decision? Why has this decision continued to be so controversial? Do you think *Roe* will be overturned?

6. How does David Wildom's story help to explain why conservative evangelical Christians became a political force starting in the 1970s? How does Wildom's decision to embrace grassroots political activism contrast with the Port Huron Statement by the SDS in Chapter 30?

7. What was President Reagan's vision of the U.S.'s role in the world?

Thirty-two

To the Twenty-first Century, 1989–2006

Ronald Reagan possessed great personal charisma and was enormously popular. He easily won reelection in 1984 against Walter Mondale. His vice president, George Bush, won the presidency in 1988, largely riding on Reagan's coattails. However, where Reagan was seen as a warm optimist, Bush often seemed patrician and distant. Bush used his presidency to advance an increasingly conservative social agenda, which included restrictions on abortion, support for prayer in schools, and deep cuts in social spending.

The Reagan and Bush presidencies saw the fall of the Soviet Union and the end of the Cold War. The Bush administration tried to capitalize on these events by positioning the United States as leader of a "new world order," the first test of which was Bush's successful international coalition to "liberate" Kuwait after its invasion by its neighbor Iraq.

In the election of 1992, voters chose Arkansas Governor Bill Clinton, a Democrat, over the incumbent president, Republican George H.W. Bush, and a strong independent candidate, H. Ross Perot. Bush had enjoyed tremendous popularity in leading an international coalition to victory against Iraq in the Persian Gulf War of 1991, but his approval ratings slid in the following year. An economic downturn and the resentment of conservatives over Bush's breaking his "no new taxes" pledge helped doom his reelection effort. Clinton ran a smart campaign, performed effectively in the debates, and promised to be a "new kind of Democrat"—advocating an overhaul of federal welfare programs, while still championing a progressive social agenda. Clinton's running mate was Tennessee Senator Albert Gore, Jr., a fellow Southern moderate.

Although Clinton had Democratic majorities in the House and Senate after he was elected, he couldn't always unite his party behind his agenda. For example, although he pushed for a major health care reform package—a drive coordinated by his wife, Hillary Rodham Clinton—it failed miserably. In the 1994 midterm elections, Republicans, led by Georgia Congressman Newt Gingrich, won majorities in both chambers of Congress for the first time in 40 years. It looked to many observers like Clinton would be a one-term president. But his handling of a subsequent budget battle with Gingrich and the Republicans one year later restored Clinton's public support, and he won a comfortable re-election in 1996 over Republican Bob Dole.

Clinton's second term proved to be even more difficult than his first. In 1998, Clinton was caught by a special prosecutor with having lied under oath about a sexual escapade with a former White House intern. Clinton's initial refusal to admit the indiscretion, and his handling of the controversy, led Republicans to call for impeachment. Although opinion polls showed most Americans opposed this drastic step, the House Judiciary Committee recommended four articles of impeachment against Clinton. Two of these articles narrowly passed the full House of Representatives in December— almost all Republicans voted for impeachment, and almost all Democrats opposed it. Included in this chapter is the text of the two articles that passed the House. In the Senate however, it would have taken 67 senators to remove Clinton from office, and neither article received more than 50 votes. Clinton emerged tarnished, but his presidency survived.

In the 2000 election, Al Gore defeated the Republican candidate, Texas Governor George W. Bush, son of the former president, by well over 500,000 votes nationwide, but, thanks to a controversial, narrow victory in Florida, Bush won with 271 electoral votes to 267 for Gore. Not even eight months into his presidency, Bush found himself having to lead the country in one of its darkest hours. On September 11, 2001, four airplanes were hijacked by well-trained Islamic terrorists, in a scheme masterminded by Osama bin Laden, and carried out by his al-Qaeda network. Two of the planes crashed into the World Trade Center in New York City, another crashed into the Pentagon, and the fourth crashed into rural Pennsylvania. The experience of one New Yorker on that terrible day, Owen Burdick, is included in this chapter.

The destruction and murder of the 9-11 terrorist attacks led to immediate calls for a strong response, with special attention focused on going after Afghanistan, where the fundamentalist Islamic government allowed terrorist training camps and gave protection to Bin Laden and al-Qaeda. Just days after the attacks, Congress voted to authorize President Bush to use military force against Afghanistan. The Senate vote was unanimous, and only one member of the House opposed it. That lone opponent was Congresswoman Barbara Lee of California. The main language of the authorization for the use of force and Lee's statement on the House floor explaining her opposition to it are included in this chapter.

In the first years of the 21st century, the growing acceptance of gay rights could be seen in the number of businesses that extended domestic partner benefits to same-sex couples, the positive portrayal of gays and lesbians in the media, and in other areas of society. However, many Americans were concerned about this trend, and social conservatives were especially fearful of the impact on the traditional family. A Massachusetts state court ruling allowing for same-sex marriage and some other local attempts to extend this right, created a strong national backlash. The final document in this chapter is from Senator Wayne Allard, a Colorado Republican, who authored a federal constitutional amendment in 2004 to define legal marriage as between a man and a woman. The proposed amendment failed to obtain the necessary two-thirds vote in the Senate, but public opinion polls showed most Americans favored such a definition of traditional marriage in the Constitution.

Thirty-two.1

George H. W. Bush, Address to the Nation Announcing Allied Military Action in the Persian Gulf (1991)

In August 1990, Iraqi dictator Saddam Hussein sent troops into neighboring Kuwait. Both countries were oil-rich, and Saddam hoped that he would be able to take over Kuwait's oil reserves and make back some of the funds he had lost during the disastrous war with Iran in the 1980s. A worldwide coalition, led by the United States, was formed to counter Iraq and push it out of Kuwait, which it did after a five-month standoff. The war was considered a success, although Saddam Hussein remained in power and the region remained somewhat unstable. In this address, President Bush announced that military action in the Gulf had begun. The president spoke from the Oval Office and his address was broadcast live on radio and television.*

Just 2 hours ago, allied air forces began an attack on military targets in Iraq and Kuwait. These attacks continue as I speak. Ground forces are not engaged.

This conflict started August 2d when the dictator of Iraq invaded a small and helpless neighbor. Kuwait—a member of the Arab League and a member of the United Nations—was crushed; its people, brutalized. Five months ago, Saddam Hussein [President of Iraq] started this cruel war against Kuwait. Tonight, the battle has been joined.

This military action, taken in accord with United Nations resolutions and with the consent of the Untied States Congress, follows months of constant and virtually endless diplomatic activity on the part of the United Nations, the United States, and many, many other countries. Arab leaders sought what became known as an Arab solution, only to conclude that Saddam Hussein was unwilling to leave Kuwait. Others traveled to Baghdad in a variety of efforts to restore peace and justice. Our Secretary of State, James Baker, held an historic meeting in Geneva, only to be totally rebuffed. This past weekend, in a last-ditch effort, the Secretary-General of the United Nations went to

* From *Public Papers of the Presidents of the United States, George Bush, 1991* (Washington, D.C.: Office of the Federal Register, National Archives and Records Service, 1992).

the Middle East with peace in his heart—his second such mission. And he came back from Baghdad with no progress at all in getting Saddam Hussein to withdraw from Kuwait.

Now the twenty-eight countries with forces in the Gulf area have exhausted all reasonable efforts to reach a peaceful resolution—have no choice but to drive Saddam from Kuwait by force. We will not fail.

As I report to you, air attacks are underway against military targets in Iraq. We are determined to knock out Saddam Hussein's nuclear-bomb potential. We will also destroy his chemical-weapons facilities. Much of Saddam's artillery and tanks will be destroyed. Our operations are designed to best protect the lives of all the coalition forces by targeting Saddam's vast military arsenal. Initial reports from General Schwarzkopf are that our operations are proceeding according to plan.

Our objectives are clear: Saddam Hussein's forces will leave Kuwait. The legitimate government of Kuwait will be restored to its rightful place, and Kuwait will once again be free. Iraq will eventually comply with all relevant United Nations resolutions, and then, when peace is restored, it is our hope that Iraq will live as a peaceful and cooperative member of the family of nations, thus enhancing the security and stability of the Gulf.

Some may ask: Why act now? Why not wait? The answer is clear: The world could wait no longer. Sanctions, though having some effect, showed no signs of accomplishing their objective. Sanctions were tried for well over five months, and we and our allies concluded that sanctions alone would not force Saddam from Kuwait.

While the world waited, Saddam Hussein systematically raped, pillaged, and plundered a tiny nation, no threat to his own. He subjected the people of Kuwait to unspeakable atrocities—and among those maimed and murdered, innocent children.

While the world waited, Saddam sought to add to the chemical weapons arsenal he now possesses, and infinitely more dangerous weapon of mass destruction—a nuclear weapon. And while the world waited, while the world talked peace and withdrawal, Saddam Hussein dug in and moved massive forces into Kuwait.

While the world waited, while Saddam stalled, more damage was being done to the fragile economies of the Third World, emerging democracies of Eastern Europe, to the entire world, including to our own economy.

The United States, together with the United Nations, exhausted every means at our disposal to bring this crisis to a peaceful end. However, Saddam clearly felt that by stalling and threatening and defying the United Nations, he could weaken the forces arrayed against him.

While the world waited, Saddam Hussein met every overture of peace with open contempt. While the world prayed for peace, Saddam prepared for war.

I had hoped that when the United States Congress, in historic debate, took its resolute action, Saddam would realize he could not prevail and would move out of Kuwait in accord with the United Nation resolutions. He did not do that. Instead, he remained intransigent, certain that time was on his side.

Saddam was warned over and over again to comply with the will of the United Nations: Leave Kuwait, or be driven out. Saddam has arrogantly rejected all warnings. Instead, he tried to make this a dispute between Iraq and the United States of America.

Well, he failed. tonight, twenty-eight nations—countries from five continents, Europe and Asia, Africa, and the Arab League—have forces in the Gulf area standing shoulder to shoulder against Saddam Hussein. These countries had hoped the use of force could be avoided. Regrettably, we now believe that only force will make him leave.

Prior to ordering our forces into battle, I instructed our military commanders to take every necessary step to prevail as quickly as possible, and with the greatest degree of protection possible for American and allied service men and women. I've told the American people before that this will not be another Vietnam, and I repeat this here tonight. Our troops will have the best possible support in the entire world, and they will not be asked to fight with one hand tied behind their back. I'm hopeful that this fighting will not go on for long and that casualties will be held to an absolute minimum.

This is an historic moment. We have in this past year made great progress in ending the long era of conflict and cold war. We have before us the opportunity to forge for ourselves and for future generations a new world order—a world where the rule of law, not the law of the jungle, governs the conduct of nations. When we are successful—and we will be—we have a real chance at this new world order, an order in which a credible United Nations can use its peacekeeping role to fulfill the promise and vision of the U.N.'s founders.

We have no argument with the people of Iraq. Indeed, for the innocents caught in this conflict, I pray for their safety. Our goal is not the conquest of Iraq. It is the liberation of Kuwait. It is my hope that somehow the Iraqi people can, even now, convince their dictator that he must lay down his arms, leave Kuwait and let Iraq itself rejoin the family of peace-loving nations.

Thomas Paine wrote many years ago: "These are the times that try men's souls." Those well-known words are so very true today. But even as planes of the multinational forces attack Iraq, I prefer to think of peace, not war. I am convinced not only that we will prevail but that out of the horror of combat will come the recognition that no nation can stand against a world united. No nation will be permitted to brutally assault its neighbor.

No president can easily commit our sons and daughters to war. They are the Nation's finest. Ours is an all-volunteer force, magnificently trained, highly motivated. The troops know why they're there. And listen to what they say, for they've said it better than any President or Prime Minister ever could.

Listen to Hollywood Huddleston, marine lance corporal. He says, "Let's free these people, so we can go home and be free again." And he's right. The terrible crimes and tortures committed by Saddam's henchmen against the innocent people of Kuwait are an affront to mankind and a challenge to the freedom of all.

Listen to one of our great officers out there, Marine Lieutenant General Walter Boomer. He said: "There are things worth fighting for. A world in which brutality and lawlessness are allowed to go unchecked isn't the kind of world we're going to want to live in."

Listen to Master Sergeant J. P. Kendall of the 82d Airborne: "We're here for more than just the price of a gallon of gas. What we're doing is going to chart the future of the world for the next 100 years. It's better to deal with this guy now than five years from now."

And finally, we should all sit up and listen to Jackie Jones, an army lieutenant, when she says, "If we let him get away with this, who knows what's going to be next?"

I have called upon Hollywood and Walter and J. P. and Jackie and all their courageous comrades-in-arms to do what must be done. Tonight, America and the world are deeply grateful to them and to their families. And let me say to everyone listening or watching tonight: When the troops we've sent in finish their work, I am determined to bring them home as soon as possible.

Tonight, as our forces fight, they and their families are in our prayers. May God bless each and every one of them, and the coalition forces at our side in the Gulf, and may He continue to bless our nation, the United States of America.

DOCUMENT ANALYSIS

1. How does President George H. W. Bush justify the decision to go to war against Saddam Hussein in the Gulf War of 1991? Is his argument compelling? Explain.

2. In the last part of his speech, President Bush mentions several U.S. soldiers by name. What is he attempting to do by including their opinions?

Thirty-two.2

Articles of Impeachment Against William Jefferson Clinton (1998)

Only three U.S. presidents have faced serious impeachment charges by Congress. In 1868, Andrew Johnson was impeached by the House and survived the removal vote in the Senate by one vote. In 1974, due to the Watergate scandal, Richard Nixon was about to be impeached by an overwhelming vote of the House, and faced certain ouster in the Senate, so he resigned. Bill Clinton's impeachment grew out of an unrelated investigation into his business dealings in Arkansas, but centered on his lying under oath about his sexual entanglement with a White House intern. The House Judiciary Committee in 1998 approved four Articles of Impeachment against Clinton, two of which passed the full House by narrow margins. In February 1999, the Senate rejected both articles, and Clinton held onto the presidency. *

In the House of Representatives
December 15, 1998

Mr. HYDE submitted the following resolution; which was referred to the House Calendar and ordered to be printed

RESOLUTION

Impeaching William Jefferson Clinton, President of the United States, for high crimes and misdemeanors.

Resolved, That William Jefferson Clinton, President of the United States, is impeached for high crimes and misdemeanors, and that the following articles of impeachment be exhibited to the United States Senate:

---

* From Library of Congress online, http://thomas.loc.gov/.

Articles of impeachment exhibited by the House of Representatives of the United States of America in the name of itself and of the people of the United States of America, against William Jefferson Clinton, President of the United States of

America, in maintenance and support of its impeachment against him for high crimes and misdemeanors.

Article I

In his conduct while President of the United States, William Jefferson Clinton, in violation of his constitutional oath faithfully to execute the office of President of the United States and, to the best of his ability, preserve, protect, and defend the Constitution of the United States, and in violation of his constitutional duty to take care that the laws be faithfully executed, has willfully corrupted and manipulated the judicial process of the United States for his personal gain and exoneration, impeding the administration of justice, in that:

On August 17, 1998, William Jefferson Clinton swore to tell the truth, the whole truth, and nothing but the truth before a Federal grand jury of the United States. Contrary to that oath, William Jefferson Clinton willfully provided perjurious, false and misleading testimony to the grand jury concerning one or more of the following: (1) the nature and details of his relationship with a subordinate Government employee; (2) prior perjurious, false and misleading testimony he gave in a Federal civil rights action brought against him; (3) prior false and misleading statements he allowed his attorney to make to a Federal judge in that civil rights action; and (4) his corrupt efforts to influence the testimony of witnesses and to impede the discovery of evidence in that civil rights action.

In doing this, William Jefferson Clinton has undermined the integrity of his office, has brought disrepute on the Presidency, has betrayed his trust as President, and has acted in a manner subversive of the rule of law and justice, to the manifest injury of the people of the United States.

Wherefore, William Jefferson Clinton, by such conduct, warrants impeachment and trial, and removal from office and disqualification to hold and enjoy any office of honor, trust, or profit under the United States.

[Article II failed in the House]

Article III

In his conduct while President of the United States, William Jefferson Clinton, in violation of his constitutional oath faithfully to execute the office of President of the United States and, to the best of his ability, preserve, protect, and defend the Constitution of the United States, and in violation of his constitutional duty to take care that the laws be faithfully executed, has prevented, obstructed, and impeded the administration of justice, and has to that end engaged personally, and through his subordinates and agents, in a course of conduct or scheme designed to delay, impede, cover up, and conceal the existence of evidence and testimony related to a Federal civil rights action brought against him in a duly instituted judicial proceeding.

The means used to implement this course of conduct or scheme included one or more of the following acts:

(1) On or about December 17, 1997, William Jefferson Clinton corruptly encouraged a witness in a Federal civil rights action brought against him to execute a sworn affidavit in that proceeding that he knew to be perjurious, false and misleading.

(2) On or about December 17, 1997, William Jefferson Clinton corruptly encouraged a witness in a Federal civil rights action brought against him to give perjurious, false and misleading testimony if and when called to testify personally in that proceeding.

(3) On or about December 28, 1997, William Jefferson Clinton corruptly engaged in, encouraged, or supported a scheme to conceal evidence that had been subpoenaed in a Federal civil rights action brought against him.

(4) Beginning on or about December 7, 1997, and continuing through and including January 14, 1998, William Jefferson Clinton intensified and succeeded in an effort to secure job assistance to a witness in a Federal civil rights action brought against him in order to corruptly prevent the truthful testimony of that witness in that proceeding at a time when the truthful testimony of that witness would have been harmful to him.

(5) On January 17, 1998, at his deposition in a Federal civil rights action brought against him, William Jefferson Clinton corruptly allowed his attorney to make false and misleading statements to a Federal judge characterizing an affidavit, in order to prevent questioning deemed relevant by the judge. Such false and misleading statements were subsequently acknowledged by his attorney in a communication to that judge.

(6) On or about January 18 and January 20–21, 1998, William Jefferson Clinton related a false and misleading account of events relevant to a Federal civil rights action brought against him to a potential witness in that proceeding, in order to corruptly influence the testimony of that witness.

(7) On or about January 21, 23 and 26, 1998, William Jefferson Clinton made false and misleading statements to potential witnesses in a Federal grand jury proceeding in order to corruptly influence the testimony of those witnesses. The false and misleading statements made by William Jefferson Clinton were repeated by the witnesses to the grand jury, causing the grand jury to receive false and misleading information.

In all of this, William Jefferson Clinton has undermined the integrity of his office, has brought disrepute on the Presidency, has betrayed his trust as President, and has acted in a manner subversive of the rule of law and justice, to the manifest injury of the people of the United States.

Wherefore, William Jefferson Clinton, by such conduct, warrants impeachment and trial, and removal from office and disqualification to hold and enjoy any office of honor, trust, or profit under the United States.

[Article IV failed in the House]

DOCUMENT ANALYSIS

1. What, essentially, are the principal charges against President Clinton in these articles of impeachment?

Thirty-two.3

Barbara Lee, Speech in Opposition to Authorizing the U.S. War in Afghanistan (2001)

Just days following the September 11 terrorist attacks, the U.S. Congress voted to authorize President George W. Bush to use military force to retaliate against those who had struck the United States and against those countries—notably, Afghanistan—who protected terrorists. Even members of Congress who were most suspicious of using military force supported this authorization. The Senate vote was unanimous, and the House vote was 420 to 1. The one vote against the measure was by Congresswoman Barbara Lee, a Democrat representing Oakland and Berkeley in California.*

H.J. Res. 64

Whereas, on September 11, 2001, acts of treacherous violence were committed against the United States and its citizens; and

Whereas, such acts render it both necessary and appropriate that the United States exercise its rights to self-defense and to protect United States citizens both at home and abroad; and

Whereas, in light of the threat to the national security and foreign policy of the United States posed by these grave acts of violence; and

Whereas, such acts continue to pose an unusual and extraordinary threat to the national security and foreign policy of the United States; and

Whereas, the President has authority under the Constitution to take action to deter and prevent acts of international terrorism against the United States: Now, therefore, be it

Resolved by the Senate and House of Representatives of the United States of America in Congress assembled,

---

* From *Congressional Record*, September 14, 2001, pages H5638, H5642–H5643, available online at www.gpoaccess.gov/crecord/.

SECTION 1. SHORT TITLE.

This joint resolution may be cited as the "Authorization for Use of Military Force".

SEC. 2. AUTHORIZATION FOR USE OF UNITED STATES ARMED FORCES.

(a) In General.—That the President is authorized to use all necessary and appropriate force against those nations, organizations, or persons he determines planned, authorized, committed, or aided the terrorist attacks that occurred on September 11, 2001, or harbored such organizations or persons, in order to prevent any further acts of international terrorism against the United States by such nations, organizations or persons....

Ms. LEE.

...Mr. Speaker, I rise today really with a very heavy heart, one that is filled with sorrow for the families and the loved ones who were killed and injured this week. Only the most foolish and the most callous would not understand the grief that has really gripped our people and millions across the world.

This unspeakable act on the United States has forced me, however, to rely on my moral compass, my conscience, and my God for direction. September 11 changed the world. Our deepest fears now haunt us. Yet I am convinced that military action will not prevent further acts of international terrorism against the United States. This is a very complex and complicated matter.

This resolution will pass, although we all know that the President can wage a war even without it. However difficult this vote may be, some of us must urge the use of restraint. Our country is in a state of mourning. Some of us must say, let us step back for a moment. Let us just pause for a minute and think through the implications of our actions today so that this does not spiral out of control.

I have agonized over this vote, but I came to grips with it today and I came to grips with opposing this resolution during the very painful yet very beautiful memorial service. As a member of the clergy so eloquently said, "As we act, let us not become the evil that we deplore."

DOCUMENT ANALYSIS

1. Does Congresswoman Lee's argument against authorizing force strike you as reasonable or dangerous? Why?

Thirty-two.4

Owen Burdick, Witnessing the 9-11 Terrorist Attack in New York (2001)

September 11, 2001, dawned as a bright, beautiful day on the East Coast of the United States, but it would soon prove to be one of the darkest moments in American history. Terrorists hijacked commercial airliners and crashed them into the World Trade Center towers in New York City, and the Pentagon in Washington D.C. These attacks killed thousands, and shocked Americans, who were not accustomed to this scale of terrorism within U.S. borders. The events were especially grim for those who viewed the events firsthand. This excerpt is from Owen Burdick, the organist and music director at Trinity Church in Lower Manhattan. For Burdick, as for so many others, it began as just a regular day.*

Narrative by Owen Burdick

It was my Birthday (September 11th) and I was on the number 4 train commuting down to Trinity Church when an announcement came over the loudspeaker that we would be bypassing Fulton Street station due to falling debris from the World Trade Center. A chef from the Marriott Hotel nearby had boarded the train up at Brooklyn Bridge in an attempt to get home. He told us that a plane had hit one of the towers. Figuring that it was a Cessna or other small craft that had simply gone out of control, we all exited the train at Wall Street expecting to see a couple of smashed windows.

The devastation took everyone's breath away as one by one we climbed the stairs to the street level. The entire upper floors were engulfed in flames, smoke billowing out in all directions, pieces of metal and glass falling to the ground below. A bunch of us watched horrified as a second jet sliced through the second tower. Up until that point we figured, or wanted to believe, that this was a commercial liner gone out of control on its way up the Hudson to La Guardia airport. The second explosion instantly confirmed our worst nightmare: this was the terrorist attack…

* From Narrative of Owen Burdick, September 11, 2001, Documentary Project, Library of Congress online, http://hdl.loc.gov/loc.afc/afc2001015.t002.

The second plane, as I'm sure you've seen from the countless television replays, didn't simply hit the building, it exploded through it. The image was a scene out of the movie "Die Hard," and the ensuing fireball and smoke, and the roar of the explosion were terrifying. The events sent many people into the church to pray and cry and just get away from the horror. Father Stuart Hoke read psalms and lead us in prayer; I was called into service to play a couple of hymns.

But after a while (being a city kid after all, from 105th Street) I said, "OK, we've praised the Lord enough; it's time to get the hell outta here!"...

A verger, David Wright, and I heard a horrendous noise and ran to the back door of the church to see what was happening. With a clear view of the South Tower, we watched as the building began to collapse. David screamed "Oh, my God!" and it marked the first time I was truly afraid. It really looked as if, from three blocks away—only two football fields—we were going to be consumed. The sound of the crushing metal, the thousands of splintering panes of glass, the deafening explosion, people falling or jumping from the building as it crumbled—it was a maelstrom, and I don't think I've ever used that word before in my life. I just keep seeing it and hearing it over and over.

After a short time, the second building (the North Tower) collapsed. The sound and wreckage were the same, and again the ground shook and the sky turned black. More debris fell on the church and still more smoke started pouring in through the leading of the stained glass windows. We sat tight and figured once the dust settled—literally—we would try to make it to the East River or head South to the ferry terminal.

In about an hour, a ray of sun was visible through the windows. The only clear pane of glass in the church is one in my office, and we went up to take a look. The only people on the street were fire fighters wearing gas masks. Occasionally, you could see civilians running for cover with rags covering their mouths. We figured it was time to move out...

No subways or buses were running, of course. There was no running water, no electricity. The city around us was dead. And it was strangely quiet. The eight to ten inches of ash and debris on the ground had the same effect as a snowstorm; all sound was deadened or muffled.

As we walked across Broadway in front of the church and looked uptown, you could see nothing but blackness in the sky, debris everywhere. We stepped over a sea of wallets and brief cases, single shoes and smoldering faxes—all "floating" within a dull white foot-high ocean of vaporized wallboard and glass....

So, with wet towels around our necks and over our mouths, we started walking. We ran into a fireman who was obviously dazed and injured. He told us that he had been blown half a block down the street and managed, somehow, to grab hold of a fence which saved his life. He said that five of his fellow firefighters—five of his buddies—had been blown away and turned into "charcoal."...

I finally made my way to Grand Central which, by 7:00 P.M., was a ghost town. I caught a train and was glad to be home. I woke up in my clothes; ash still covered my shoes.

DOCUMENT ANALYSIS

1. How does Burdick's account of his experience on 9-11 compare with what you remember of that day?

Thirty-two.5

Wayne Allard, Testifying in Favor of the Federal Marriage Amendment (2004)

*Remarkable gains were made by gays and lesbians in American society, beginning in the
1970s. By the first decade of the twenty-first century, a growing movement to allow for same-
sex couples to enter legal marriage won a state court victory in Massachusetts, and other states
were considering legal changes to legalize gay marriage. This angered supporters of traditional
marriage, and led to the swift passage of laws and state constitutional amendments in many
states defining marriage in strictly heterosexual terms. Wayne Allard, a Republican Senator
from Colorado, authored a constitutional amendment in 2004 to define marriage nationwide
in such terms. Despite overwhelming approval in the House, and support from President
George W. Bush, the measure failed to win the 2/3 vote necessary in the Senate.* *

Thank you Mr. Chairman. I appreciate the Committee allowing me to be with you
today to discuss marriage and a possible amendment to the Constitution to define
and preserve this institution....

Without much academic examination most of us understand the historical, cultural, and civic importance of marriage. Marriage, the union between a man and a
woman, has been the foundation of every civilization in human history. This definition of marriage crosses all bounds of race, religion, culture, political party, ideology
and ethnicity.

As an expression of this cultural value this definition of marriage has been incorporated into the very fabric of civic policy. It is the root from which families, communities, and government are grown. This is not some hotly contested ideology
being forced upon an unwilling populace, it is in fact the opposite. The value and civil
definition of marriage is an expression of the American people, expressed through the
democratic process our Founding Fathers so wisely crafted.

---

* From Senator Wayne Allard, Senate Judiciary Committee Testimony on S.J. Res. 30, the Federal
Marriage Amendment, March 23, 2004, online access www.senate.gov/member/co/allard.

In 1996 Congress thoughtfully and overwhelmingly passed the Defense of Marriage Act (DOMA). DOMA passed with the support of more than three-quarters of the House of Representatives and with the support of eighty-five Senators before being signed in to law by then President Bill Clinton.

The Defense of Marriage Act was designed to allow states to refuse to recognize the act of any other jurisdiction that would designate a relationship between individuals of the same gender as a marriage. Thirty-eight states have since enacted statutes defining marriage in some manner, and four states have passed state constitutional amendments defining marriage as a union of one man and one woman. These state DOMAs and constitutional amendments, combined with Federal DOMA, should have settled the question as to the democratic expression of the will of the American public.

Unfortunately a handful of activist judges have recently determined that they are in a position to redefine the institution of marriage. A few state courts, not legislatures, have sought to overturn both statute and common perception of marriage by expanding the definition to include same gender couples.

State court challenges in Arizona, Massachusetts, New Jersey and Indiana may seem well and good to colleagues concerned with the rights of states to determine most matters, a position near and dear to my heart. These challenges, however, have spawned greater disrespect, even contempt, for the will of the states than any of us could have predicted.

The State of Nebraska provides the most stark example of this. Seventy percent of Nebraska voters supported an amendment to the state constitution defining marriage as a union between a man and a woman—seventy percent. This amendment has since been challenged in federal court. In early March the Attorney General of Nebraska testified before a subcommittee of this body that he fully expects the duly amended constitution of his state to be struck down—ruled un-Constitutional—by a federal court. This is what we have come to and this is where we are headed. The will of voters, in the Nebraska case an overwhelming majority of them, undone by activist judges and those willing to use the courts to bend the rule of law to suit their purposes.

The courts are not alone in this subversion of the will of the people. Local activists who want to ignore state law are culpable as well. To date 4,037 licenses for marriage have been issued [to same-gender couples] in San Francisco, California....California is one of the thirty-eight states that have enacted a DOMA law, a law selectively ignored by a handful of public officials. Couples from forty-six states have taken advantage of the issuance of licenses in San Francisco and returned to their home states....

In November I proposed an amendment to the U.S. Constitution to define marriage as a union between a man and a woman and leaving all other questions of civil union or partnership law to the individual state legislatures....Yesterday, in response to much debate and deliberation in the Senate, I reintroduced this [Amendment]...to make our intent more clear. Numerous critics have propounded the false notion that we have far greater restrictions in mind and it is my hope that our technical changes will serve to clear the air of this charge. The policy goal has been and will continue to be to define and preserve the historic and cultural definition of marriage, while leaving other questions to the respective state legislatures.

DOCUMENT ANALYSIS

1. Why does Senator Allard argue that a constitutional amendment to define marriage in traditional heterosexual terms is necessary?

Chapter Study Questions

1. How is Bush's "liberation" of Kuwait viewed now since U.S. involvement in Afghanistan and Iraq?

2. If you had served in Congress in this era, how would you have voted on impeaching President Clinton, authorizing the use of military force in Afghanistan after 9- 11, and the Federal Marriage Amendment?

3. How do you think history will judge the attempt to impeach President Clinton?

4. Owen Burdick's experience in New York on 9-11 was terrifying, but even those who lived far from New York or Washington felt the shock of the surprise attacks. Do you think Americans will ever feel as safe as most did on September 10, 2001?

5. Given the growing acceptance of gays and lesbians in American society, why do you think the prospect of legal marriage for same-sex couples elicits such strong negative reaction?

Credits

Grateful acknowledgment is made for permission to reprint:

CHAPTER 30

Page 225. From Curtis Sitcomer, "Harvest of Discontent," *The Christian Science Monitor*, September 8, 1967. Reprinted by permission from *The Christian Science Monitor*. Copyright © 1967 by the Christian Science Publishing Company. All rights reserved.

CHAPTER 31

Page 250. From Donald E. Wildmon, *The Home Invaders* (Wheaton, IL: Victor Books, 1983), 7–8, 44–7. Copyright © 1985 by Scripture Press Publications, Wheaton, IL 60187. Reprinted by permission.